THE CLASSICS OF GOLF

Edition of

F. G. TAIT
A RECORD

by

John L. Low

Foreword by Herbert Warren Wind

Afterword by Ross Goodner

Foreword

Shortly after the British Amateur Championship was inaugurated at Hoylake in 1885 by the Royal Liverpool Golf Club, John Ball, Jr., a quiet, modest young man whose father owned the Royal Hotel hard by Hoylake's seventeenth green, came to the fore. He had already made his mark in the game: at seventeen, he had entered the 1878 Open championship, at Prestwick, and had finished in a tie for fourth. In 1888, also at Prestwick, he broke through in the Amateur by defeating John Laidlay, of the Royal & Ancient Golf Club of St. Andrews, 3 and 2, in the final, and began his incredible record of winning that championship eight times in all. He won it in 1890, at Hoylake, again beating Laidlay in the final; in 1892, at Sandwich, where he defeated his fellow member of Royal Liverpool, Harold Hilton, 3 and 1; in 1894, at Hoylake, edging out Mure Fergusson, of the R & A., 1 up; in 1899, at Prestwick again, where he beat Freddie Tait, of the R. & A., on the 37th; in 1907, after an eight-year drought, at St. Andrews, with a convincing 6-and-4 victory in the final over C. A. Palmer of the home club; in 1910, at Hoylake again, thumping A. C. Aylmer, of Sidmouth, 10 and 9, in the final; and in 1912 for the eighth and last time, when he defeated Hilton, his old rival, 4 and 3, at Prestwick, a course he invariably played well.

Harold Horsfall Hilton, who entered the lists at eight in the boys' competition at Hoylake, also had a remarkable career. Before he won the first of his four Amateur championships, Hilton, an engaging man with an exceptional golf mind, had taken the Open championship at Muirfield in 1892 and at Hoylake in 1897. He did not capture the Amateur until 1900, when he won at Sandwich. He repeated the next year at St. Andrews. In the final he met John Low, of the R. & A.—and, incidentally, the author of this book—and finally subdued his tenacious opponent, 1 up. He didn't win the Amateur again until 1911, when he led the way at Prestwick. (That year Hilton traveled to the United States and carried off our Amateur championship at the Apawamis Club, in Rye, New York. In the final, he defeated Fred Herreshoff on the first extra hole when his second shot, which he played with a spoon, bounced either off the bank to the right of the green or off a rock, and finished nicely on the green.) Hilton won his fourth and last British Amateur in 1913, at St. Andrews. He turned forty-four that year.

John Ball and Harold Hilton's lengthy careers so occupy one's mind when he reads about the golden years of British amateur golf that most of *the other talented amateurs of that day are lost in the shade. All except one, Freddie Tait, of Scotland. Tait appeared on the scene in the 1890s and rose quickly to the top. A prodigious driver, he had grown up on the Old Course at St. Andrews and, not surprisingly, was a master of the long chip and run and a marvelous putter to boot. He also had a gift for playing stunning recovery shots from extraordinarily difficult positions, and this made him a foe to be feared in match play. He could hold his own with Ball and Hilton, and many of their matches were memorable ones. From my early reading, I remember that Tait, the idol of Scotland, was a very fine man whose only shortcoming was a tendency to play his bagpipes in the streets late at night and wake up the whole neighborhood.*

I learned more about Frederick Guthrie Tait in the summer of 1984, under the best possible circumstances. For one reason or another, I had arrived at St. Andrews a full week before the opening round of the British Open and had too much time on my hands. My old friend Laurie Auchterlonie apparently sensed this, for, when we were sitting in the library in his home on Pilmour Links late one afternoon, he reached around and came up with a copy of "F. G. Tait—A Record", by J. L. Low. "Here's an old book you may not know which I think you might like," Laurie said as he handed it to me. I was surprised how quickly I got into the flow of the book, which was published in 1900, and how much I enjoyed it. Having time on my hands, being at St. Andrews, and popping in each day on Laurie and his wife Bea may account up to a point for the pleasure I found in the book, but I believe that a person interested in golf and golfers will react similarly whether he reads it stuffed inside the New York subway or taking life easy on a slow boat to Oban.

"F. G. Tait—A Record" tells the reader a good many things about Freddie Tait other than his winning the British Amateur in 1896 and 1898, and his finishing top amateur in the 1896 British Open. A rugged six-footer who took deep pride in being a Scot, there was a certain magic about him not unlike Bobby Jones'. Apart from being a golfer, Tait was a professional soldier, a graduate of Sandhurst. On October 2nd, 1899, after standing 4 down on the tee of the twenty-third hole, he defeated his great rival, John Ball, 1 up in a 36-hole match at Lytham St. Annes. Three weeks later, on October 22nd, 1899, he boarded the steamer "Orient" at the Tilbury docks, near London, along with the officers and men of the Highland Brigade of the Black Watch, bound for Capetown and the Boer War. On December 11th, he was wounded leading his company in an attempt to force the Boers from their position at Magersfontein. He recovered well from his wound—he had been hit in

the thigh bone of his left leg. On January 10th, Lt. Tait rejoined his company in the Magersfontein area. On February 3rd, they moved westward down the Riet River and arrived the following day at Koodoosberg Drift. Lt. Tait was killed that day in a reconnaissance operation. A soldier in his company described the action in a letter he wrote to Lt. Tait's mother: "Just as we finished, he [Lt. Tait] said, 'I think we'll advance another fifty yards, and perhaps we will see them better, and be able to give it them hot.' We all got ready again, and Lieutenant Tait shouted, 'Now, boys!'. We were after him like hares. The Boers had seen us, and they gave us a hot time of it. But on we went. Just as our officer shouted to get down, he was shot. I was just two yards behind him. He cried out, 'Oh! They have done for me this time.' I cried up to him, 'Where are you shot, sir?' and he said, 'I don't know.' He had been shot through the heart, and never spoke again."

John L. Low, an able Scottish golfer and a close friend of Tait's, wrote this book in 1900. He received the fullest possible cooperation from Tait's family. There have been few biographies in which key letters have been so available and which reveal so much about the writers and the receivers. Among these is a letter written by Tait to his mother two days before his death. Low's biography has an introduction by Andrew Lang, at that time a well-known man of letters who had long been associated with St. Andrews. The book is a tribute to Tait, the man and the golfer. All Scotland loved him, and one can readily understand why. They admired the way this stalwart man attacked a golf course, his informal manner during a match, his consideration for his opponents, and his obvious pride in his country. He had all the proper accessories for a national hero, down to his dog Nails, one of whose parents was probably a Bedlington or, if not, an Irish terrier.

In peace and in war, Tait also embodied the fundamentals of character that the Victorian age prized so highly: devotion to family, friends, duty, honor, and country. Most readers of this book, I think, will begin to read the section that describes Tait's role in the Boer War as something they will just skip over. However, I believe that few will be able to do this. The detailed account of Tait's role in the war has an arresting quality about it, and the reader is as deeply moved as he is when reading such classics as "The Red Badge of Courage" and "All Quiet on the Western Front." Today, more than ever, we look at war as a needless waste of lives which accomplishes nothing, but it is impossible not to be stirred by the valor of individuals in earlier times when a man's conduct was directed by another code.

Freddie Tait came from a family of some prominence. His father, a graduate of Edinburgh University, became professor of mathematics at Queen's College, Belfast, and later professor of natural history at Edinburgh University. It was he who chose St. Andrews as the spot where the family would spend its summers. He amused his sons—all three of them were excellent golfers—by his lifelong efforts to arrive scientifically at the initial velocity of a golf ball struck by a first-class player.

Freddie began to play on the links at St. Andrews when he was seven. At fourteen, he began to keep a diary in which he recorded the details of his matches. (Extracts from his match book between 1896 and 1899 form Appendix II in this book.) He joined the R. & A. in the spring of 1890, when he was twenty. That summer he won the club's Calcutta Cup competition with a 77, the lowest round ever played on the Old Course by an amateur. On July 11th, 1893, he became famous overnight from one end of Britain to the other when he drove the green on the two-level 341-yard thirteenth hole at St. Andrews. We know that his tee shot carried two hundred and fifty yards and that the ground was frozen, so the ball must have landed on the upper level of the fairway and rolled the rest of the way. He had a 76 on that round. In February, 1894, Tait broke the previous record score for the Old Course by holing it in 72. He also set a new course record of 72 for Carnoustie that year. When he was not at Sandhurst or on military duty in England and Scotland, he annually played in both the Open and the Amateur. (Appendix I consists of newspaper and magazine accounts of his matches in the Amateur from 1892 on.) Low covers Tait's golfing career thoroughly. He is undoubtedly at his best in his superb analysis and appreciation of Tait's style of play. I was struck by one sentence in particular: "Apart from the beauty of his manner of hitting the ball, there was something very pleasant to watch about the light-hearted, very pleasant way in which he acted when engaged in a match. A good golfing temperament is as important as a good golfing style, and Tait was blessed beyond most men in this respect."

A word about John L. Low. To begin with, he was an accomplished player who three times was in a position to win the Amateur. In 1897, he reached the semifinals at Muirfield and was unlucky to lose to James Robb on the twenty-first hole. In 1898, at Hoylake, he met Tait in the semifinals, and went down to defeat on the fourth extra hole after Tait had hung on with a succession of his celebrated recoveries. In 1901, when the championship was again held at Hoylake, Low made his way to the final but was beaten on the last hole by Hilton. There was no question that Hilton *was the better shotmaker, but Low, who could putt with the best of them, carried the match to the last green. Bernard Darwin writes about John Low in the book "The Oxford and Cambridge Golfing Society." Edited by Eric Prain and published in 1949, the book is made up of contributions by many of the members of that significant body, which was founded in 1898. Darwin paints a vivid picture of Low, the O. & C.G.S.' first captain: "To John Low, I venture to think, more than to any other man we owe what we like to think is the particular and characteristic atmosphere of the Society. No one could blend in more perfect proportion a proper seriousness with friendliness and conviviality; no one could try harder or relax more completely when the fray was over. Indeed, in using the word 'fray', I am offending against one of his principles, since he once reproved me for writing of a match as a 'fight'; however hard, it must never be more than a game. In his own way, a certain gravity always likely to break into happy little spurts of merriment, he was a great enjoyer and imparted this intense enjoyment not only to his followers, but to our kind hosts."*

The Oxford and Cambridge Golfing Society, whose team was made up of graduates of the two universities, played a testing schedule of matches in the British Isles and now and then abroad. As captain, Low was responsible for the lineup of the team, a task that required considerable tact. A well-to-do man, Low never pushed himself hard as a golfer or as a writer, though he was gifted at both pursuits. His best-known book, "Concerning Golf," which was published in 1903, is made up of articles he had written for Athletic News magazine. The most popular piece in the collection is "How to Go About Buying a Putter," which has been reprinted in many golf anthologies. Darwin reminds us of one other contribution to golf by Low: "Incidentally, the world owes to him rather than to America the graded irons, now universal. He, I believe, first conceived the notion of having one favorite iron head copied in various degrees of loft, though he never carried the system to the extent of the vast armories now deemed essential."

Ross Goodner, who has kindly provided the Afterword, was born in Beaver, in the Oklahoma Panhandle, a good distance from St. Andrews. A great reader, he and a group of friends in that town of fifteen hundred people, discovered P.G. Wodehouse and Damon Runyon when they were in high school, but it wasn't until Goodner entered the University of Oklahoma, in Norman, that he bought his first golf book. Browsing in the college bookstore, he spotted Bernard Darwin's "British Golf" lying on a table amid a miscellaneous array of books on sale at bargain prices. Today, in the

Goodner's library of four thousand books, Ross has a sub-treasury of over five hundred golf books.

Goodner's first job after his graduation from college was as a copy editor for the Daily Oklahoman, *in Oklahoma City. He also covered a few golf tournaments. In 1962, he came East to work as a copy editor for the New York* Times. *He wrote on the side. In 1966, his first book was published: "The 75 Year History of Shinnecock Hills Golf Club". Goodner joined the staff of* Golf *magazine in 1966, and later became its editor. Since 1977, he has been affiliated with* Golf Digest *magazine, and currently serves as Senior Editor. His second book, "Golf's Greatest", was published in 1978. It is made up of biographical sketches of the first thirty-five players and other luminaries inducted into what is today the PGA World Golf Hall of Fame, in Pinehurst, North Carolina. Goodner is currently working on a book which will celebrate the centennial of the official founding in 1893 of the Chicago Golf Club, which that year opened this country's first eighteen-hole course in Belmont, Illinois.*

Herbert Warren Wind

F. G. TAIT

A Record

The profits accruing from the sale of this book will be devoted to the Black Watch Widows' and Orphans' Fund.

yours ever
F. S. Keith

F. G. TAIT

A Record

𝔅eing his 𝔏ife, 𝔏etters, and 𝔊olfing 𝔇iary

JOHN L. LOW

WITH AN INTRODUCTION BY ANDREW LANG

" The good die first,
And those whose hearts are dry as summer dust
Burn to the socket"

𝔏ondon

J. NISBET AND CO., Ltd.

21, BERNERS STREET

INTRODUCTION.

———✦·I·✦———

M R. LOW has invited me to write my
reminiscences of the late Mr. Frederick
Tait. I comply out of affection for his
memory; though, unhappily, my acquaintance
with him was but slight. That, knowing
him so little, and meeting him so rarely as
I did, I yet felt the warmest regard for him,
is a proof of his singularly winning nature.
This proof is, indeed, the most that I have
to offer to a record of his brief life, a life of
real beneficence, for he brought sunshine
wherever he came and a reflection of his
own constitutional happiness.

Our additions to the well-being of the
world rise not so much from what we do as

Introduction

from what we are, and the most ardent friend of his species may do less for it than the man or woman who merely shines upon it with a radiant presence. To do *that* was the unconscious virtue of Freddie. Genius, we know, has been defined as "an infinite capacity for taking pains." It is rather an infinite capacity for producing the right effect without taking any pains. All manner of painstaking is vain, says St. Paul, "if I have not charity," by which he means universal goodwill. That was Freddie's quality: you had only to look at his kind, strong, friendly face, and honest eyes, to see that he was full of goodwill. A child would "lay his hand, unasked, in thine," Lord Tennyson says of his friend: and man, woman, and child had this spontaneous confidence in the friend of so many of us, whose face we shall not see, whose voice we shall not hear again, "till dreams depart and men awake."

He was a young man, a soldier, an athlete, in the fulness of joyous vigour, and I was—at the opposite pole. But, odd as it may seem, I had exactly the same sentiment to

Introduction

Freddie as, when at school, I used to have for a big, kind, football-playing elder kinsboy, if the word may be coined. He was so strong, so good, so jolly, so devoid of conceit, despite his immense popularity, and fame on the Links. It was on the Links at St. Andrews that I generally saw him, and a happy hour it was for many in that wintry little town when we heard that Freddie had come to lighten the murky days of December or January. You saw his broad, sunny smile brightening on you from far away, above his broad shoulders and un-dandified dress. I stop to "gaze across the glooming flats" of the sodden Links, and seem to see again him who is now but the brightest of the shadows that haunt this place of many memories. Bruce and Wallace, Culdees and grim Covenanters, the frail, wandering ghost of the exiled Henry VI., Knox in his vigour and Knox in his decline, the stern Regent Moray and the harmless Lyon King-at-Arms whom he burned; they are all among our haunting shades, with the Queen in her glad youth, and Chastelard, here condemned to die for her, and her

7

Introduction

French valet in like case, and the great Cardinal in his glory, and the anxious eyes of Mariotte Ogilvy, and Montrose in his boyhood—a thousand characters of immortal memory, with the same shroud around them all. But he who died in Africa, glad and kind as he was brave till his latest breath—he, too, will not be forgotten; he it is, next to one other, younger, and as brave and kind and good as he, whom I must remember best and long for most.

It was rarely except on the Links that I saw Freddie. It was my custom, and that of several others, to walk round and watch his play at golf, but I never even saw him compete for the Medal, or in any greater contest than a match over both Links with Andrew Kirkcaldy. We used to make little bets with him, in ordinary matches, that he would not do the round under seventy-eight, or some such figure, and we were apt to lose our half-crowns.

At first, his extraordinary driving was the chief attraction, but he later aimed more at accuracy, and drove much within his powers.

Introduction

I remember his coming into the Club and asking whether it was worth while to measure a drive he had made. He had, in fact, "overpowered" the Heathery Hole, the thirteenth as you come in, on the right-hand course. The drive has been disputed, and I only narrate what I remember. Perhaps my recollection is inaccurate. He was playing behind his brother Willie, and, when the brother and partner had played their second, Freddie's ball flew over their heads, and lighted on the long, narrow table-land which there crosses the Links. Freddie, on approaching the hole, could not find his ball, and, I think, gave up the hole, and then found his ball about "hole-high." The day was of a light frost, brilliantly sunny, and with the faintest flicker of air, no breeze. I remember seeing Mr. Tait measuring the distance to the place where the ball was found, and I think the whole extent was about 350 yards, the "carry" being about 250 yards. Probably there is a more authentic record than my memory supplies.

Freddie became, as is well known, a master in every department of golf. He

Introduction

was not very careful, and usually smoked,
laying down his briar-root pipe on the grass
when he was making a stroke. His resource was wonderful. I remember his
making a beautiful approach with one foot
in and one out of a steep bunker, while
his ball trembled on a blade of grass in
the sand on the brink. Perhaps the last
time I ever saw him, his ball lay on thin
ice in the Scholar's Bunker. He walked in
over the boots, for the ice was a mere film,
and flicked his ball on to the green, over
the slight declivity which stops so many
an approach.

The best round I ever saw him do
was 72 : he was playing, I think, with Tom
Morris and Mr. Hull. The record previously was 73, and though he might have
been down in 71, he left himself an awkward shortish putt, on a difficult sticky
green, for 72. When he had holed out
he said, "That putt took a year off my
life": so great was the nervous tension.

These are trivial anecdotes. One day
his game illustrated the feebleness of human

Introduction

evidence. He was playing in the Monthly
Handicap, and winning easily. But at the
hole beside the burn, coming in, he putted
to run up a hill, and roll back to the
hole. Forgetting that this was a solemn
occasion, he replaced his ball, played
his putt over again, and holed. Several
people were looking on, and someone said
that the putt was not orthodox. Then
arose a dispute as to what he had done.
A spectator, a townsman unknown to me,
maintained with so much conviction that
the putt was all right, that neither Tom
Morris nor myself could venture to say
exactly what had happened. Our critical
memories were submerged in that of the
earnest townsman. However, Freddie remembered, and explained — and lost the
handicap. In weighing historical evidence
as to more important events, one is occasionally reminded of this little incident.

One had no special forebodings when
Freddie said good-bye, and went to take his
part in the unhappy war. When the bitter
news came of Magersfontein, it was currently
reported in St. Andrews that Freddie had

fallen. That element of the gloom was presently dissipated, and no calamity could have been less expected than the newspaper reports of his death. There was no official news for several days, and St. Andrews had begun to hope again, when the newspaper correspondents mentioned particulars which hardly admitted of doubt. We had supposed that his Magersfontein wound would have made it impossible for him to take part in a rapid march. Then the worst was confirmed beyond doubt, and these days of anxiety were over.

Hundreds of the finest young men, of both parties, have fallen, and the end no man foresees. All of these, in every rank, had friends to whom they were as dear as Freddie was to us. But none had more friends than he : who was so widely known, and, wherever he was known, was loved. His memory does not rest on his athletic prowess. Dozens of lads are acclaimed by the world of play, but he would have been as much endeared to those who knew him, if he had never handled a club. His golf merely made him known to a larger circle. I never heard a word

Introduction

said against him, except a solitary complaint that, in the lightness of his heart, he played pibrochs round the drowsy town at the midnight hour. What would we not give to hear his pipes again ? For himself, a soldier's death, sudden and painless, was not the worst of fortunes. His memory lives among the glories of the Black Watch.

BEATI MORTUI QUI MORIUNTUR IN DOMINO.

A. LANG.

ALLEYNE HOUSE,
    ST. ANDREWS,
        December 3, 1900.

AUTHOR'S PREFACE.

THE publication of this Memoir has only been rendered possible by the kind co-operation of Lieutenant Tait's family. I acknowledge most gratefully the assistance they have given to me and the graciousness with which they have done everything in their power to help my efforts. To Mr. A. G. Tait I am especially indebted. He has been my co-worker throughout, supplying me with information and furthering in every way the work I have undertaken.

I acknowledge also the kindness of Mr. H. H. House of Malvern College, who revised my proofs.

Some of the photographs reproduced have come into my possession without the names of the artists who produced them; I regret therefore that I am unable to thank them personally for their work.

I am indebted to Mr. Walter Stone for his excellent photo, which I have used as the frontispiece of this book, and to Mr. W. Dod and Mr. Buchardt for the snapshots they have allowed me to use. Mr. Leicester Harmsworth and Mr. Garden Smith have greatly assisted me in matters of reference. To everyone who has helped me I tender my grateful thanks.

J. L. L.

St. John's, Surrey.
October 1900.

15

CHAPTER I.

INTRODUCTORY.

I F any excuse be required for this attempt
to put on record some of the events of
the life of Lieutenant F. G. Tait, it must
be sought for in the expediency, nay, almost
the necessity, of the case.

Few lives so short have been followed
with such interest by so large a circle of
friends and admirers—the story of Scottish
Sport contains no more familiar name, the
tradition of Scottish Arms no braver son.

The wide-spread interest which centred
round him, and will continue to centre round
him, as long as the national game of golf is
played, made it necessary that a Record of
his feats should be published as a source of
reference for golfers of the present and the
future.

Lieutenant Tait was however more than
a famous golfer; his golf was indeed but

F. G. Tait

the medium which brought so many within
the reach and influence of his charming
personality.

In writing a memoir of one so recently
dead, the writer is apt to be influenced by
a fictitious charity which may endanger, and
finally banish truth, turning what should
have been biography into mere eulogy. The
maxim " De mortuis nil nisi bonum," if
carried out to the full, would make history
impossible. Appreciating this fact I will try
before everything in this sketch to be true;
and the nearer the truth the more pleasant
will the portrait be.

I am fully conscious also that I write
for two quite different classes of readers,
namely, Tait's personal friends—and they
are many—and secondly, those who followed
his career with interest from a less intimate
standpoint. It is for the first of these classes
that I shall primarily write, and it is from
them that I shall expect most sympathy and
indulgence. They will forgive what is poor
and unworthy, knowing that all has been
attempted only with the one idea of pre-
serving a memory which we mutually esteem.
The smaller details of schoolboy and soldier
life will hardly interest the general reader,
but he will, I trust, pardon their inclusion
for the sake of those who may care to dwell
on them.

A Record

Lieutenant Tait's life was not one of any very stirring incident. It was the life, the young life, of a soldier serving in this country until called upon for—or, rather, volunteering for—service in South Africa; yet there was no one better known or more liked in Scotland, and this fact is in itself significant, for it shows the power that an amiable personality, coupled with honesty and simplicity of character, may, almost unconsciously, wield over many men. It is an influence too subtle to be defined, yet too strong and certain to be gainsaid.

This power and influence Tait possessed, and it makes him of interest altogether apart from his brilliant achievements as a golfer.

In the following pages an endeavour will be made to sketch his short life, and also to give in some detail a record of his greater athletic feats.

In reading those letters of Tait's which I have been able to collect, I have at times experienced a feeling of vividness with regard to him which nothing else could have given. Regarding myself as only one of many who would enjoy this sense of closer recollection I will publish those letters which seem most to reflect him to us. They are not put forth as the best of his literary efforts, but rather with a view to giving some echo of his life and character.

F. G. Tait

If this simple record aids in any way to keep fresh the memory of a brave, light-hearted manly soul in the minds of those who knew him, or to suggest something of his worth to the less favoured, these pages will still be but a small tribute to a much-loved friend..

A Record

CHAPTER II.

——◆◆◆——

EARLY DAYS.

Professor Tait, whose father was private secretary to the Duke of Buccleuch, was born at Dalkeith in 1831, and educated at the Academy and University of Edinburgh.

After leaving Edinburgh he proceeded to Cambridge, where he took the highest honours that scholarship could achieve, graduating as Senior Wrangler and First Smith's Prizeman. In 1852 he was elected a Fellow of his college, Peterhouse, and in 1854 was appointed Professor of Mathematics at Queen's College, Belfast, where he remained until 1860, when he was elected to the chair of Natural Philosophy at his old Edinburgh home.

Throughout his forty years of Edinburgh work, Professor Tait has, during the times of university vacation, found such congenial

F. G. Tait

recreation on the links of St. Andrews that his life has become more and more bound up with the sister university town. A man of many interests, with a keen insight into human character, and an intense delight in things humorous, he found in golfers and their game much to amuse and interest him. The philosophy or lack of philosophy of the players he played with, or watched, supplied the Professor with a feast of fun, and even the ball as it was lashed through the air or along the ground was for him no mere toy, but a projectile whose antics had meaning, a meaning indeed worthy of study and discovery.

Added to this the air of St. Andrews was especially suited to his health, and acted as a tonic after the long work of the Edinburgh Session. Thus it was that Professor Tait went to St. Andrews, and growing to love the place the better as years went on, he handed on this love to his children.

FREDERICK GUTHRIE TAIT was the third son of Professor Tait, and was born in Edinburgh on the 11th January 1870. During the winter months, when the University was in residence, the Tait family lived in George Square, Edinburgh. The square encloses a quaint old garden, common to the houses surrounding it, and this garden is used as the pleasure ground of the dwellers in the

A Record

square, and the playground of their children. Here then in winter, and on the sands at St. Andrews in summer, young Freddie disported himself, no doubt much after the simple manner of folks of very tender years. In the George Square garden there are many trees, dark and naked indeed in winter, but still trees, and as such dear to children. Little boys do not look upon trees from an æsthetic point of view—as things to be gazed at and admired; they regard them rather as things to be climbed, and as suitable ground-work for the carving of names and initials.

Freddie was boyish in the best and manliest sense of the word, and it follows, therefore, that there were few trees in that garden he did not climb, few smooth-barked ones which did not bear his name.

One of his early playmates—now resident in Monte Video—writes of those early days at George Square as follows :—

Freddie and I were constant companions, and I much regret that I cannot give you any reminiscences of him worth publishing. Our chief amusement when together was erecting mud forts in the gardens and then bombarding them with small cannon, and afterwards blowing them up with underground mines. We also delighted in playing tricks on the gardener. Freddie was a most popular boy, and was greatly respected by the others on account of having his name cut on more trees in the square than any other boy.

F. G. Tait

Here indeed we have all the attributes of a youthful hero and boy leader. What boy could resist following the owner of cannon, especially when he was armed also with a reputation for tree-climbing and every form of boy-delighting mischief ? But most thrilling of all must have been the honour of being chosen to join in a gardener-baiting expedition under such a leader. On these occasions the command is not entrusted lightly to anyone anxious to take it. The affair is of too much moment for a luck-and-pluck policy, and the chance of capture and the strong right hand of the horticulturist are not risks to be faced without trepidation. That Freddie was the chosen leader in all such escapades I have heard from several sources, and this pre-eminence must have been thrust upon him ; for any desire to push himself forward was utterly foreign to his character.

At St. Andrews, and at the age of five, Freddie laid down the wooden spade and the sand-bucket, and took up in their place a little club of wood. This tiny weapon had but little form and no lead ; still it was the rude forefather of clubs destined in the same hands to do mighty deeds in after years. Freddie had however even before this early date taken an interest in golf *balls*, if not in golf *clubs*. An elder brother of his had

" FREDDIE."

A Record

noticed that his stock of balls was gradually diminishing day by day. No explanation could be suggested, and no clue as to the culprit discovered. One day however it was noticed, when mention of the lost balls was made in the course of conversation, that a look of superior knowledge and intelligence came over little Freddie's countenance. Freddie had given himself away and was at once placed under *surveillance*. Soon after he was seen wending his way to the garden, bearing a ball in each hand ; he was watched, and caught in the act of carefully burying them. Freddie was not however working after the fashion of our canine friends,—planting the balls in a place of security that at his coming again he might find them safe and sound ; his scheme involved a more advanced sense of economic law. He was moreover acting to some extent on the strength of a fact he had experience of, only he was unaware that this fact was incapable of universal application. He had seen the gardener both planting potatoes and reaping his harvest and noted the multiplication ; so the youthful culprit turned out after all to be, not an embryo burglar, but only an experimental philosopher.

From golf on the sands with a leadless club Freddie advanced in his golfing career, until, at the age of seven, he began to play on the long links with children of his own

F. G. Tait

age. Practising from early in the day until dusk, he soon improved under the tuition of his father, who was wont to be on the links long before the breakfast hour. Probably owing to his father's advice, Freddie learned to putt with a cleek, and those who remember the Professor's putting in those days will easily understand the reason of the pupil's early success.

Freddie's high spirits frequently led him into mischief, but mischief of a more or less harmless nature.

One Sunday—whether because the subject of the discourse was beyond his grasp, or because his mind on this particular day desired lighter and more humorous food, I cannot say—Freddie laughed, and that aloud, just at the time when a boy of eight years old is expected to be listening calmly and attentively to the ecclesiastical word of advice. The late Master of Peterhouse, Dr. Porter, was at the time a guest at Professor Tait's house. At his instigation poor Freddie was made the object of a conspiracy of terror. A plot was laid for him, and owing to his tender years he fell into the midst of it. Next morning's post brought the culprit two letters—the first from Mr. Tuttiett, the rector of the church in which the offence had been committed, and the second from no less a person than the late

A Record

Dr. Charles Wordsworth, the Bishop of St. Andrews. The letters were of course forgeries, and had been written by some friends, guests of the Taits. Freddie was young and unsuspecting, and the epistles completely deceived him and threw him into a state of no small consternation. Here is the first of the terror-striking letters.

Monday,
26th August, 1878.

My dear Sir,

It was with inexpressible pain that I observed your irreverent conduct in my church on Sunday evening last. I intend calling a vestry meeting to-morrow at noon, that we may decide what steps it will be necessary to take in the matter.

I remain,
Yours faithfully,
LAURENCE TUTTIETT.

P.S.—May I suggest that a handsome donation on your part towards the Church Cushion and Hassock Fund might possibly improve your position with the vestry?

P.P.S.—Should you care to avail yourself of the friendly hint contained in my postcript, it might be as well to send your contribution before noon to-morrow.

L.T.

Now Mr. Tuttiett was the meekest of men, and this letter alone would not perhaps have had sufficient effect on the interrupter of sermons. Far otherwise was it with the

F. G. Tait

second missive, for Dr. Wordsworth, though there was nothing but charity and goodwill to men in his character, had so commanding and majestic an appearance and was even at that time so powerful and athletic a man, that the threat of corporal punishment at such hands was enough to frighten the lad indeed. Thus ran his letter :—

Bishopshall,
Monday,
26th August, 1878.

Sir,

As I was approaching the sixteenth head of my discourse on Sunday evening, my attention was arrested by an unseemly tittering proceeding from a pew in front of me. I have since ascertained that you are the delinquent, and I beg to inform you that I shall, on the first opportunity that presents itself, administer *personal chastisement* with a *very thick stick,* that invariably accompanies me when I take my walks abroad.

I remain,
Yours episcopally,
CHARLES WORDSWORTH,
Bishop of St. Andrews.

Freddie was of high spirit and hated to be corrected, and his temperament did not brook interference. Still, there was the big stick and the strong arm of ecclesiastical authority to be reckoned with, so in his extremity he sought counsel of his friends, who, while accentuating his fears by their

A Record

appearance of sincerity, advised him to write to the bishop a letter of apology. This Freddie did, though the letter of course never reached the episcopal eye. Three days of fear and trembling passed, and on the fourth came the following :—

Bishopshall,
30th August, 1878.

Sir,

I beg to acknowledge the receipt of your communication of Tuesday last. For the last three days I have given my best consideration to the appeal for mercy therein contained. I must admit that the penitential spirit in which you have written has done much to mitigate the severity of my feeling towards you, and should your present disposition continue, there is a probability that you may yet escape the condign punishment of your offence. I must however warn you that, should you repeat your misconduct, you will most certainly become acquainted with a *very* MUCH THICKER stick than the one referred to in my first letter. I have only to state in conclusion that I shall keep my eye well fixed next Sunday morning on a certain pew in the side aisle.

I remain,
Yours episcopally,
CHARLES WORDSWORTH,
Bishop of St. Andrews.

The Bishop had by this time been told of the jest, and thoroughly entered into the spirit of the fun. He indeed asked if he

F. G. Tait

could do anything to help the conspirators,
and remarked to one of the forgers, "Shall
I frown on the lad if I meet him."

His kindly letter however set Freddie's
mind at ease, for it was now no longer necessary for him to watch with fearful eye for
Dr. Wordsworth with his rod of chastisement
in hand. I cannot say if there was any very
lasting improvement in Freddie's conduct,
but that he was truly grateful to the supposed
leniency of the prelate is proved by the following extract from his will, written shortly after
the events just described :—

I leave my ring to the Bishop of St. Andrews,
in grateful remembrance of his kindness to his
penitent son in 1878.

Freddie commenced at a very early age
to make use of the divine weed, and many of
his contemporaries remember, with more
vividness than pleasure, the circumstances of
their failure to keep pace with him in the
practice of the narcotic habit. He was
always a great smoker, and at one time never
had a pipe out of his mouth when playing
golf. During the last two or three years of
his life he gave up, to a great extent, the
custom of smoking while playing, though I
do not know if his total consumption of
tobacco really decreased.

After having been some time at a pre-
paratory school Freddie went to the Edin-

A Record

burgh Academy in the winter of 1881. His class master was the late James Carmichael, and under his charge he remained for two years, another great athlete, H. J. Stevenson, being among the instructed ones.

Although Freddie never won the class medal, he always received his share of praise from his master, while his class-mates held him in high honour as leader in everything which was dear to the schoolboy love of adventure. His interest in the Academy was sustained throughout his career, and one of the very last things he did before sailing for South Africa was to wire to Edinburgh to ascertain how the Old Boys' football club had fared in their match with the Watsonians.

It is the usual custom at the Academy for each class to form itself into a club, which meets once a year to discuss old days and a dinner together. Many of the boys, years after they have left school, travel from all parts of the country in order to be present at this function. Each year a new chairman is elected, and in January, 1900, Freddie's turn would have come to take the seat of honour. The call to arms came however and he was unable to undertake the duties, but he wrote to say that all being well he hoped to be present at the next meeting in January 1901, when he would be able to give his old friends his experiences of South Africa. It is one of the sad but necessary features of such gatherings that time makes gaps in every circle, and the new faces can never take the place of the old; Freddie's bright face and cheery laugh will no more bring joy to the social board, but his memory will be long cherished by his old Academy schoolfellows.

Freddie from his earliest days was intensely keen on all out-door sports, and during his first year at the Academy he played with much pride in the 7th XV. and the 8th XI.

In the spring of the years 1882 and 1883 Freddie took part in the golf competition for Academy boys under 15 years of age. The play was one round of Musselburgh Links, and he made the following scores—54 in 1882 and 61 in 1883. In the former year Freddie was successful in gaining the second prize—probably his first golfing victory.*

He left the school while still a very little boy, and of course never received his football or cricket colours, but his loyalty to the old place he never lost, and in later years when at Edinburgh University, or later still, when quartered with the Black Watch at the Castle, he was wont to express the greatest satisfaction when the Academy had beaten any of their formidable school rivals.

---

* I am indebted to his "caddie," Mr. G. H. Lindsay, who was one of Freddie's class fellows, for this interesting record.

A Record

At St. Andrews Freddie early made the acquaintance of the sea, and soon became an expert swimmer. His bathing-place was of course at the far famed " step rock," where the water, varying from shallow to deep, is suitable for all classes of bathers. Freddie was not long in making good his claim to be allowed to bathe on the " deep side," and his joy was great when he at last swam across the " step," a distance of some 100 yards, and felt himself for the future master of the situation.

In the summer of 1882 Freddie is seen in a new light; for, although his Diary with details of all his matches does not commence until 1884, still in this summer he first began his habit of noting down his scores. The boys he played with were Norman Playfair (now Captain in the King's Own Scottish Borderers), John Stewart (now Captain Stewart), and Ernley Blackwell, and they no doubt proved worthy antagonists. Scores written on old envelopes, with the remark, " Round in 105; played very fairly," or " Round in 110; not at my best," are still extant, and are indicative of his early methodical habits. When a stroke might have been saved, he makes a note of the circumstances for future guidance. It was in this year 1882 that he first succeeded in going round under 100, and his satisfaction at this

F. G. Tait

feat is proved by the remark, " Round in 98 ;
played splendidly." His style in those days
was extremely neat, and many good judges saw
a brilliant career before him. Mr. Macfie was,
I fancy, the first really great player he played
with, but Freddie was of course at that time
in receipt of very liberal odds.

Playing constantly under the able tuition
of an elder brother, himself a crack player,
and in practice always playing seriously, it is
little wonder that he turned out to be the
brilliant player of later years. Freddie began
to keep an account of his matches in 1884,
and never departed from this habit up to
the end, his last match of importance being
against Mr. John Ball at St. Anne's, shortly
before he sailed for South Africa.

What I have said about his early play
will be sufficient to justify the remark which
Tait made in later years to the Czar of
Russia, when that august personage ques-
tioned him about his golf : " *I took to it seriously
when I was eight years old.*"

"ALEC" AND "FREDDIE."

A Record

CHAPTER III.

———◆◆———

SEDBERGH.

May 1883 — December 1886.

MAINLY on the advice of Bishop Sand-
ford, at that time rector of St. John's,
Edinburgh, and a great friend of the Tait
family, Freddie was sent to Sedbergh School
in the May Term of 1883.

Schoolboy life at any of the large Public
Schools of England is a record of work and
play, differing but slightly for one boy or
another. The boys being thrown by the nature
of school discipline and the system of school
routine into clubs and classes, have in a
measure to sink their own individuality and
become immersed in the whole life of the
school. From *their* point of view, indeed,
there are incidents and experiences of great
moment ; for it is just when things are actual
and present that they look big.

Time changes the perspective, and afterwards on looking back one day seems to have
been much the same as another, and we
cannot understand why we could really have

F. G. Tait

thought it important whether we played foot-ball for our house or not, or whether our report read "conduct good" or "conduct inclined to be rowdy."

But small details, even when, as must needs be, they are of a common-place nature, are often of interest when they concern one whose memory we hold dear. At the risk of appearing to some to be trivial, I will tell some of these little things.

Freddie's life at Sedbergh was simply that of a happy schoolboy doing his best at work and at games, for school or house. It is fourteen years since he left the Yorkshire school, and masters and old boys remember him as a bright, manly boy, keen at work and play, fresh of face and strong of limb, a fine example of what the old school could produce.

At the end of his first year, Mr. Mackie, his house-master, wrote: "He is a thoroughly jolly boy, with any amount of backbone developing itself."

Freddie had no great liking for the study of the dead languages, Greek, indeed, being quite annoying to him. "Greek is awful muck; I do not think I shall ever be able to do it," he writes to his brother Alec in his second term, and he did not subsequently change his mind in favour of the ancient authors.

A Record

The small pleasures of school life were however his, and he enjoyed them when they came to him, as in the shape of a present of eggs from his aunt. " I shall have grand breakfasts and teas now for a long time with your eggs," was his way of expressing his thanks—words which showed an anticipatory pleasure in a simple, but thoroughly excellent and satisfactory form of enjoyment.

His whole letter is so characteristic that I give it in full :—

Sedbergh,
9 *March*, 1884.

My dear Aunt Jane,

The eggs came yesterday, and there was only one a little bit broken. I am glad to hear that you thought my report was good. What does the governor think of it ? Our house played Hart's house on Wednesday, and licked them by one goal and four tries to nothing. The team was barring the fellows in the First Fifteen in each house. I had one place kick, and kicked a goal—the only one we got, because the wind was rather strong, and it was difficult to kick straight.

I hope you are well. I shall have grand breakfasts and teas now for a long time with your eggs. Did you get the postcard ? It is a very nice day ; I will have a jolly walk this afternoon from 2 till 4.30. Tell Edith to be quick with the patterns * ; if she wants to get a good one, get 283 ; it is a pipe-rack ; it will do very well for the Bishop. I

---

* The patterns referred to were for fretsaw work.

F. G. Tait

was at tea with Mr. Quick, the minister here—he asks out four boys out of each house at a time. We had a very good tea.

So with love to all,
Yours affectionately,
F. G. Tait.

Thanks very much for the eggs. They are a very welcome present.

His mind was already set firmly on his future profession, which he was keenly anxious to enter upon as soon as possible. Writing to his mother in April, 1884, he bemoans the fact that he is not yet full enough of years to enter the Army. " I wish I was about four years older, and I could easily get into the Army, now that there is going to be a war with Russia." Britain's time for fighting, like Freddie's, was however not yet come, and the schoolboy had to wait many years before he could prove to the full in his country's cause the " good backbone " which was in him.

In the same month—April, 1884—an incident occurred which in many ways was the most significant in his school career. It showed Freddie, perhaps for the first time in his life, brought face to face with a great crisis, suddenly called upon to do the right thing—to act, in short, the man's part. While on a walk in the Yorkshire Fells he saved a schoolfellow named Craggs from

A Record

drowning, and showed exceptional presence of mind and courage. The adventure took place near the junction of the Rawthey and the Dee, some two miles from the school; the spot is well known to Sedbergh boys as "Lord's Dub." I have never heard Tait mention the incident, and during his life he would not have permitted the facts to have been published; but now he can be allowed to tell the story in his simple schoolboy way, just as he told it in a letter to his brother at the time :—

Last Sunday after I had written my letter, D——and I were out for a walk and we went to cross the river at a place where it was about 6 feet across and it was between two rocks about 6 feet above the level of the water, and all the big river was crowded into the little place. Of course the current was very strong and D—— and I jumped across and got across all right. There was another fellow in our house who was there and thought he would try it, so he jumped across and his foot slipped, and down he went with the waterfall and he went right under the water. As the place is about 10 feet deep and the waterfall pressing the water down from the top, he stayed under a good long time. So as soon as D—— saw it, he began to shout like anything for help, and as there was nobody there it was of no good, so I stood still and waited till he came up, and before I could get at him down he went again, but the next time when he came up I climbed down the rock to the side of the water just below the fall, and when he came up the second time I caught hold of his hand and began to lug him out. But he was such a weight that he nearly dragged me in, but I got D—— to take my other hand, and with his help we lugged him out quite insensible, and as he had lost his hat I gave him mine. We had to take him home about a mile and a half, it was very hard; as soon as we got him home we took off all his clothes and put him into bed and went and pulled all the rugs off the other beds and made him warm. Then Mrs. Mackie came up and gave him something hot to take, and he is all better now. . . . The place is a very dangerous place for anyone to cross, even if they can swim, because the rocks go almost straight up from the water. I do not know at all how I got down the side because it is so slippery, a lot of people have been drowned in it—three boys from the school within the last 20 years, and a cart and horse, and two people, and a father and son from Kendal, so the boy Craggs had a lucky escape. Can you find any small brass guns in the house; I tell you where I think there is one, in my tool chest in the press in your room. . . .

It is quite a simple story, and Freddie does not seem to attach any great importance to his brave act, and it would seem, indeed, that "the small brass guns" were uppermost in his mind. That his conduct really showed rare courage and was in every way remarkable on this occasion, I have heard from his master, Mr. Mackie, who regarded Freddie's action as a great one.

A Record

In a letter of thanks written at the time, Mrs. Craggs says :—

The more I think of the gallant rescue of my boy, the more I feel how thankful I ought to be to you. Such presence of mind in anyone so young is seldom called forth. . . .

The whole story is suggestive and indicative of a very marked phase in young Tait's character, and one which developed itself as his years increased. Tait was never quite at his best until he was " cornered "; the bigger the job the better did he do it; he succeeded just at the moment when one would have expected anyone else to fail. In later years as a golfer this was one of his great characteristics, namely, his ability to rise to the occasion; to do a great thing when all looked hopeless; to snatch a victory out of the fire. It was a quality which, had his military career not been cut short, would have helped him to show the courage and resource, if need be, of a Baden-Powell.

Each July Freddie took his prize in Mathematics and French, these were his favourite subjects; Euclid especially seemed to meet with his favour. He was keen to do well in his work, keen especially that the home circle should get a good " report " of him at the term's end. When writing home week by week, he would tell where he stood in his form and what prospects of gaining a prize

F. G. Tait

or getting his remove were before him. Always methodical by nature, he early started to keep a diary, a small book full of little notes as to cricket, work, and items of school news. A new cook came to his house, and Freddie at once started to weigh up her ability by detailing her week's menu. All went well for six days, but on the seventh the report concludes with a dreadful description of the haddocks which she supplied for breakfast, "rotten" being the mildest and least suggestive epithet applied to the fish.

In 1886 he received his First Fifteen colours for football, and earlier in the same year was tried for the Eleven, but failed finally to get a place. His keenness for all games was intense, and he would count the days that had to be lived before the next cricket or football match. When quite a little boy, and not yet playing in the school or house matches, his heroes were taken from the playing fields of Sedbergh. Earliest and chief among these great and almost inaccessible deities was Charles Toppin, who had at that time just left Sedbergh for Cambridge. In Freddie's view, the idea of anyone attempting to play the bowling of so great a man was almost irreligious. Writing to his uncle, Dr. Porter, the late master of Peterhouse, and for many years the popular

A Record

treasurer of the Cambridge University Cricket Club, he says: " See that Toppin gets into the eleven, he can bowl any man in England in four balls." Toppin, of course, got into the eleven, and was in his day one of the best fast bowlers in England. Freddie watched his hero's progress, and after the 'Varsity match of 1885 we find him writing to his brother :—" Cambridge won after all, and Toppin won it *too ;* and he is also playing for the Gentlemen *v* Players at the Oval." There is an air of triumph about this. He seems to say: " I told you that if anyone could win this match *my* man alone could do it." Later on he writes home to say : " Toppin is going to play for the old boys at the end of the term, so we won't get many runs." He was a devoted Sedberghian, and long after he left the school he watched the doings of old Sedberghians in the arena of life or sport with steadfast interest.

Freddie also managed to introduce a little golf into Sedbergh ; at least the appliances were imported. A boy at school had some clubs, so " two golf balls " were asked for from Edinburgh, and duly arrived, together with some " ginger and chocolate " all doubtless welcome. None of these gifts were however destined to last, for the ginger and chocolate met the fate which must always attend such popular visitors at a Public

F. G. Tait

School, and the golf-balls were lost during the first day's play.

Nothing has up till now been said about Freddie's golf during this Sedbergh period. In truth, it has been purposely omitted owing to a desire to keep the golfing side of his life, and especially the greater events of it, separate from his true life-story. It is not, however, possible, nor indeed desirable, for the two stories not to intertwine to some extent. In order to place them in their proper environment, the golfing incidents must find some place in the biographical side of this memoir. Chronological fitness demands this, and true portraiture requires it still more. We must look at Tait with binocular vision if we would get the best view of his life and character.

Were we to represent him as caring for nothing but his work when at school, and with no thought but for his profession when in the army, we should be giving a false picture of the boy and the man.

Tait perhaps even more than most boys, preferred football and cricket to Latin and Greek, and as a soldier he never pretended that a barrack-square parade was always more congenial to him than a day on the links or the moors. His schoolboy chapter would therefore be incomplete without a passing reference to his golf during his later Sedbergh days.

44

A Record

The summer holidays of 1886 were spent at St. Andrews, and Freddie played golf nearly every day. About this time he commenced to keep a record of his matches in a small book suitable for the purpose, and his record for the holidays reads—" Played 89 matches from July 31st till 17th September ; won 50, lost 24, halved 15. Holes won 281, lost 53." At the end of the record of each match it was his custom to make some comment on the play, and these remarks are very candid, and to all appearances just. In his criticisms he does not spare himself, his partner, nor his opponents, but deals out praise and censure with a level hand. In a match against himself, and presumably included among the " halved " rounds, he says, " Played as bad a round as possible ; " and again, " Never played worse, with the exception of a few iron shots."

Freddie includes his opponent when he writes of one match, " The characteristic of the game was the bad play of both." It is to his partner that he alludes when he says " The play of Mr. Blank was feeble in the extreme." In another match when Freddie and his partner won by 12 holes, one of their opponents " sulked and went away four holes from home " ; there is no further record of play with this gentleman—his retirement from the sphere of Tait's golf was final, as well as undignified.

45

F. G. Tait

Some idea as to the strength of his game at this time may be obtained from the fact that with the aid of six shots he could play and beat Mr. A. F. Macfie in two matches played on Aug. 30th, 1886. At the same odds he also defeated Captain W. H. Burn a few days later, but lost to his brother Jack, who conceded Freddie four strokes. Young Tait's better rounds averaged a little above 90, but on one occasion he records a round of 86, probably his best at this period. In matches Freddie at this time played about level with Mr. Norman Playfair, Mr. Heriot, and Mr. Boothby, all afterwards fine players, the last named, indeed, at his best having few superiors.

Enough has been said to determine Tait's golfing status at the end of these Sedbergh days, enough to enable us to watch from this point onwards the progress of his play.

In December, 1886, Freddie said farewell to Sedbergh. He was in the Fifth Form, and, though always a steady worker, had not shown any exceptional ability as a scholar. His school life had been a happy one. Frankness of disposition and joviality of temperament—the latter often showing itself in the form of practical jokes and little schoolboy escapades, and the whole toned and influenced by an intense love of home and a great affection for his parents—form the leading features of his character at this

A Record

time. Freddie's nature was always affec-
tionate, and this was probably the keynote
of his subsequent popularity. He seemed to
like most people with whom he came into contact—to see the good in them, to understand
the weaker side as well—and as a result
of this amiable view of life his acquaint-
ances, as well as his friends, were irresistibly
drawn to him. He left his school to enter
upon his bigger life without an enemy, and
already with a crowd of friends.

Behind and above a certain seat in the
dining-hall of Mr. Mackie's house at Sedbergh hang two photographs. The seat was
Freddie's, and the one picture represents him
as he was in his early Sedbergh schooldays,
with that bright, almost mischievous look
which all Old Sedberghians of his time will
remember. The other photograph is taken
some fifteen years later; it is the picture of
the young soldier, ready to start for the
Front. But the two are almost the same in
feature and expression, for in the man no
charm of youth has disappeared; there has
been no change, only development. Tait
was indeed still a Sedbergh boy in spirit,
fresh and young and strong, rejoicing in
to-day and planning some sport for to-
morrow, when he entered on his life's last
term of service for school, for country, and
for Empire, in South Africa.

F. G. Tait

CHAPTER IV.

EDINBURGH AND SANDHURST.

1887-1900.

THE first six months of 1887 Tait spent at Blackheath, where he "coached" with a view to entering Sandhurst, but was unsuccessful in the examination, which was held in July. It was then determined that he should enter the Army as a University candidate, and he accordingly went to Edinburgh University in October.

From July to October the Tait family were at St. Andrews, and from a golfing point of view the months are interesting, as showing a marked improvement in Freddie's game. He is now able to play Mr. Macfie at the reduced odds of four shots, and he plays his brother Jack on even terms, and scores his first victory over him. The elder brother however took a terrible revenge on his youthful opponent a few days later, when he beat

[*Photo by Hill & Saunders.*

F. G. TAIT AS A SANDHURST CADET.

A Record

him by a pocketful of holes. His matches, as was the good habit in those days, were mostly foursomes, and he had the advantage of playing more than once against Jamie Anderson, probably the finest of all iron players. " Anderson played beautifully," Tait writes in his notebook, and of the afternoon round he says, " Jamie Anderson played even better than in the morning." His influence on Freddie's game must have been beneficial, though it is to other sources that we must look for the development of Tait's style ; but as the place for such discussion is not here, we will leave it to its proper place and follow him to Edinburgh.

To enter Sandhurst as a University candidate from Edinburgh, it was necessary to pass the " Examination of Candidates for the Army." The subjects which Tait took up were Mathematics, English Literature, and Latin. Mathematics and English Literature he passed in March, 1888, and in October completed his preliminary examination by passing in Latin.

Tait enjoyed his Edinburgh days, and entered into the full life of the University with great enthusiasm. He joined the University Company of the Queen's Edinburgh Volunteers, and in July, 1888, he went to " camp out " with them at Earlscraig, near Elie. He naturally became a member of the

F. G. Tait

University Golf Club, and was more or less successful in prize-winning, gaining the gold medal of the club at North Berwick in July, 1889. Among the best-known of his Edinburgh friends were Mr. Ian McIntyre, Mr. H. J. Stevenson, and Mr. James Currie. Mr. James Currie has recently been appointed principal of the new Khartoum College, and Mr. Stevenson and Mr. McIntyre are household names wherever Rugby football is played.

With Mr. Ian McIntyre he entered *con amore* into all sports, from cricket to rat-catching. Writing of Tait's University days, Mr. McIntyre says :—

The recollection of the individual days and hours that I spent with Freddie at the University is indistinct, but the nett result was a strong and sure affection for him, which only grew the stronger and more sure the more I saw of him.

We see, then, the same impression left at the University which was left at school—the same affection gained, the same power of attraction shown. It is the dominant *motif* of a life which was not without much music in it ; it is a *motif* which we shall find increasing in power throughout each scene.

In 1888 Tait played a lot of golf; more than 120 matches are recorded in his match-book. On July 31st we find the record of a match with Mr. Norman Playfair, which Tait

A Record

lost by 7 :—" Driving very poor. Put a ball through a man's hat and had to pay 5*s*." In the afternoon, however, Tait seems to have kept the line better, for he beat his opponent by 5 holes, and no further casualties are reported. The moment Freddie made the almost fatal shot just recorded Norman Playfair shouted out—" You've got him "— and so he had. Freddie was somewhat annoyed at having to part with the five shillings, and took that king of kindly counsellors Old Tom into his confidence in the hope that he would gain from his old friend some consolation. But Tom could not be persuaded that Freddie was the injured party; his thought was rather one of gladness that the feat had been accomplished without any *real* injury. He saw that Freddie's driving needed more " control," so he replied : " Ah, Master Freddie, ye may be vera thankful that it's only a hat and no an oak coffin ye hae to pay for."

It has been recorded of Tait that :—

During his boyhood, when he came over to St. Andrews for the holidays, he was regarded by contemporary youngsters as a suitable object of the hero-worship often characteristic of that age. It is narrated by some of these, with sentiments of befitting reverence, how he was the hero of three remarkable exploits in the course of one day, to wit,

F. G. Tait

firstly, how he drove a ball through a man's hat ; secondly, how he drove a long iron shot up to the sixth hole green—how the ball pitched in the hole and remained there ; thirdly, how, having lost a knife while pottering about in the sands in the morning, he went down late in the day, when the tide was up, waded about, and, feeling something with his foot, discovered that the knife had got inserted between two of his toes.

It seems almost a pity to spoil so good a story by being hypercritical, and to wrench the tale from the realms of romantic tradition only to place it in the cold light of history. But lest there be some who doubt the facts as presented to them in hearsay form, let them know of a truth that these things were so. I have not the details of the knife incident, but have already set forth the facts of the punctured hat adventure, and trust that they are circumstantial enough to put to the blush all doubters.

Of the third feat we have abundant proof as to date and circumstances. Tait was playing with Mr. Macfie on August 2nd, 1888, and his note on the match is as follows—

A fine match all through. F. G. T., round in 86. Out, 5 6 5 6 4 3 6 3 4=42. In, 4 3 5 5 6 5 6 5 5=44. Total, 86. Remember 6th hole ! A full iron fell into hole and stuck. Extraordinary.

We might add with our old friend the schoolmaster, " Prodigious ! " The evidence

A Record

therefore goes to show that these feats *were* accomplished, though not on the same day, nor when Tait was a schoolboy, but such discrepancies, apologists would tell us only prove the truth of the narrative ; in this case, however, no proof is needed. The match just recorded has something more of interest in it than the incident at the sixth hole. It was, I believe, the first time that Tait played Mr. Macfie on level terms, and on this occasion he halved the morning round and gained the second round by one hole. Mr. Macfie had however just very slightly the best of it in subsequent matches during this year. The two played many matches together from the time when Tait received his six strokes, until, as Mr. Everard says, " the odds of a third became a vanishing quantity so far as Mr. Macfie was concerned, or for that matter anybody else." Though Tait differed almost entirely in style from Mr. Macfie, we are inclined to think that he learned something of his grace and accuracy of hitting from the latter's beautiful play.

After the autumn spent in St. Andrews, and his subsequent success in his October examination, Tait, toward the end of the year, proceeded to Rouen, where he studied French for six months. He boarded with a French family in the old cathedral city and enjoyed the companionship of Mr. A. S. Wingate, and

F. G. Tait

Mr. Arthur Houston, now in the Indian Staff Corps, who were also studying with a view to the Sandhurst examination. Mr. Wingate afterwards joined the Gordon Highlanders, and was killed on the fatal day of Magersfontein.

Writing in February to his aunt, Mrs. ——, from Rouen, Tait gives some description of his impressions of the place.

I thought perhaps you might like to hear a little about the place. I don't know whether you have been to Rouen or not, but at any rate I will give you a short description of it. It is a very interesting town, for many reasons. All the churches are splendid, and the cathedral is magnificent. The spire of the cathedral is made of iron, and you can see all round about when you are going up—not like most spires, where you are almost in total darkness all the time. The height of the spire is 450 feet. The river runs through the middle of the town. There is a good deal of shipping here, and large vessels can come up as far as Rouen. Sunday is a great day here; everyone is out on the streets or in the *cafés*. It is needless to say that they are not strict Sabbatarians here; in fact, it is the usual thing to go to the theatre or play cards in the evening. The family I am with, however, are a little more strict. They always go once to church, and very seldom go to the theatre on Sunday; they play cards on Sunday, but not with us. The roads about Rouen are rather pretty, with trees on each side like an avenue, and absolutely straight. The family here certainly try their best to make you learn French.

A Record

The old lady sometimes is exceedingly funny, and has some very amusing stories about the Prussians. The Prussians, as you no doubt know, captured Rouen in the late war, and stayed there for about five months, during which time the inhabitants had to supply them with food. According to the old lady's account, the first night the Prussians arrived they turned her out of bed, and made her run about the house all night to bring them things to eat. Each Prussian arrived with about four drawing-room clocks, and various other articles which he had stolen. The Prussians, on the whole, seem to have had a very good time of it at Rouen; they lived like kings, broke into the cellars, smashed the furniture, played on the pianos, danced and sang all night. This is Madame's version, but I think it might be better not to believe quite the whole of it.

I had a most amusing letter from Alec the other day, written in a style which equalled Macaulay.' He dwelt at length on the happy days of our childhood, and on the manly sports at which we used to play together, etc.

Yours affectionately,
F. G. Tait.

P.S.—Thanks for present.

Writing a little later (February 25th) to his mother, he is principally concerned with his work for the Sandhurst examination.

My Dear Mother,

I got your letter all right; the book arrived on Friday. I think you are right about living with Jack, as I will have his help in the evenings. The examination begins on the 21st of June, and that

leaves eight weeks four days from the 23rd of April.
I think the eight weeks will be sufficient to
strengthen my Latin and Mathematics. I shall be
very glad to come up for a few days to Edinburgh.
I shall be delighted to see Fred Paton and show him
over the place.

I don't know what my expenses will be ; send me
money, and I will be careful of it. The special
period of History is not the whole of that book, but
there is an ordinary paper set as well, which comprises all English History. I have read very carefully from Henry VII. to James II., which is a
period as large as the one you sent me—about 700
pages. The Seine has overflown, and there is a
river running down the middle of the streets.

Yours affectionately,
F. G. Tait.

In June 1889 Tait went up for his examination, and on August 6th he received notice
that he had passed, being placed fifth among
the University candidates.

During July and August Tait was playing
every day at St. Andrews, and his golf had
improved some three or four shots as compared with the previous summer's work. Mr.
Everard, who had previously given him odds,
now finds it hard work to cope with Freddie
on even terms, and indeed out of about sixty
matches which he played, the only player
able to record a victory was Mr. D. I. Lamb,
who, on two occasions, was able to lower the
colours of the all-conquering young golfer.

A Record

Mr. Lamb was just at that time at his very best, and quite one of the most brilliant of amateur players.

In this year, 1889, the average for the four scratch medals of the Royal and Ancient Club was just under 90, and as Tait was doing rounds of from 81 to 90 (often 85 and 83), he was already quite in the first rank.

Tait went to Sandhurst in September 1889, and remained there until he passed out with special honours in riding and military administration in July 1890. Writing to Mrs. Tait on his arrival, he describes his first impressions of the place.

I suppose you know that Lindsay and I dined with Mr. —— at the Palace Hotel. The train to Edinburgh was an hour late, and the engine which was intended to take the train from Granton to Edinburgh was unable to get up the slope near Abbeyhill; however, with the help of another we succeeded in reaching Edinburgh. As Lindsay and I had each a considerable amount of luggage, especially Lindsay, we lost another quarter of an hour in getting it. We met Mr. —— at the Caledonian and went off to dinner, and, as you may well know, we dined pretty well. Curiously enough, he did not consent to travel in the same compartment, so we had to part company for the journey, except when we saw him getting out at every station we stopped at to get a drink. We got into a carriage with a very religious individual, who sang hymns, etc., all the way to Preston. This was exceedingly entertaining at first, but the service was too long, so on several occasions we fell asleep, and generally on awakening he was still at it.

I went to breakfast at the Ormans, and spent the rest of the time till 2 o'clock in visiting Lax. On arriving at Camberley we found about 500 cabs and other vehicles drawn up to receive us. Orman and the other fellows in our carriage being old birds knew how to do it, so about a dozen of us hired the bus and had a cheap and comfortable drive. The first thing I had to do was to report myself to the adjutant and then to the captain of our company, whose name is Gould-Adams.

The same evening I made the acquaintance of a lot of the seniors, all friends of Orman. I also met a good many fellows who had been at Wolffram's with me. The next day the two fellows in my room and myself went down the village to see about furnishing our room. Everything here is done by hiring, so we hired a carpet for 5s. 1d., curtains for 4s. 1d., and two splendid long easy chairs, and some other necessaries such as tea, sugar, and methylated spirits. The reason why everything is hired is this: no one ever has the same room two terms running, for you are generally put in a three-room at first, and then the second term you get a single room.

The work here is fairly stiff. . . . The fellows here are a very decent set, and the seniors treat us (the juniors) very respectably.

At Christmas, 1889, he was promoted to the rank of corporal, and in the same term received his colours for football. He played

A Record

in the XV. during the season 1889–90, and was one of the best forwards in the team.

Before Tait's time golf had been unknown at Sandhurst, so he laid out a short course for his fellow cadets, and instructed them in the ways and mysteries of the sport.

In a letter to his brother in Madras, written in Freddie's most racy style, he says :—

I have not had the pleasure of writing to you for some time, but as you know that the gentleman cadet is a hard-worked individual, with little or no spare time, I daresay you will overlook my want of zeal in not finding time to write.

I have just arrived from Sandhurst, and hope to be gazetted in two or three months' time. I have applied for foreign service, so possibly I may come across you one of these days.

The Duke of Cambridge inspected us on Tuesday last, and I need hardly add that he was absolutely charmed with our parade, bearing, and general knowledge of military matters. Referring to our drill, he said that it was unequalled by the best troops in the British Army, and was the best that he had ever seen at Sandhurst.

This, he said, reflected great honour, not only on the adjutant, but also on the under officers and "corporals"!!! I won't know how I have passed out for two or three weeks yet, but I did entirely to my own satisfaction in every paper except one. I have no doubt that you imagine that my ability

F. G. Tait

to acquire knowledge of all military matters is about equal to my ability in learning Latin ; but there you are mistaken, for even now I could command an " Army Corps."

About a month ago, Willie, Uncle John, and I went for a two days' excursion on the Thames. Willie was not what you would call a finished oar, but towards the end of the second day he did not upset the boat so often ; his steering was good on the whole, except on two or three occasions, when he tried to run us over a weir. Uncle John was more often in the stern than in any other part of the boat, and from that position would occasionally remark, " Now then, Willie, here comes a critical party, row in your best style." This exhortation usually ended in Willie catching a crab and doing his best to capsize the boat. However, we managed to come to the end of our journey without any other mishap than that Willie smashed his row-lock.

No more time.

Yours,

F. G. TAIT.

The letter reflects young Tait at this time better than any descriptive writing could do, for it indicates his plans and exemplifies his humour.

Tait joined the Royal and Ancient Club in the spring of 1890, and, after leaving Sandhurst in July, spent nearly three months at St. Andrews, competing for the Calcutta Cup, the Jubilee Vase, and the Autumn Medal.

A Record

The Calcutta Cup Competition started on Tuesday, August 5th, and on the previous Saturday, in a match with Mr. Macfie, Tait not only won by 4 holes, but beat all previous amateur records by holing the course in the low score of 77. Records change with great rapidity nowadays, but what was best at the time must always be good, if we consider it in its proper historical position. The early feats of navigation are not really made small because a floating hotel can now cross the Atlantic in five days. The heroes who won the Olympic Crown are not to be counted less famous than the athletes of modern England or America, though their records would look poor if a comparison could be made.

Tait himself cut his 77 down to 72 in the course of a few years, but he was doubtless as much pleased at the time with the one performance as with the other. Be this as it may, this 77 was very noteworthy, and most prophetic—to use the word in its baser sense—of what young Tait was capable. In the Calcutta Cup Tournament he was also at his best, defeating Mr. J. H. Blackwell, who conceded him a start of 1 hole, by 5 up and 4 to play, and Mr. Laidlay, who gave him 2 holes, by 4 up and 3 to play. These were great performances, and though Tait was beaten in the

F. G. Tait

semi-final by Mr. Nimmo, who received
4 holes start, his first competition must be
considered a great success. Soon after this,
in a match of two rounds, the brothers
Tait defeated the brothers Blackwell, the
strongest combination that could be brought
against them, by 1 hole. A fews days later,
Andrew Kirkcaldy played the best ball of
the Taits, and won at the last hole; Mr.
Alec Tait was, it must be remembered,
little more than a boy at this time. Playing for the Jubilee Vase, Tait reached the
final, only to be beaten by Mr. Bethune,
who was in receipt of 7 strokes. In the
Medal round, he did not, however, show to
such advantage, going out well enough in 43,
but requiring 52 for the homeward journey;
the last 8 holes cost 47, though but a few
days earlier he had a score of 29 for them;
the last-named score must however have
been on the reverse course.

A Tournament, open to all amateurs,
was held at North Berwick, in the beginning of October, and Tait entered along
with many of the best players in Scotland;
England also being represented by Messrs.
Hilton and Molesworth. Tait reached the
semi-final, when he was beaten by Mr.
David Anderson at the last hole. The
players were all even, but Tait, with a
long shot, got behind the club maker's

A Record

shop, and required two shots to clear, losing the hole and the match. Mr. Hilton ultimately won the tournament. This fact is interesting, as it was probably the first time that Tait and Hilton saw each other play ; they were about the same age—Hilton a month or two older—and were destined to have a series of great encounters, out of which Tait emerged with extraordinary success.

F. G. Tait

CHAPTER V.

THE LEINSTER REGIMENT.

October 1890—June 1894.

ON the 28th October, 1890, the young cadet was gazetted to the 2nd battalion of the Leinster Regiment, the 109th Foot.

During the months of October and November he remained in Edinburgh, getting his kit in order, and making what preparations were necessary for joining his regiment. He had applied for foreign service, and hoped to join a regiment on duty in India. This, however, was not to be, as the 2nd battalion of the Leinsters was quartered at Shorncliffe camp, near Folkestone, where Tait joined them on November 29th.

Tait had greatly improved as a Rugby football player during his Sandhurst days, and while waiting in Edinburgh he eagerly seized the opportunity of playing with the Edinburgh Wanderers, one of the best teams in Scotland. He was one of the "hard working type" of Scottish forwards, who have been

A Record

the making of the Rugby game in the North, and knowing the great traditions of the game he was keen to act well by them. As showing what manner of player he was it may be of interest to quote the opinion of no less an authority than Mr. Ian McIntyre, President of the Scottish Rugby Union, and at that time captain of the Wanderers Club. Writing of his play in 1890 he says :—

It is my deliberate opinion that at that time he was one of the very best forwards playing in Edinburgh, if not in Scotland. I cannot to this day understand how it was that he was passed over in the selection for the "Inter-City." One match in particular I remember against the Watsonians at Myreside, where he fairly excelled himself, and was the best forward on the field.

Seldom after this period had he any chance of developing this side of his athletics, but for all that his interest in football never slackened. Scotland never played an International Match that Tait did not follow keenly, and when he subsequently joined the Black Watch he never missed an opportunity of encouraging the regimental team both in their practice games and in their cup ties.

Tait's stay at Shorncliffe was but a short one, as his regiment left in the middle of February for Aldershot.

I liked Shorncliffe very much (he writes to his brother) ; there was always plenty to do. I got

F. G. Tait

some very good duck shooting on some government ground within a few miles of camp. Sandwich was quite close, and I could always get good men to play with. The work at Shorncliffe was not nearly so hard as at Aldershot. I believe Aldershot is about the only place in the kingdom where they go in for soldiering properly. We often have night marches, fire alarms in the middle of the night, brigade parades, divisional days, and any amount of battalion parades. I like the work very much, but the only objection I have to Aldershot is that there is absolutely nothing to do after your work is done. The links are awfully bad, so the only amusement I get is to go long walks, and consequently I am at present feeling very fit. I hope to be able to get leave for the Spring Meeting and Championship at St. Andrews in May. I suppose you have any amount of golf and shooting in India. We go out in the end of '92. I believe the Laird gave a lecture in London the other day on the Lanark and Ayrshire Railway. I do not know whether it was a success or not. I know neither *The Times* nor *The Referee* had any account of it. I expected " Mustard and Cress " might make some slight allusion to it.

Alec is, I hear, going up for his examination. He wants to pass, as, curiously enough, he does not want to have another year with Prof. ——. How is old Tim ——? Give him my kind regards, and ask him if he remembers the thrashings he used to give me at St. Andrews. The drill season is going to begin here soon, so we will get to know the Long Valley very well.

A Record

I think when we go out to India we are going to Agra.

Tait did not, however, manage to get to St. Andrews for the Amateur Championship of 1891, which Mr. Laidlay won, beating Mr. Hilton in the final after a tie. But he was able to play for the St. George's Cup at Sandwich, and finished third to Mr. John Ball, jun., whose winning score was 174. Tait, who played with Mr. Hilton, scored 183, and his partner 187; ten strokes were required for the seventh hole in the morning round, owing to a low tee shot, which caught the top of the bunker, otherwise Tait's round of 91 would have been excellent as the scores went.

As a boy he had been very keen on shooting, and spent many a day up the Fifeshire Eden after duck, plover, or snipe. At Aldershot he turned his attention to rifle shooting, and soon became quite on the " scratch mark." In August he writes :—

We have a big competition coming off in a week or so among the officers of the regiment for a silver cup; seven rounds at 200, 500, and 600 yards. I beat them all the last time, and hope to repeat the performance again.

In the regimental cricket eleven his batting average stood second, viz., 20·5 per innings. Tait, in truth, entered into all sports with equal enthusiasm, if not always with equal success.

F. G. Tait

In September Tait was at St. Andrews for the Autumn Meeting, but with a score of 91 he was clearly not at his best; Mr. Alexander Stuart and Mr. R. B. Sharp were the winners.

The Open Championship was played for in October, and won by Hugh Kirkcaldy in a gale of wind, in the grand score of 166—Tait was 182, and many good players far more. Kirkcaldy's play on this occasion was very fine, and indeed compares favourably with the low scores of later years.

After thirteen months of regimental work at Shorncliffe and Aldershot, Tait got a short leave, which he spent at Edinburgh.

He returned to Aldershot, and entered again with zest into his service life. In April, to his great joy, he obtained leave to play for the first time in the Amateur Championship at Sandwich. He played in the event in the following month, but was at the time quite out of practice, having been unable to get any satisfactory play at Aldershot. He was defeated in the second round by Mr. F. A. Fairlie.

As a result of his match with Mr. Fairlie, a return took place in June at Wimbledon, which was at that time Mr. Fairlie's home green. Tait won the thirty-six hole match by two, his first round being a 76, the half round being accomplished in 34—a record at that time.

A Record

Tait was meanwhile full of enthusiasm about his regiment and their doings. With special pride he wrote to his father to tell him of the honours conferred on his men :—

I have had the great honour conferred on me of carrying the Queen's Colours on Monday, when Her Gracious Majesty comes down to lay a foundation stone and review the Aldershot Division. We are very much pleased just now, as our Regiment has not only been called upon to furnish the " Guard of Honour " (a great feather in our caps, as there are 10 Battalions of Infantry here), but also to supply the music during the ceremony of laying the foundation stone. I need scarcely say that a better selection could not have been made, as we have produced a hundred splendid men who average about 5 feet 10 inches, and led by three officers—average 5 feet 11 inches—not so bad for the junior Regiment in the Service ! !

And again, writing a little later to Mrs. Tait, he says :—

Yesterday was a great day for the Prince of Wales' Leinster Regiment. We won the Tug of War for teams of 10 men (total weight not to exceed 120 stone) open to the Army. We also won the Officers' Tug of War open to the Army. We pulled over a team averaging nearly a stone a man heavier in the final. We got a splendid cup, and the men got £10. I may as well mention that the Tugs of War, both officers' and men's, are considered the best events to win. Our band marched all round the camp (with a huge man carrying the cup) playing

F. G. Tait

the Regimental March. Our manœuvres begin in a short time now. The Army Rifle Meeting comes off next week. I have the honour of being a member of the Regimental Team. I expect Willie here one day this week.

His brother duly came and spent a day at Aldershot, much to Tait's joy. In the evening he was induced to play whist with the strictest and most serious players of the regiment, and "led off," as Freddie put it, by dealing out *five* hands. The situation must have been a fine one, and it was just such an one as to appeal to Freddie's sense of humour. He told the story often, and it lost nothing in the telling.

Tait was still anxious for foreign service, and with regret he writes in July, 1892 :—

I don't believe we are going out to India for two years, so I am seriously thinking of applying for a transfer to the other battalion, which will soon be on its way to Burmah, where there would be a chance of a little revolver practice, and a chance of getting a "medal." I have no doubt, however, that Gladstone will find something for us to do before long.

The latter part of the year 1892 Tait was quartered at Hythe, in Kent, where he went through a course of musketry instruction. This he thoroughly enjoyed, and was, moreover, very successful in his work, coming out third in rifle shooting, and equal first with the

A Record

revolver. While there he found time on Saturdays to break the records at Deal, Folkestone, and Ascot, and was only prevented from scoring a win in a handicap competition by the tender attentions of an enthusiast, whom he describes with almost Horatian satire.

He has walked round with me about six times, and has had a duplicate of every one of my clubs made, and as he is particularly pleased with my driver, he is going to order half-a-dozen. He came round with me at Deal when I was playing for a competition the other day, and after every decent shot I made he said, " That is a very good shot, but I was twenty yards past that yesterday." I may as well tell you he plays about the same game as Mr. ——. I happened to do the first hole in three, which is equivalent to doing the third hole at St. Andrews in the same number, when he remarked, " That is not bad, but you ought always to do it; I do it five times out of six." This style of thing went on all the way round.

It is a pretty description of a not yet obsolete class of bore, and Freddie knew them well when he met them.

At the end of 1892 Tait paid a short visit to Edinburgh, and thence he went to St. Andrews and to Newcastle, in North Ireland. At Newcastle he broke the record with a score of 76, and at St. Andrews, on 11th January, 1893, he made his famous

F. G. Tait

record drive of 341 yards, with a carry of about 250 yards. Tait was driving to the thirteenth hole at St. Andrews; there was no wind, but the ground was frozen. Mr. Guy Grindlay was his opponent.

So much has been said and written about this shot that I will not trouble the reader with any of my personal views on the subject. It will be of more interest to hear Tait's own account of the performance, and to note in what light he regarded it. Writing at the time he said—

> I enclose you a cutting from the *Daily News* of Monday, January 16th, by Andrew Lang, on a drive made by me on my 23rd birthday. No doubt you will say, as the Governor said: "Stuff! Humbug!" but the fact still remains. The Governor will be very much annoyed about the article, as he wrote not very long ago an article to *Golf* proving conclusively that it was impossible to carry more than 190 yards on a calm day, unless you exerted about three times more energy.

It should be pointed out that at the time Professor Tait wrote the article which Freddie alludes to, he had not made his important discovery as to the effect of under-spin on the flight of a golf ball. In his celebrated article published in *Nature* he says—

> I shall consider the flight of a golf ball in a dead calm only, and when it has been driven fair and true without any spin.

A Record

Young Tait regarded the record drive and the talk about it as a nuisance, for writing from Aldershot in February he says—

I wish I had never made that drive at St. Andrews; everyone I meet here at once begins asking about it. I had a letter from a man Clarke at Ascot asking me to come and play golf with him. He said at the end of his letter—" I drove a ball last Tuesday 480 yards with a slight breeze behind, ground on the hard side, and slightly down wind. This was measured accurately by my brother (price 5s.)." This is the sort of chaff I have been getting lately.

On returning to Aldershot, Tait found that most of the best men in his company had been drafted out to India.

We are now left with a lot of boys, and we are a long way under strength, and two thirds of the regiment are recruits.

This is the first hint that Tait let fall that he was not satisfied with his life at Aldershot and desired change. This sense of dissatisfaction and desire for change grew upon him, until at last he could think of nothing but his chances of obtaining an exchange into one of the Highland regiments.

This feeling, or rather change of feeling, was the result of several different ideas working together in his mind towards the same end. His captain, for whom he had a great regard, was about to leave the regiment, and,

73

as we have seen, he himself had lost the best men in his company. Over and above all this there was a strong and natural desire to be connected with one of the Scottish regiments. Tait was very anxious to see some active service, and hoped by joining a Highland regiment to do so. Writing to his father he urges this point.

I know very well that the only way to get on now is to see some fighting, and you will no doubt have noticed that whenever there is any fighting to be done, and there is a Highland regiment anywhere near, it is invariably sent.

There were, however, many difficulties in the way of an exchange, and it was not until June, 1894, that Tait joined the second battalion of the Black Watch.

In July, 1893, indeed, there seemed a good chance of Tait working out his plan, but the officer with whom he hoped to exchange had to wait until he received his promotion, and this was long delayed. The exchange would also involve loss of "leave" for the year, as Tait would have to join his new regiment immediately on leaving the Leinsters. This prospect did not trouble him, for he cheerily remarked: " In any case leave is of small consequence when you have the honour of belonging to a regiment like the 73rd."

Tait played for the Spring Medal at St. Andrews in 1893, and was placed fourth. He

A Record

won the bronze medal at Prestwick in the Amateur Championship, being beaten by Mr. Laidlay after a tie, and in September he won the second medal at St. Andrews with the fine score of 80 ; but of these events I will write more fully in their proper place. The Division played a match at Crookham under trying circumstances—rain and snow—and the loss of seventeen holes by their tail man making the day rather a failure.

A day at Ascot was more successful, Tait winning several prizes. This style of golf was not, however, congenial to him, and he writes of his performances almost with shame.

I did not want to play at all, as I consider that sort of thing " pot-hunting." The members, however, insisted on my playing, and I won by about twelve strokes.

Early in February, 1894, Tait spent a few days at St. Andrews, and signalised his visit by breaking the record of the green with a score of 72.

In the Amateur Championship, which was held at Hoylake in April, he again reached the semi-final, being defeated by Mr. Mure Fergusson by five up and four to play. Tait, however, won the first medal at St. Andrews in May with a score of 83, and at Sandwich he greatly distinguished himself in the Open Championship, and also in a tourna-

F. G. Tait

ment in which amateurs and professionals competed. In this last-named event he was only defeated by the subsequent winner after a tie, in a match in which the luck was decidedly against him. Two days later, much to his joy, Tait received a telegram to say that he had been gazetted to the Black Watch, which regiment he immediately joined at Barry Camp, in Forfarshire.

As a parting gift to his old regiment, Tait presented them with several volumes of the Badminton Library. In a letter of thanks the colonel and officers say—

> The present will be most useful to us, and we shall always value it as having been given by you. We all unite in good wishes for your future.

Though Tait never loved the Leinster Regiment with the same patriotic affection which he felt in later days for the Black Watch, enough has perhaps been said in this chapter to show that he took a real pride in their successes, and while with them exhibited that true *esprit de corps* which was inseparable from his nature.

Throughout his short military career Tait was always adored by the men he commanded. In a letter written to Professor Tait, after his son's death at Koodoosberg, Sergeant Malone tells what the men of the Leinster Regiment thought of their officer—

A Record

Dear Sir,

With feelings of deepest regret I read of the death of your son Lieut. Tait, who was my Company Officer in the Leinster Regiment, during his stay in the Regiment. He was one of the best officers we ever had, and was loved by all the men in the Company, including myself; I was indeed most deeply attached to him. Please accept my deepest sympathy in your sad bereavement.

Yours respectfully,

THOMAS MALONE (Sergeant).

At the end of this first chapter of soldier life, we hear again that *motif* of love which dominates Tait's whole life-story.

F. G. Tait

— ◦◦◦ —

CHAPTER VI

WITH THE BLACK WATCH.

THE first six weeks of Tait's life with his new regiment, the 73rd, or second battalion of the Black Watch, were spent at Barry Camp, in Forfarshire, where his men were under a course of instruction. The change that Tait had made was one he had been hoping for, and looking forward to, for some time, and the repeated delays which had occurred in connection with his transfer only tended to strengthen the delight he felt, when at last he found himself connected with the grand old Scottish regiment.

From Aldershot he brought with him a friend, whom it will be necessary here to introduce to any reader who may be unfortunate enough not to have already made the acquaintance of " Nails." Nails was so closely connected with Freddie in everything he did during the last half dozen years of his life, that not to mention him would be a grave injustice to the dog, and an omission which

[*Photo by Marshall Wane.*

LIEUT. F. G. TAIT, 1896.

A Record

his late master would never have pardoned.
Nails, then, is a terrier in every inch and
every pound of his 35-lb. body. In no class
would he receive even a highly commended
card at a dog show; but he is a good dog
all the same. One of his parents or grand-
parents must have been a Bedlington, for
Bedlington is the dominant note in his personal appearance. There are evidences also
that an Irishman must at some time or
other have been connected with the family,
and here our diagnosis of his origin must
stop.

If I have cast some shadow of a doubt on
the purity of Nails's pedigree, it is not with
the object of belittling his character as a dog
and a friend. His ancestors may indeed have
been the flower of ancient dog families, who,
disregarding the rules of the Kennel Club,
determined to sink all old-fashioned clan pre-
judices and intermarry. This perhaps is the
kindlier way of looking upon the actions of
the good dog's forefathers, so we will adopt it.
Nails himself was good and true—true to his
master, and true to his name, a hard customer,
a true friend to man, and a deadly enemy to
all the rest of the animal world, not excepting
his own branch of the canine race. Tait loved
his dog and loved him to the end. His letters
from South Africa always contained some
reference to " my son Nails," as he was wont

to call him, regarding himself as in some way standing *in loco parentis*. When killed at Koodoosberg, a scrap of paper was found in Freddie's pocket; it was the little letter from Nails to his " father " which will be found reproduced in its proper chronological connection.

Tait enjoyed his stay at Barry immensely, as may be gathered from the following letter :—

Barry Camp,
Near Carnoustie,
Forfarshire,
20th July, 1894.

My dear Mother,

We are having a most excellent time here. We work all the morning from about six to one, and golf all the afternoon. It is very healthy work.

Nails is in great form, and has been made an honorary member of our mess, which means that he is allowed to come into it whenever he likes. I may mention that this is a favour granted to very few dogs. He has made great friends with everyone. The other day I was playing a match with Livingstone and MacFarlan, and I took him over to Livingstone's Militia Regiment on my way down to the links. We played two rounds, and at the end of the last round he disappeared somewhere. That night I dined with Livingstone's Regiment, and up to that time I had seen nothing of Nails. Livingstone was a little late for dinner, but when he came in he told me that Nails had come round to his tent when he was dressing, and had made himself quite at home; he also told me that he had brought Nails

A Record

round to the ante-room. When we came out of dinner we found Nails lying down on the best sofa, wagging his tail, and quite at home. I wanted to turn him out, but all the Militia officers insisted on his staying. I think he knows everyone in camp now. I am thinking of coming to St. Andrews for the Calcutta Cup if I can get away, and I should like to bring a very nice fellow called Murray for the week if you can find room. The weather here is excellent; I am about as fit as I have ever been. I played a great foursome the other day—Macfarlan and I against the two Simpsons. I did not play very well, but the Simpsons are very hard to beat on their own dunghill; they beat us by three. We are going to take them on again next week. You might find out when the entries for the Calcutta Cup close, and you might also ask the governor to send some money to Cox and Co., as the regimental people have sneaked about three months of my pay for regimental subscriptions. You might also tell him that his article in *Golf* of the other day is being read with great interest by all the people here and at Carnoustie. I have not been able to make any experiments, as I cannot find anyone with a stop-watch; but I will have some more trials at St. Andrews, when the Governor will be there to superintend.

Yours affectionately,
F. G. Tait.

The "trials" referred to were in connection with the experiments that Professor Tait was making at that time with a view to ascertaining the initial and subsequent velocity of

F. G. Tait

a golf ball. The matches with the Simpsons, Bob and Archie, resulted in grand tussles, honours being about easy at the end of the series. Captain Macfarlan, Tait's partner, will be well remembered at Carnoustie and elsewhere as a beautiful player, who only required more practice in order to be quite in the very first rank. He was, during Tait's first years with the Black Watch, perhaps his greatest friend in the regiment, and his death at Magersfontein robbed them of one of the most kindly of men, a true sportsman and a good soldier.

In a match against Lieutenant Macfarlan Tait beat all previous records at Carnoustie with the wonderful score of 72. Those who know the course will best appreciate the value of the performance. The following account of the round taken from the *Dundee Advertiser* gives the particulars of the score :—

Those who have witnessed Lieutenant Tait's brilliant play in the recent foursomes, in which, partnered by Lieutenant Macfarlan, he held so close Bob and Archie Simpson, will not be surprised to learn that yesterday he made two new records for the Carnoustie course.

All lovers of golf in the district were anxious that Mr. Tait should play a round single-handed, and this he did yesterday, his opponent on the occasion being Lieutenant Macfarlan. Both were in grand form, and although Macfarlan did the round in the fine score of 78, he was beaten by

A Record

Tait by five holes—the total of the latter being 72. Hitherto Archie Simpson has held the record with 73. But Tait made another record, for his score for the first nine holes was 33, which is two strokes below the previous best. From his detailed score it will be seen that on the outward journey no hole cost him more than 4, and he had three of them in 3. Coming homeward he still played magnificently, but 5's at the sixteenth and seventeenth holes spoiled an otherwise faultless round.

To such a strong golfer as Tait, both are very easy 4's, and, had he managed them at that figure, his total would have been 70. The details of the scores of both players are as follows :—Lieutenant Tait : Out, 4 3 4 4 4 3 4 3 4=33; in, 4 5 4 3 5 4 5 5 4=39=72. Lieutenant Macfarlan : Out, 4 3 5 3 4 4 5 4 4=36: in, 5 5 5 5 5 4 4 5 4=42=78.

After a six weeks' stay at Barry, Tait went with his regiment to Edinburgh Castle, where he remained for two years. His success as a marksman while in camp is recorded in the following short note written just before he left :—

> Barry Camp,
> Near Carnoustie,
> Forfarshire,
> 26 *July*, 1894.

My dear Mother,

I think we are coming back to Edinburgh on Saturday next. We have been having awfully bad weather lately. My bed was just like a puddle last night. I met Ronald Burn yesterday here, and I told him to enter my name for the Calcutta Cup.

F. G. Tait

I hope to be able to get away, only I am not certain yet. If I can get away I will bring Murray with me. We played the Simpsons again the other day, and beat them. We hope to have a return to-morrow. I shot very well, I was the best shot of my company. The penny bull's eyes made the men shoot up like blazes. My captain will have to pay four or five pounds for "bull's eyes." I am rather tired of playing golf at Carnoustie, as every round I play I have a crowd of a hundred or more.

Yours affectionately,
F. G. TAIT.

Tait played for, and won, the Calcutta Cup, even though penalised to the extent of two holes. In the semi-final he was drawn against his brother Alec, and in the final he beat Mr. W. Gordon, to whom he conceded seven holes start. Mr. Gordon had halved with Tait in a previous round, but in the end, Freddie playing grand golf won cleverly by two up and one to play.

Nails did not have such a successful visit to St. Andrews, for after a most protracted struggle with the dog of a neighbour, which match indeed he won, he was ignominiously "kicked out" of the city. It was no doubt thought that the presence of so pugnacious an inmate might bring discredit to the house of the Professor; at any rate Nails had to go. Freddie always took the greatest interest in Nails' prowess, and chuckled when he heard of any of his special pugilistic feats.

"NAILS."

— " The poor dog, in life the firmest friend,
The first to welcome, foremost to defend,
Whose honest heart is still his master's own,
Who labours, fights, lives, breathes for him alone."

A Record

This year, 1894, was one of great golfing success for Tait. Not only did he make his famous record score of 72 at St. Andrews, of which an account will be found in the Appendix, but he also won the first Medal at St. Andrews in May, the Bronze Medal in the Amateur Championship, took the first place among the amateurs in the Open Championship, won the Calcutta Cup, and finished up by winning the Autumn Medal with a record score of 78, and the Glennie Medal with a record score of 161. This is an extraordinary series of successes, and I have always thought that this was perhaps Tait's very best year, not even excepting 1896, when his play at Sandwich and elsewhere created such a sensation.

In a letter written to his brother Jack from Edinburgh shortly after his arrival at the castle, Tait speaks with great pride of his new regiment—

The Castle,
Edinburgh,
27 *August*, 1894.

My dear Jack,

Thanks for your letter. I am awfully pleased with my new regiment in every way. A splendid lot of officers, N.C.O.'s and men, and in my humble opinion out and away the finest regiment in the service. The only drawback is that it is a trifle more expensive, but as the Laird said the other day, " Never mind, Freddie, you will only owe a

F. G. Tait

little more next time." This was after I had won the Calcutta Cup from the "owe 2 holes" mark, and he and I were talking over the expenses of a military life. I have been playing a good game lately, and I am glad to say that I can drive a straight and fairly long ball. I am sorry to say that poor dear old Archie Stewart is dead. He died on the same day as his sister; I have forgotten her name. He certainly was one of the best. I have heard nothing of Bob lately. I will be pleased to send you a photograph, even after your insolent remarks about dressing myself properly.

The Calcutta Cup you will be glad to hear is now on the mess table, and looks very well. Nails, I am sorry to say, got kicked out of St. Andrews by the Governor after he had got over the wall, and left the dog next door for dead. I meant to go over to St. Andrews next week to play for the Jubilee Vase, but as I hear I am to owe 4 or 5 strokes I am going to sit tight till the Medal. Our old Colonel has just left us; he was a capital chap. One night after I had come back from St. Andrews I took him into the mess-room to show him the cup; he was very pleased with it and said, "Well, Tait, I do not know of anything that we cannot win," and then catching sight of a very impudent 2nd Lieutenant he said, "Well, ——, what cup are you going to win for us?" "I don't know, Colonel," said ——. "Well, I think I can tell you," said the Colonel. "What, sir?" said ——, awfully pleased. "The championship of the army for downright cheek."

A new paper called *The Golfer* has been started in Edinburgh a week or two ago, I was interviewed to-day; I will send you a copy. Alec is going to play in the Jubilee Vase, I hope he will make a good

A 5 AND A 4 FOR 78. ST. ANDREWS (September) MEDAL, 1894.

[Photo by W. & D. Downey.

A Record

show. I was over at Barry the other day putting my company through their annual course of musketry, and I played a good deal of golf with your old friend Bob Simpson. He asked very kindly after you, and told me a lot of amusing stories. He is a most excellent man. We have a brother of David Macfarlan's in the regiment, a very fine fellow and an excellent golfer. We played six rounds against Archie and Bob, and won three each, only unfortunately we agreed to play the last four rounds as two 36 hole matches, and although we each won 2 rounds they beat us on each 36. I know a very good chap in the 48th—Trent by name. Alec has just been up here, and has sneaked my best "iron" to try and win the Vase.

Yours ever,
F. G. TAIT.

The Autumn Meeting of 1894 at St. Andrews was a very notable one. The Right Honourable A. J. Balfour was captain, and the gathering was the largest on record. The golf also was first rate, Mr. Leslie Balfour and Mr. Laidlay were both round in 80, but Tait went two better and finished in the grand score of 78. The details of his score were: Out, 4 6 4 3 6 4 6 3 4 = 40; in, 4 3 4 4 5 5 4 5 4 = 38 = 78.

The dinner after the competition was equally memorable, and places had to be balloted for, so great was the demand for seats. Mr. Balfour made an excellent speech, and the subsequent speakers, no doubt recognising that they could not equal the right

F. G. Tait

honourable gentleman in the quality of their orations, tried to surpass him in the quantity. Tait's speech was, however, the best and the shortest. He upheld the principle of leading trumps when in doubt, the necessity of using a niblick when in a bunker, and maintained that the chief end of the diner was to enjoy the repast rather than discuss irrelevant subjects.

After his St. Andrews triumph Tait returned to Edinburgh, remaining at the Castle until the autumn of 1896, when he went to Ballater to act as one of Her Majesty's guard. Of Tait's life at Edinburgh Castle I know but little. It was simply the life of a young soldier, doing the routine duties of his military calling, and looking forward with pleasure to the days of leave which he could spend at St. Andrews and elsewhere. It is a sad thought, moreover, that the sources of information as to his doings when in the Black Watch are not available. All his comrades in arms have gone forth to do their duty in a distant land, from which many, alas, will never return.

Tait's enthusiasm for sport found vent on the football field, and we find him playing, and playing well, for the Edinburgh Academicals during the early part of the season 1894–95. The regiment had one of the best football teams in the army, but the

A Record

soldiers pursued the round ball, not the oval one. This fact did not prevent Tait from being the keenest supporter of the team during their successful progress in the competition for the Army Cup. Meanwhile what little golf was going was of a character not likely to be of much service as practice for future matches. A sloping roof projects southward from Edinburgh Castle, and of an evening Tait and a brother enthusiast would go forth on to this strange tee with a few old balls. From this lofty plateau the balls were driven, and fell to earth, I know not where; it may hap on the house roofs, or perchance on the head of some passer-by, who, greatly wondering, would no doubt take the apparently heaven-sent missile home, and detail to incredulous friends the circumstances of its capture.

The beginning of 1895 saw the formation of the New Luffness Golf Club, and Tait greatly interested himself in the new venture, being one of the first life-members to join the club. The first medal was played for in April, 1895, though a professional meeting had taken place earlier in the year. The course, now one of the finest in Scotland, was then some-what in the rough stage, so that the score with which Tait won, viz., 76, must be con-sidered an exceptionally fine one, beating as it did all previous professional records by six strokes. This was the first time that he had

F. G. Tait

ever played on the course, and his score has never been beaten. Tait kept up his interest in the New Luffness Club, and in July, 1898, when they entered for the first time for the East Lothian Cup, he was one of their winning team.

During 1895 Tait played so well that his comparative failure in some of the big events of the year is the more remarkable.

At the Spring Meeting at St. Andrews he won the second medal after a tie with Mr. A. Stuart at 85. Mr. Laidlay finished no less than seven strokes to the good of these two, but then his score was a phenomenal one. There was a strong north-west wind, and the greens, as is often the case at this season at St. Andrews, were very keen and difficult. Mr. Laidlay's score of 78 was perhaps therefore, under the circumstances, up to this time the best of this great player's scoring performances. I say "up to this time," not because he has done better for a St. Andrews Medal, but because he has since put on record a 73 for the Tantallon Medal, which is, I venture to think, the best score, amateur or professional, which has ever been made in a real contest with the scoring card and pencil as chief spectators.

In the Amateur Championship, which followed hard on the St. Andrews Meeting, after starting favourite and playing grand golf

A Record

against Mr. Stuart and Mr. Laidlay, Tait fell before Mr. John Ball. In the Open Championship, which was also held at St. Andrews, he hardly did as well as might have been hoped, though in the tournament held on the following day on the new course, he came out first of the amateurs, being 3 strokes worse than Herd, the winner, and a stroke better than the future champion, H. Vardon.

During the summer months spent in Edinburgh, Tait was distinguishing himself on the cricket field, playing for the Grange C.C., a club which included many of his old school friends. September found him again at St. Andrews, and found him in his best form. He played for and won the Jubilee Vase from the " owe 3 " mark, a unique performance. In the course of his victorious career he played Mr. F. A. Fairlie, to whom he conceded 1 stroke, Mr. Jim Blackwell, Capt. Stott, then his brother Alec, and finally Mr. T. Jeffrey, who received a half from the winner. Tait played grand golf all through the tournament, though physically far from well on the first day. His win was, as usual, very popular, and among many messages of congratulation came a characteristic telegram from his father's old fellow worker—

Our congratulations to you and Mrs. Tait. Hope Alec is not too much cast down, nor Fred

F. G. Tait

uplifted. Suppose he will be made brevet-major, and the Victoria Jubilee Vase inscribed on Black Watch colours.—KELVIN.

Although on the great Autumn Medal day Tait returned the sound score of 83, he was only one of eight who had equalled or bettered that figure, so good was the scoring. However, in the following month, Tait won the Scratch Medal at the New Luffness Club on a windy day with a score of 86, and in the afternoon, in a match against the best ball of Mr. Armour and Mr. Mitchell Innes, he went round in 79, beating the formidable combination by two holes.

In the beginning of 1896 Tait spent his two months' leave shooting in Aberdeenshire, and afterwards golfing at St. Andrews. The following letters, the first two written to his brother in India, and the third to Mrs. Tait, throw some light on his golf and the further development of the series of experiments in which Tait assisted his father. At this date, and indeed long before, when with the Leinster Regiment, Tait was anxious for foreign service, and it is probable that had he not obtained a staff appointment he would have gone to India in 1897.

2 January, 1896.

Dear Jack,

I hope you are fit. I wish you a happy New Year, and many of them. The governor and I had a very successful day at college. We think we have at last arrived at the truth about the initial velocity of a good drive (220 feet a second). I am on leave for two months. I am going off to shoot with a brother officer in a day or two. My class dinner comes off soon ; I am in the chair, so I fancy we will have a good night. I am learning the pipes, and am getting on first class. I told Mrs. Lang the story of the old lady who was had up for assaulting her husband (biting a piece off his nose). The judge who tried the case remarked that it was a most painful and disgusting case; but as the lady did not appear to have any previous conviction against her, all he could do was to bind her over to keep the peace. She replied she was very sorry she could not, as she had given it to the cat.

Mrs. Lang enjoyed this story immensely.

Yours ever,

F. G. Tait.

38, George Square,
Edinburgh,
15 *January*, 1896.

Dear Jack,

As I am at present staying at 38, G. S., and have not very much to do, I thought I might send you a few lines. I have just come back from Aberdeenshire, where I had an excellent week's shooting. I was staying with one of our fellows, the Master of Sempill. We had very good sport; any amount of partridges and rabbits, and a few pheasants. I am going to St. Andrews next week, to stay with another of our lot who has got lodgings there for a week or two—Macfarlan, by

F. G. Tait

name. He is a brother of the great David MacF. The one in my regiment is an excellent golfer, and one of the finest drivers I ever saw. He is a very powerful fellow, over 6 feet 3 inches, and has a most perfect swing. He and I are going to take on any two at St. Andrews. When we were at Barry, two years ago, he and I had some splendid matches against the two Simpsons. We played six rounds, and we each won three. The last time I saw old Bob Simpson he was asking very tenderly after you. I think he is an excellent fellow; I get all my clubs from him now. The governor has been making a lot of experiments lately at college. He has now finally settled that the initial velocity of a really good drive is about 240 feet a second. I don't think I will waste any time in explaining how this result was arrived at, as you never were much good at either natural philosophy or mathematics.

Macfarlan and I did all the driving. The governor has written a long article on the subject, which will appear in the *Badminton Magazine* for March. I think I will come out to India in another year or so and join our 1st Battalion. Our 1st Battalion is at present at the Cape and Mauritius, half at each. In March they go to India, unless there is likely to be any fighting with the Boers. My present Battalion is going to York some time this year. Billy has improved in his singing, but it is still dreadful. The St. Andrew Square masher is a great authority now on every subject, and I am sorry to say the poor old governor has a bad time of it between him and Kilbirnie. I hope you will be back for a bit next year or this year. I believe you want to play the

A Record

best ball of Rolland and myself. I do not know where you got your information from about heeled mashie shots in my 72 round; I never heeled a single one (*Golf*, February 16, 1894).

I am getting on first class on my chanter, and will be able to play a tune on the pipes by March. 38 ought to be fairly lively between me and Kilbirnie.

Yours ever,

F. G. TAIT.

Royal and Ancient Golf Club
of St. Andrews,

31 *January*, 1896.

My dear Mother,

I will be back in time for dinner to-morrow night (Saturday). I want to have another lesson on the chanter on Monday. I expect I will go back to St. Andrews on Tuesday or Wednesday. We have been having great fun over here, and very jolly weather. Macfarlan and I have played twice against Jim Blackwell and Willie Burn, winning the first by 4 and 2, and the second by 5 and 4. On the second occasion we came back in 34; which, I believe, has never been done before. The holes were very long, so that it is really a magnificent performance. 4 4 3 4 4 4 3 4 4 = 34.

The short hole in we just lay on the lip for 3, and they knocked us in, so we might almost call it 33. We took 44 to go out, unfortunately. Total, 78. We also played Jim Blackwell and Macfie three matches. Lost the first by 2 at the last hole; won the second by 1, and the third by 6 and 5. I have enjoyed myself immensely, and I

F. G. Tait

am very sorry that the Macfarlans cannot stay any longer. You might have dinner at six to-morrow, as I have to go out after. Macfarlan has been playing very well the last few days. I have just had a 3-ball match with him and Jim, and beat them both at the burn; the former by 2, the latter by 3.

Yours affectionately,

F. G. TAIT.

1896 is known among golfers as "Tait's Year," principally on account of his grand play at Sandwich in the St. George's Vase and Amateur Championship, both of which events he won. His play at Sandwich will be more fully put on record in the Appendix, but two scores which he made in the spring of this year are very worthy of note. On March 22nd he went round Muirfield in 73, his score being made up thus:—Out, 3 5 4 4 5 4 4 5 4 = 38; in, 4 4 4 4 4 3 4 3 5 = 35. Just before leaving for Sandwich he played an even more remarkable round, this time at North Berwick. His score was 74, and those who know the length and difficulty of the extended course consider this one of his greatest scoring feats. His figures were:—Out, 4 5 4 3 4 4 4 5 3 = 36; in, 4 4 4 4 4 3 5 6 4 = 38; total, 74. On the following day he beat Sayers by 8 holes; Ben's remark at the conclusion of the round fairly summed up the situation—"Beaten by 8 holes on my own green; it's no possible but it's a fac'."

A Record

Tait played at the May Meeting at St. Andrews, but without success. He was, however, in grand form in the Open Championship at Muirfield, where he finished third to Vardon and Taylor.

In the amateur event, Tait defeated one after another all the crack players of the day—Mr. Hutchings, Mr. Laidlay, Mr. Ball, Mr. Horace Hutchinson, and Mr. Hilton. He went from strength to strength, and apparently seemed to play better each round, his play in the final being absolutely perfect.

Writing of this match, his opponent, Mr. Hilton, says :—

I never remember witnessing finer golf than that displayed by Mr. F. G. Tait in the final round at Sandwich. His driving, although probably not quite as long as of yore, was infinitely more accurate than what we have been accustomed to associate with the name of the champion; in fact, for my own part, I have never yet seen more accurate play both from the tee and through the green. He has always had the reputation of being a good putter, and he certainly did not fail to act up to that reputation, his holing out at two or three yards being marvellously correct; in fact, it was golf of the finest order, and the sensational part of the performance was almost lost in the machine-like accuracy with which the holes were played one after another.

Tait's triumph at Sandwich was received

F. G. Tait

with immense satisfaction at Edinburgh Castle; colonel, officers, and men all entering into the joy, which was quite national. The Championship Cup was added to the other trophies which decorated the mess table of the Black Watch, and Tait's popularity, if possible, increased. He was elected an honorary member of the Burgess Golfing Society, and played several matches on their new green at Barnton, notably a three-ball match with Mr. Armour and Mr. Gray as opponents, in which he lowered the record of the green with a score of 76.

Instead of the annual visit to St. Andrews in September—a visit he never, with this exception, missed for about twenty years—Tait went to Ballater to act as one of Her Majesty's guard at Balmoral. The life at Ballater suited him admirably, and he always looked back on the six weeks he spent there as among the happiest days of his life. Tait had had no great experience of the gentle craft of angling, and certainly had never thrown a fly upon the waters with the hope of securing a salmon. Notwithstanding his inexperience, he turned out to be an excellent disciple of the great Isaac, and landed many and good fish, being indeed the most successful fisherman on the water which the Queen so kindly reserves for the officers on duty at Balmoral.

[Photo by Mr. Milne.

F. G. TAIT AT BALMORAL, 1896.

A Record

During his stay at Ballater he met the Czar of Russia, to whom he was presented as the hero of the Scottish national game; but the following letters, fortunately preserved, give the best insight possible into his life at the Queen's Highland home :—

The Barracks,
Ballater,
20 *September*, 1896.

My dear Mother,

Thanks for your letter. We will be awfully busy here this week with the Czar. The band and pipers are here, and another fifty men, also a troop of the Scots Greys. Great preparations at Ballater for the Czar; electric light and flags, and all sorts of things. Sir W. Brooks is going to give me my first head. I had a jolly day partridge shooting with Bogie Hamilton at Skene; we got twenty-five brace. I have met the Duke and Duchess of York, both very nice and pleasant. I hope to get two or three more days' stalking yet. Lord Glenesk always gives his heads away. This is an awfully expensive place; we have got to do so much driving, and a lot of dining out to be done.

The Czar comes at seven o'clock on Tuesday evening. I hope there will be no bomb throwing anywhere near us, as the wrong people are generally hit; personally I would rather be killed by a golf ball. If I get a good salmon I will send it to you. Please send me some calling cards. I don't think Lieutenant Tait will win the King William IVth Medal this year. Tell Alec to stick in and win. Willie might win the handicap if he has not to use his heavy iron too much.

F. G. Tait

I hope Edith will win the Ladies' Medal. Hope Uncle John is fit.

Yours ever,

F. G. TAIT.

The Barracks,
Ballater,
25 *September*, 1896.

My dear Father,

I thought you might like to hear of my interview with the Czar. We dined at Balmoral with the Household on Wednesday night, and after dinner we were presented to the Queen and the Czar. The Queen was very gracious, and spoke to us all. Five of us went over from here. Our three selves and two officers of the Scots Greys—very nice fellows. Balmoral is nine miles from here. I was introduced to the Czar (or rather presented) by the Duke of Connaught, as the Champion Golfer of Scotland. He did not seem to know much about the game, but he soon picked it up. I spoke to him for ten minutes or so. He was exceedingly pleasant to talk to. He is short, very much like the Duke of York both in figure and face. I should say that he was a very timid and nervous man. We have just received an order to go to Balmoral and write our names in the Queen's birthday book.

I had a great day's fishing on Tuesday before the Czar came. I killed five salmon, weighing 22, 14, 12, 7½, and 6½ lbs.; that is our best day so far. Up to now we have killed twenty-nine. The Queen gives us four miles of the Dee. To-morrow we shoot partridges with Keiller (of Dundee fame). We expect some more stalking soon. Please tell

A Record

the old lady to tell Gordon that I will be "took" here for the golfing picture. Dining with the Household I sat next Sir Arthur Bigge, and during dinner about twenty telegrams came in from all parts of the Kingdom, and one from Egypt and one from Lord Salisbury. He seems to answer all the Queen's telegrams. We met the Queen's doctor, and all sorts of people. I hope Alec will win the medal this year. If you see Macfie you might tell him that I am now an awfully keen fisherman. No more time. Just off to Balmoral.

Yours ever,

F. G. TAIT.

The Barracks,

Ballater,

My dear Mother, 11 *November* 1896.

Thanks for your letter. We leave here on Saturday morning, Bruce and Cameron by the early train. I come on with a sergeant and a man later on. I remain here after them to hand over the barracks, etc. I get to Edinburgh about 5.15 in the afternoon.

We dined at Balmoral last night, and were again presented to Her Most Gracious Majesty. She was good enough to speak to us all. Personally, I had quite a nice little chat. She can make herself very pleasant, and she certainly did last night. I had a long chat with Sir James Reid, he is a very jovial fellow. No more time. Will look you up if I have time on Saturday.

Yours affectionately,

F. G. TAIT.

When Tait returned to Edinburgh he found his regiment about to leave for York, and, probably not without a sigh, he turned his back for a time on Scotland and her fair capital.

Tait remained at York until the end of 1897, and during his stay there made many friends. Chief among these were two young Lieutenants, Mr. A. G. Wauchope and Mr. N. N. Ramsay. Tait had many interests in common with them, and these three were fast friends to the end. All three were keen sportsmen, and devoted to every form of game. Ramsay, indeed, was a fine all-round athlete, and will be well remembered by all old Wyke-hamists as one of the best football players the school has turned out. He was no mean golfer, and, like Tait, took a great interest in pipe playing and Highland dancing, in which latter art he was quite an adept. Tait worked very hard at the bagpipes, and whenever he had a chance he went to the meetings of the Pipe Club in Edinburgh.

In the beginning of 1897 Tait was on leave in Scotland. There was hard frost in January, so hard that golf was impossible for a time. Tait, however, got his fun out of curling instead.

Writing to his brother Jack, he gives some account of things during his leave—

Edinburgh,

My dear Jack,   *27 January*, 1897.

I hope you are fit. The old lady has asked me about fifty times to-day if I have written

A Record

to you, so I hope to be able to answer yes to the fifty-first time. I came up here on the 14th of this month for two months. Up till now I have only played one day's golf, as there has been a lot of snow and frost. I have had about a week's curling. I am very fond of the game, but a week at a time is quite enough for me. I like curling in the country, where you meet a lot of ploughmen and gardeners, and that class of people, and then you get plenty of excitement. Down at Coates' Club, where I have been playing (just behind the Grange Field), you only meet judges and lawyers, and business men and that sort of crowd.

I am getting on first class with the pipes. I can play five marches now. I have just read the old lady's letter to you; I see she has not got the spelling of my best march right. " Glendaruel " is the name. My other tunes are—" The 79th's Farewell to Gibraltar," " The Portree Men," " Pibroch of Donnil Dhu," and " Jenny's Bawbee."

I am learning a strathspey called " Brechin Castle," and another march, " The Earl of Mansfield."

Willie had a go at my chanter last night; I think he is going to start again. Jolly for the governor and old lady. The old man is gradually getting broken in to the pipes as he was to my dog " Nails." I am going to Prestwick and St. Andrews for a week or two when the frost goes. The Welsh Match is off for Saturday. The English Union has made A. J. Gould a professional, because he accepted a testimonial (nothing like such a large one as Grace got). Wales won't play without Gould, and so the match is off until the matter is settled. Wales are good this year. We have got a capital forward team for them however. I think we ought to win all right. We expect to get some capital cricket at York this summer. I am very keen, but I shall not play until I have got the serious golf off my hands.

The last time I saw Bob Simpson he was asking very tenderly after you, and wanted to know when you were coming back, and all that sort of thing. I suppose you will be back this year for six months or so. It will do you good to have a month or two at St. Andrews, golfing, and a dip at the Step Rock every now and then. You will then have a chance of playing the best ball of Andrew Kirkcaldy and myself.

The Amateur Championship is earlier this year, and is to be played for at Muirfield (a course I hate like poison), last week in April I think. The Open just a fortnight later.

Hoping to see you sometime this year.

Yours ever,
F. G. TAIT.

Tait went to Manchester to see the International Football Match in 1897, and in a characteristic note written on his return to York, he expresses his disgust at the poor play of his countrymen.

Infantry Barracks,
York,
21 *March*, 1897.

My dear Mother,

Many thanks for your letter. I have not got over that football match yet.

I never saw any Scotch forward team play so badly.

A Record

The English team played very well, especially the quarters. We are very busy here. I have been up at six every morning except one since I came; rather a change from Edinburgh life. I had a day at Ganton yesterday, and played well. Young Wauchope came with me. Colonel very fit. When we reported ourselves the morning after we came back from leave, he said, " I am very pleased to see you all back again." The last two days have been perfect here. Sorry I did not see the governor before I left; hope he is fit.

Hope to have another day's golf this week.

Yours affectionately,
F. G. TAIT.

Tait's remark in this letter that he had "played well" on the previous day at Ganton, hardly describes sufficiently what took place. As a matter of fact, we know from other sources that he did the round in the extraordinary score of 68. The course was, however, rather shorter than usual, so that the score of 70, which he made just before the Park and Vardon match, is held to be the accepted amateur record.

At Luffness, Tait won the Scratch Medal with a score of 78; and at St. Andrews he tied with Mr. Leslie Balfour Melville at 84. This tie had to be played off in August, the first attempt having resulted in honours being again easy; at the third time of asking, however, Tait was victorious.

In the Amateur Championship he was

F. G. Tait

beaten by his old friend and opponent, Mr. W. Greig, but in the Open Championship he was in grand form, and finished third to Mr. Hilton and Braid.

At York the Black Watch Cricket Eleven were having a successful season, winning 33 matches and losing 9. Tait stood second in the batting averages, with a record of 523 runs made in 27 innings, giving him an average of over 19.

The last two months of 1897 Tait spent in Scotland on leave, and proceeded at the beginning of 1898 to Aldershot, where he went through six months gymnastic training with a view to qualifying for a staff appointment. He describes his shooting and golfing exploits in the following brotherly letter:—

> 38, George Square,
> 28 *October*, 1897.

Dear Jack,

I hope you are fit. I am on first leave just now—that is to say, 15th October to 31st December. I had a week with a fellow, Ramsay, in my regiment, who comes from Alyth in Perthshire. We had some capital shooting. I killed a capercailzie (I hope that is the correct spelling).

I am going to stay with a man, Kerr, at Luffness House for a few days. He manages the tramways all over the country, and is consequently called "Tramway Kerr." A little later on I am going to stay with him, and help him shoot his covers.

A Record

I made an awful mess of the last 3 holes on the Medal day last September. I have not been playing enough this year. I can play 15 holes very well, and 3 very badly. I ought to have finished in 77 at the very most. I don't care much about the scoring game.

I am getting on very well with the pipes; I think the old man is beginning to appreciate their strains. Old Bob Simpson always asks for you; he is a capital chap. He has a very fine business now, and is getting very fat. I suppose you are entitled to a year's leave now. Come back next year and play Rolland and me for a year's pay!

If you come across the 42nd, look out for Major Wiltshire, Major Burton, and F. D. Murray.

No more time,

Yours aye,

F. G. Tait.

While at St. Andrews, in November, 1897, Tait played several very notable matches; a 4-ball match in particular, with Mr. Edward Blackwell against Andrew Kirkcaldy and Willie Auchterlonie, is especially noteworthy. The amateurs played most brilliant golf, thrashing the professionals by a pocketful of holes, and in the first round establishing what must be a record for this species of golf. Their figures were: Out, 5 4 3 4 4 4 4 1 4 = 33; in, 3 4 3 5 5 4 4 4 4 = 36; total, 69. The eighth hole was done by Mr. Blackwell in one stroke, and I have no doubt he paid the full penalty.

On January 1st, 1898, Tait migrated to

F. G. Tait

Aldershot, where he remained, with the exception of several golfing excursions, until the end of June. At St. Andrews he was unsuccessful, but at Hoylake he was in grand form, and regained the Championship Cup, a most popular win. On the eve of starting he writes to his mother—

17, Grosvenor Road,
Aldershot,
16 *May*, 1898.

My dear Mother,

I am off to Hoylake on Friday, so I shall have Saturday and Monday for practice. I have been playing much better, so I hope to do myself justice this year.

I have been offered a gymnastic appointment already by Colonel Napier, the Superintendent of Gymnasia for the Army. Not bad for Frederick, considering that I have not got my certificate yet. I have accepted the billet; it is at Colchester. I suppose I shall go there in July, unless the War Office disapproves, or Colonel Andy cannot get on without me. As I said before, the gymnastic billets are the best in the army; I don't mean in pay, as there is practically no difference (because while you are away from your regiment you still have to pay regimental subscriptions, etc.), but you are entirely your own master and run your own show. I intend to have a model gym.

If you have any message for Janion send me a letter here, to arrive not later than Friday morning.

No more time,

Yours affectionately,
F. G. TAIT.

A Record

And after the Cup was played for and won, he writes the following notes on his victory—

17, Grosvenor Road,
Aldershot,
2 June, 1898.

My dear Mother,

I ought to have written to you long ago, but I have had so many things to do and think about that I have only just started to get through a most awful quantity of correspondence.

Many thanks for all your letters. I had some very narrow shaves, but I played very well with the exception of that fatal day, Thursday. I was feeling very ill, and I really never began to play with Low until I was 1 down and 3 to play.

I broke my driver in the middle of the round, and I drove all over the place with the other one. I played any amount of bad shots, but I can assure you that I also played some fairly good ones at the end.

I played four of the best shots that I have ever played in the last part of my round with Low.

In the final I was as fit as a fiddle, and played well up to form.

If I can get three days I shall go to Prestwick, but it is doubtful. Hope you are all very fit.

Yours affectionately,
F. G. Tait.

Almost as interesting as the Championship was the match played at Hoylake between the local club and the Tantallon Golf Club of North Berwick. The result of the match and

F. G. Tait

a short account of Tait's match with Mr. Ball, taken from the *Scotsman*, are worthy of a place in this record of Tait's doings—

TEAMS.

Tantallon.		*Royal Liverpool.*	
F. G. Tait	5	John Ball, Jun.	0
G. L. Dalziel	0	H. H. Hilton	3
W. B. Taylor	0	J. Graham, Jun.	14
Dr. Lawrence Gray	0	C. E. Dick	7
T. T. Gray	0	Charles Hutchings	6
Duncan MacLaren	0	F. A. Fairlie	5
C. Whigham	0	R. S. Hilton	2
T. Lorimer Campbell	0	H. A. Farrar	8
D. M. Jackson	0	E. Spencer	1
E. R. Turnbull	0	H. Holden	2
H. H. Harley	5	E. D. Prothero	0
W. T. Armour	0	W. Crowther	3
Oliver Thomson	0	J. Hornby	2
W. G. Bloxom	0	W. C. Glover	14
Total ...	10	Total ...	67

Majority for Royal Liverpool, 57 holes.

Last year at North Berwick it was given to Mr. Ball and Mr. Ross to lead the way; to-day Mr. Ball had as his opponent Mr. F. G Tait. A meeting between two such players would at any time be interesting; a double significance attached to the tussle between them on the eve of the Championship. A few holes were sufficient to show that Mr. Tait was at the very height of his game. He made a grand start by winning the first hole, where he ran up beautifully, in 4. Mr. Ball, however, took the second in rare style in 3, and squared the game. From this point the Scotsman, playing with great brilliancy, dash, and judgment, gradually established

A Record

a substantial lead. So faultless and effective was his game, that at the turn he had 4 holes in hand. Coming home the game was of a more even character. At the 11th hole Mr. Tait played a perfect stroke from the tee, and might, had he required it to win, have had a 2. A 3 was sufficiently good to secure him the hole. This made him 5 up, and though he lost the fourteenth he won the next, and with three halved holes to complete the round he was five up at the finish.

The scores were:—Mr. Tait—4 4 5 3 4 4 4 5 4 5 3 4 4 6 5 6 5 5=80; Mr. Ball—5 3 6 3 5 5 5 5 4 5 4 4 4 5 6 6 5 5=85.

If in the second stage Mr. Tait did not place anything to the credit of his side, he did not allow his opponent to gain any advantage. With Mr. Ball in improved form, as compared with the early part of the day, their game was of a closer character than was that in the first round. It was remarkable as a finished exposition of golf, and as an indication of the great capabilities of the players. In the first instance the advantage lay with Mr. Ball, and at the turn he was 2 holes to the good. This lead he held, despite the efforts of Mr. Tait to wipe it off, until the fifteenth hole. He lost the sixteenth, however the second last was halved, and Mr. Tait won the home hole, where the Hoylake player was stimied and tried unsuccessfully to loft. Accordingly the match was halved.

Mr. Ball's score for the round was 78, made up as follows:—6 4 5 3 4 4 3 5 3 4 4 4 3 5 4 6 5 6=78.

Shortly after these events Tait won the St. George's Cup at Sandwich for the second time. He and Mr. Mure Fergusson were all square and one to play, the latter lying close to the hole while Tait was at the far edge of the green. Tait ran down a long putt, while Mr. Fergusson, missing his for the half, must be deemed on this occasion a most unlucky man.

Tait went to Prestwick for the Open Championship, and finished fifth with a score of 315. He also went to Colchester as Inspector of Gymnasia for the Eastern District, but only remained there a few weeks, for in August he was appointed to the Scottish District, much to his satisfaction and the joy of his northern friends.

His headquarters were at Maryhill Barracks, Glasgow, and the other stations he had to superintend included Hamilton and Ayr in the Western District, Perth, Stirling, Edinburgh Castle, Piershill (Edinburgh), Glencorse (Edinburgh), Fort George, and Inverness. His duties included two visits a year at least to each of these centres, and a yearly inspection with the Colonel commanding at Aldershot. Tait took up his residence in Glasgow in October, his usual custom being to spend from Monday till Friday there, and the " week ends " golfing or shooting, generally in the Edinburgh district.

At the end of the year he was a guest at Luffness House and Gilmerton, where he assisted at the covert shooting. He had in July renewed his connection with the New

A Record

Luffness Golf Club, and led the team to victory in the County Cup already referred to. The Cup is played for by a team of four from each club, and two foursome matches are played to decide each round. Tait was partnered with Mr. Armour, and the other couple were Mr. T. T. Gray and Mr. A. M. Ross. In the first round they drew a bye, in the second they beat Dirleton Castle, in the third the Honourable Company, and in the final defeated the Tantallon Club by 4 holes. Tait, with his usual modesty, would take no credit for his part in the victory, but gave his partner all the praise, and it must be said that Mr. Armour gave him most able support. In the following year Tait was persuaded to play for the Tantallon Club, but his team were defeated in the first round.

At St. Andrews Tait tied with Mr. Leslie Balfour Melville for the Second Medal at the Autumn Meeting at 82 strokes; and on playing off, won with an almost perfect round of 78, his outward half being 37.

Just before this, Freddie and his brother Alec engaged the two great Hoylake players, Mr. Hutchings and Mr. J. Graham, junio , in a big match over two rounds of the St. Andrews' green. The Taits gave a grand display, fairly running away from their opponents; giving them, as Freddie termed it, an

F. G. Tait

"awful twisting." This was not owing to the bad or even indifferent play of the Hoylake men, but simply because the Taits played the best foursome game that has ever been played on the time-honoured course.

One of their rounds easily beat all previous records, and their rivals had the somewhat unremunerative consolation of having been spectators of a wonderful performance. This round required only 74 strokes. Here are the details: Out, 4 6 4 4 6 4 4 3 3 = 38; in, 3 2 4 5 6 5 4 4 3 = 36. "I did quite well, but 'the young un' did more than his share" was Freddie's characteristic remark at the end of the round.

Meanwhile, Tait had been studying hard at his profession, and we find him writing to his brother about his future military prospects—

38, George Square,
Edinburgh,
10 *November*, 1898.

Dear Jack,

The old lady has insisted on my writing to you, and as I am the only one who never causes her any trouble, here goes.

I finished my examination for promotion to-day; I think I have examined the examiners all right. My new billet suits me very well, and the work is much more interesting than ordinary regimental work. I hope to be a captain within the next two years. Bullen Smith, the man that exchanged with me, is now a captain. I don't envy him at all. I

A Record

was at the University for an hour to-day with the governor, driving golf balls for him. He thinks that he has now fairly settled the whole thing; 215 feet a second he makes out to be the initial velocity of a golf ball. As far as I can remember, he got the initial velocity at one time nearly up to 400 feet a second. His theory is *underspin*.

Next week I am shooting five days with a pal of mine, John Kerr, at Gilmorton and Luffness. We shall get about 600 head a day for six guns. I met a Major Miller Wallnutt,* in the Gordon Highlanders; he said he knew you well. He seems a very nice fellow, and is a fine big chap.

I have had a fairly successful golfing season this year, and I hope to do better next year, as I ought to be in better practice.

Benjie and I did a 74 two days before the Medal, and gave two Hoylake fellows, Graham and Hutchings, an awful twisting.

"Strive to cultivate," &c.,†

Yours ever,
F. G. Tait.

In the beginning of the following year Tait received the news that he had passed his examination with honours in tactics, and was therefore qualified to receive his promotion whenever his chance should come.

---

* Major Wallnutt was killed at Ladysmith during the Boers desperate attack on Waggon Hill, Jan. 6th, 1900.

† This was a reference to a favorite dictum of the Rev. A. K. H. Boyd, which had impressed Freddie and his brother Jack. It ran: "Strive to cultivate humility, you need it sadly."

F. G. Tait

The first two months of 1899 Tait spent in the ordinary duties of his appointment, and in golfing on odd days at Muirfield and Luffness. He was able to get a day or two's curling at Tillicoultry, and also at Gilmerton, and in the beginning of February he visited St. Andrews twice; once for a few days' golf, and once in order to attend the meeting of the Rules of Golf Committee. Tait was one of the prime movers in the last revision of the rules, and his suggestions were always most valuable. When the question of a Golf Union arose in England he took a firm stand against the idea, and when later the whole matter was complicated and nearly bungled by the action of the weaker brethren in the Royal and Ancient Club, Tait was one of the ringleaders, who saved the club from adopting a cowardly half-way course. His love for his mother club was very great, and he always used his immense influence to forward her best interests, his shrewd good sense always prompting him to advocate the better policy for her to pursue.

In the beginning of February Tait played a rather peculiar match at Muirfield, when he undertook to play the best ball of three well-known players. As the match turned out they might have taken half-a-dozen more into their combination without having the best of it, for Tait won by about 12 holes

A Record

on the 36 hole match. This match is rather unique, and the result goes to show that there is not always safety in numbers, for probably the "three" do not play up to their form, owing to carelessness, and the absence of that feeling of responsibility which puts men on their metal. Tait, however, did the two rounds in something like 73 and 77, which no doubt had a good deal to do with the verdict.

In the middle of March, Tait paid a visit to the gymnasium at Aldershot, where he saw a lot of his old friends in the Black Watch. While South he visited Oxford with a team of Lothian golfers, captained by Mr. R. H. Johnston, but the visit was a disastrous one for the Scots, the Oxonians beating them very easily. On the following day, March 11th, Tait had the pleasure of seeing Scotland beat England in the Rugby International Match at Blackheath. At the May meeting at St. Andrews Tait played perfect golf, carrying all before him with a grand score of 80.

The Amateur Championship at Prestwick was played at the end of May, and Tait was throughout a hot favourite, though he was hardly up to his best form at the time. In the match against Hoylake, the particulars of which will be found below, he played well, but in several of the rounds in the Championship his play was very uncertain. In his match with Mr. Hilton he played excellently, his putting being quite up to his best, but in the second half of the final he seemed to fall away from the good game he had played in the morning. I do not think that he was quite fit at the time, and he was also rather "over-golfed." I remember him lying down on the sofa before he had finished his lunch on that final day, and complaining that he felt very tired, a most unusual thing for him to do. However he soon regained his form, and playing wonderful golf won the St. George's Cup with a record score of 76 and 79. This 76 was one of the finest rounds he ever played, the tees being very far back, and the weather being most unfavourable for low scoring and in marked contrast to the following days on which the Open Championship was held. In this latter event Tait was easily first among the amateurs, though but seventh in the whole field.

In July the great Park-Vardon match was played, and Tait refereed for Park, both at North Berwick and at Ganton. Tait had confidence in Park's ability to pull off the match, and was greatly disappointed with the result. Tait, John Ball, and I stayed with Mr. Broadwood at Scarborough for the Ganton half of the match, Tait being the life and soul of the house party. Tait and Park played Mr. Ball and Vardon a 36 hole match, but

A Record

lost by five. In a letter to his brother he
comments on these events—

Western Club,
Glasgow,
12 *July*, 1899.

Dear Jack,

Thanks for your letter. I played fairly badly
all through the championship except against Hilton.
I have now knocked him out of the championship
five times, and licked him once in a Club Match,
Tantallon *v.* Royal Liverpool. I don't think I
would have lost to John Ball if I had not got so
many up in the morning. I was 5 up at the
14th hole, and I thought the whole show was
over, and played the last four very slackly. I
have learnt a lesson, however, which I hope to
remember. I left the amateurs a long way behind
in the St. George's Cup, in which I played a real
hot game, but I did not keep it up in the Open
Championship.

Your golf balls were sent off about the 20th of
May. I played with that particular kind of ball
in the Amateur Championship. I think they are
as good as you can get. It is desperate hard to
get a good ball just now I find.

I was one of the umpires in the first half of
the Park-Vardon Match the other day at North
Berwick. Park drove badly, otherwise he might
have been a hole or two up. His putting was very
fine, however. I have just applied to be allowed
to go out to the Transvaal in the event of my
regiment being sent on active service. I think
business is meant this time. This billet of mine
suits me fine, but I don't want to miss a chance

F. G. Tait

of active service. I suppose we shall see you early next year.

Strive, etc.

Yours ever,
F. G. TAIT.

A description of the Tantallon Match and Tait's encounter with Mr. Hilton, is here appended.

Tantallon *v.* Hoylake, 20th May, 1899. The following were the results of the first round, which consisted of singles—

FIRST ROUND.

Royal Liverpool.		*Tantallon.*	
Mr. H. H. Hilton	o	Mr. F. G. Tait	2
Mr. J. Ball, jun.	o	Mr. J. E. Laidlay	2
Mr. J. Graham, jun.	2	Mr. R. Maxwell	o
Mr. C. E. Dick	1	Mr. A. W. Robertson	o
Mr. R. H. Dun	2	Mr. W. B. Taylor	o
Mr. A. C. Blain	o	Mr. C. F. Whigham	8
Mr. H. A. Farrar	o	Mr. J. M'Culloch	6
Mr. R. Goold	o	Mr. C. L. Dalziel	8
Mr. E. Spencer	5	Mr. Josiah Livingstone ...	o
Mr. J. Hornby	o	Mr. H. H. Harley............	1
Mr. W. C. Glover	5	Mr. H. M. Brown............	o
Mr. W. Dod	o	Mr. G. H. Law	1
Total ...	15	Total ...	28

Majority for Tantallon, 13 holes.

The first couple, the Champion (Mr. F. G. Tait) and Mr. H. H. Hilton, struck off punctually at one o'clock, by which time the weather had brightened up. Formerly Mr. Ball used to be the first card of the Royal Liverpool Club, but this year the ex-Open Champion, who has lately been playing in his best form, was in the premier place; and as the two

A Record

are typical representatives of first class golf, the match naturally attracted the great majority of the spectators, about 500, including a good many ladies, following the players round the course. Though Mr. Hilton has twice won the Open Championship, he has never annexed the amateur blue ribbon; and for this fact Mr. Tait has a good deal to account, Mr. Hilton having fallen before him on no fewer than four occasions, most notably in the final at Sandwich, when so many heroes had succumbed in former stages. If Mr. Hilton could on this occasion disappoint the evil genius which seems to dog his footsteps when he meets Mr. Tait, it was felt that his chances of being successful next week would be rosy. This, and the international character of the match, gave piquancy to its otherwise interesting nature. The spectators were not disappointed, for the play on both sides was excellent, and the little weakness which eventually led to Mr. Hilton's new defeat was on the putting green, where he several times failed to give the ball a chance; a weakness unknown to his opponent, who seems always to act on the golden maxim, "Never up, never in," and who on the green really missed nothing, while several times his holing out from a distance was quite phenomenal, one native being heard to remark, after Mr. Tait's three successive 3's at the fifth, sixth, and seventh holes, "It's no gowff at a', it's jist miracles." The Champion made rather a bad start by visiting the railway, a mistake which he repeated in the afternoon, and which caused Charlie Hunter to remark, in his pawky style, "I think he maun hae shares in the company." Mr. Hilton therefore drew first blood in 4. At the second hole the Champion half stimied his opponent, to whom he had to play the

F. G. Tait

odd; but Mr. Hilton managed the stroke, and secured a half in 3. Both had fine lies in front of the Cardinal, but Mr. Tait's second had an advantage, as it was on a straight line to the hole, and a fine pitch and equally fine putt won for him the hole in 4—a stroke below par. The fourth hole was lost by Mr. Tait, chiefly owing to the watery nature of the green, which made the ground soft. and shortened what would have been a good pitch. Both got nicely over the Himalayas; but Mr. Hilton, by weak putting, lost this to his opponent's 3. The match thus again stood square. Then, with a brilliant approach and putt, Mr. Tait secured the Elysian Fields again under par in 3, following this up with another fine approach and putt at the Railway hole. Monkton was halved in 5. At the end hole Mr. Hilton should have reduced the lead against him, for, after a grand second, Mr. Tait was in the bunker which guards the hole; but Mr. Hilton's approach and putt following were both weak, while Mr. Tait's recovery was so good that he got down in 5 to 6, and at the turn stood 3 up. At the tenth hole Mr. Hilton holed a long putt for 4, which, with a hearty cheer from the crowd, seemed to hearten him a little, for he also secured the homeward Himalaya, and was now only 1 down. The Duke was halved in a ding-dong style in 5, but at the thirteenth hole Mr. Tait, after a great second, holed out in 4 to Mr. Hilton's 5, and raised his lead to 2. The fourteenth was halved in an orthodox 4, and then, in going to the fifteenth, Mr. Hilton came to grief in the bunker to the left, which has been the scene of many hard words. This was finely carried by the Amateur Champion, thus showing that the hazard is not, as some call it,

A Record

unfair, but a test of good swiping. The Cardinal's back was a pretty half in four, and in ordinary phraseology Mr. Tait here won the match by 3 up and 2 to play; but the bye had to be added to the general result, and in this the Alps, where both played short in their second, fell to Mr. Hilton in 5, Mr. Tait having given his long putt rather too much in trying for a 4, leaving himself too much to do. The last hole was halved in 3, and this left the Champion 2 up on the round. The details of the scores were:—Mr. Tait : Out, 6 3 4 5 3 3 3 5 5 = 37; in, 5 5 5 4 4 4 4 6 3 = 40; total, 77. Mr. Hilton: Out, 4 3 5 4 4 4 4 5 6 = 39; in, 4 4 5 5 4 5 4 5 3 = 39; total, 78.

THE FOURSOMES.

Royal Liverpool.		Tantallon.	
Messrs. Hilton & Ball	0	Messrs. Laidlay & Tait ...	0
Messrs. Graham & Dick ...	3	Messrs. Maxwell & Robertson	0
Messrs. Dun & Farrar	0	Messrs. McCulloch & Brown	3
Messrs. Blair & Dod	0	Messrs. Whigham & Dalziel	3
Messrs. R. Goold & Hornby	0	Messrs. Taylor & Law......	4
Messrs. Glover & Spencer...	1	Messrs. Livingstone & Harley	0
	4		10

Majority for Tantallon on foursomes, 6 holes; majority on match, 19 holes.

Tait's next golfing expedition was to St. Andrews, where, notwithstanding a 4 holes penalty, he won the Calcutta Cup, playing with great power throughout the competition.

F. G. Tait

He was, however, unable to win the Jubilee Vase, his handicap of "owe 5" being too much for mortal man to strive against, unless indeed, the hitherto honourable term " scratch " has fallen from its high estate. True, he had won the Calcutta Cup owing 4 holes, but it is easier for a player of Tait's power to give 4 holes on the new course than 4 strokes on the old. The Autumn Medal, however, fell to him with the good score of 81, and with it the Glennie Medal for the third time with the fine aggregate of 161. Mr. Edward Blackwell should at least have equalled this 81, had he not had the misfortune to have his ball kicked into the road at the 17th hole by a stupid spectator. No one, however, least of all Mr. Blackwell, will do any thing but rejoice at the fact that Tait was enabled to finish his great golfing career victoriously on the green he loved so well.

Tait played his last great match against Mr. John Ball at St. Anne's on Monday, October 2nd. The match is so interesting for many reasons, that I give the account of it written by Mr. Hilton at the time. It was, alas, the final of a series of great struggles between two of the greatest golfers and finest sportsmen the world of sport has produced. Tait won by 1 hole, and so avenged his defeat in the championship. He had a great admiration for Mr. Ball and for his golf, and the

[*Snapshot by E. A. Burchardt, Esq.*

EDWARD BLACKWELL AND F. G. TAIT ABOUT TO START
FOR HIS LAST MEDAL ROUND, September 1899.

A Record

feeling was, one may be sure, fully reciprocated.

Mr. Tait, having had only one opportunity of playing over the links previous to the actual encounter, was naturally at a slight disadvantage, but St. Anne's is a links which does not materially favour the home player. The distances are not difficult to judge, and in most cases the approach can be played well up to the hole. He was certainly handicapped, in that the breeze—a strong one too—was blowing from an exactly contrary direction to that in which he played his preliminary round, but that this did not seriously interfere with his game was proved by the excellent judgment he displayed in gauging the distances in his approaches. When the players started there was a strong wind from the north-west, which, however, is a favourable wind for the course, as it aids the player on the narrow outward journey. After the first hole had been well halved in 3, Mr. Tait drew first blood at the second with the aid of a pretty 4, Mr. Ball being very short with his second, driving into the railway. At the third hole Mr. Tait was never in sight of a half, while another sliced tee shot was mainly instrumental in losing him the fourth. At the fifth Mr. Ball ran down a longish putt for 2, and thus stood 2 up. Mr. Tait had an excellent chance of reducing the lead at the sixth, but was faulty in his approach from the edge of the green, and allowed the opportunity to slip, a compliment which Mr. Ball returned at the seventh, a four-foot putt for a win in 5 proving too much for him. Faulty in distance from the tee to the seventh, Mr. Tait was short in his approach putt, and Mr. Ball had no difficulty in increasing his lead to 3, only to lose the ninth through being far too much to the right with his second, and obtaining a very bad lie in consequence, leaving him 2 up at the turn.

From a slightly pulled tee shot to the tenth Mr. Tait was punished, and never making up his leeway, once more found himself 3 down, whilst the eleventh enabled Mr. Ball to add another to his lead, Mr. Tait being again in trouble from the tee. He recovered one of his losses at the thirteenth, a magnificent tee shot of fully 230 yards eventually resting within two feet of the hole, Mr. Ball, making a splendid bid for a half, only just failing to hole his short pitch on to the green. After three uneventful halves, Mr. Tait once again reduced the lead by the aid of a brilliant 3 at the sixteenth hole, but lost the seventeenth chiefly through a very badly sliced tee shot. He made amends for this, however, by taking the last in 3, and so stood 2 down on the round, the approximate scores being: Mr. Ball, 78; Mr. Tait, 81.

The afternoon round opened in favour of the Amateur Champion. He easily annexed the first, his opponent being wide from the tee; whilst Mr. Tait was hard pressed for a half at the second; a four-yard putt doing the needful. Useful putts after indifferent approaches resulted in a half at the third, but a faulty approach cost Mr. Tait the fourth; Mr. Ball, as in the morning, playing the hole perfectly. The fifth was well halved in 3, a similar result being achieved at the sixth; but at the seventh Mr. Tait gave his opponent no chance, as he holed his approach, thus accomplishing a hole of over 500 yards in three, and this bit of sensation seemed to act as a tonic to him, as from this point

A Record

he never really looked back, as after a half in 3, he secured the ninth in a perfect 4, this leaving him in the same position as he stood in the morning round, viz., 2 down.

After the tee shots had been played to the tenth, the hole looked like going to Mr. Tait, but whereas Mr. Ball, from a half-topped tee shot, was lying comparatively well, Mr. Tait was unexpectedly found badly trapped in the extreme end of the bunker, and eventually Mr. Ball secured the hole, and once again stood 3 up. Going to the long eleventh, Mr. Tait considerably outdrove his opponent, but eventually had to be content with a half, a similar result being achieved at the twelfth, where again Mr. Tait had a putt for the hole. At the thirteenth Mr. Ball stimied his opponent, who however deftly manipulated the stroke, and secured a half, leaving Mr. Ball 3 up with 5 to play, generally a fairly secure position, but not secure enough on this occasion, as the sequel proved. An error of judgment was mainly instrumental in losing Mr. Ball the fourteenth, as, taking a cleek for his second, he was very short, whilst at the fifteenth Mr. Tait had much the best of the tee shot; Mr. Ball eventually making a bold bid for a half, which was, however, ineffectual. One up and 3 to play is not as pleasant as 3 up and 5 to play, at least, from the St. Anne's point of view. But worse was to come, as Mr. Tait, playing the sixteenth to perfection in 3, brought matters on a level footing, whilst the seventeenth appeared likely to go the same way, as Mr. Ball was weak from the tee, and gave his opponent an opportunity, which he just failed to take an advantage of, with the result that the match stood all square with 1 to play. Mr.

F. G. Tait

Tait's tee shot was a long one, but wide of the line, and found a resting-place in the bunkers on the right. On the other hand, Mr. Ball was well on the line, and as he followed it up with an excellent approach within seven yards or so of the hole, Mr. Tait's chance did not appear rosy. He was lying hard and clean in the bunker, however, and playing the stroke to perfection, reached the green a few feet further away from the hole than Mr. Ball. His approach putt was not one of his best, but it left him within three feet of the hole. On the other hand, Mr. Ball, who was lying in a small cup on the green, was woefully short, and failing to get his fourth down, gave Mr. Tait an opportunity of avenging his narrow defeat at Prestwick, which he did not fail to take advantage of, and so ended one of the best matches ever fought out on a golf green.

On the play, a halved match would have been a fitting determination, as, whereas Mr. Ball undoubtedly played the steadier golf, as he had done at Prestwick, Mr. Tait's efforts in the last half of the second round deserved at least a half, if not the match.

For a long while, in fact, well into the second round, Mr. Ball more than held his own in the long game. But Mr. Tait, who seemed to gain a new lease of life at the turn of the second round, had considerably the better of the wooden club play in the later stages, his driving being quite reminiscent of old days. It was an excellent match, played in true sporting spirit, and the only fault to be found is that such games do not occur more frequently.

From St. Anne's, Tait went to Cowshill, in the county of Durham, for a week's grouse driving, and returned to Glasgow on the day of the declaration of war in South Africa.

Tait had applied for leave to join his regiment in case of active service, and now made every effort to get rid of his staff appointment in order to rejoin the Black Watch, and his friends were able to bring such strong influence to bear, that his resignation was sanctioned on October 18th. He was shooting at St. Fillans at the time, but started off immediately for Glasgow, and left Edinburgh on the following evening. Two days were spent at Aldershot in getting his kit ready, and after a delay of nearly two days more, during which his steamer, the " Orient," lay befogged at Tilbury, Tait finally started for South Africa on October 24th, 1899.

Such is the outline of Tait's life, traced through its principal events. We may here pause a moment to look a little closer into the man himself, and guess at the elements which made up so lovable a character. As a boy, Tait was impulsive and high-spirited almost to excess. He was always trying to do his best, and hated to be corrected. At school he was a champion of what he thought to be right and just ; and, even as a small boy, did not hesitate to tackle boldly a master, who seemed to him to have treated a boy unfairly. He was very quick-tempered,

and could not brook being ordered about in
any way.

The following story, told me by Mr. F. P.
Lemarchand, the old Oxford blue, of Freddie's
Sedbergh days, is illustrative of this—

I remember once having a great row with him
over nothing. I was looking after a lot of boys
bathing, Freddie, or "Connie," as he was always
called at school, amongst them. He refused to
leave the water when I told them all to come out.
At last I said, "Look here, young Tait, if you
don't come out I shall give you a good hiding."
Instantly he fired up, and said, "If you do, I shall
fetch a policeman, and give you in charge!" I
fear that the comic side of the remark seized me,
and that I burst out laughing.

Tait and Mr. Lemarchand were always
the greatest friends, and often in after years
laughed together over the episode of the
policeman.

Long after this, when Tait was a member
of the Royal and Ancient, he had been
playing with Mr. David Lamb, and found
that one of the holes had been cut in a place
which was quite unsuitable for the purpose.
A suggestion made to one of the men in
charge of the green bore no fruit, so in the
evening, Tait, with Mr. Lamb as aider and
abettor, went forth armed with a hole-cutter,
determined to take the matter into their own
hands and remedy the evil. This they did,

A Record

and provided for themselves and the golfing public a suitable goal for their efforts on the following day. The Green committee of the club did not, however, take the same philanthropic view of the case, and considered that the act was in some way derogatory to their dignity. Mr. Lamb, as one of the most distinguished members of the club, could not lightly be called in question for his actions, and the authorities also knew from experience that they were likely to come second best out of any discussion in which they had him for an antagonist.

An apology was demanded, but Tait would hear none of it. Some of his friends, however, wished to settle the dispute, which was really of no serious nature at all, and counselled him to get a legal "chum" to write a diplomatic letter which would put things straight. To this Tait agreed, and the letter, which was of an apologetic nature, was drawn up ready for signature. He read the letter through, and then read it again. "This," said Tait, "looks to me very like an apology," and with this remark he put the letter aside. This incident illustrates the same trait in Tait's character—the determination to stick to a line of conduct once adopted, and see the thing through at all costs. His public school and military training however softened down this side of his disposition, so that in later years, if it was present in him, he never allowed himself to show it. Tait was however always a man of strong opinions, and entertained strong likes and dislikes; not the least of the latter was his disapprobation for long sermons. He held the view that a man who had 104 opportunities of preaching in the year, ought to confine himself strictly to the twenty minutes limit. He was, moreover, not deeply versed in matters theological, so it is possible that some sermons did not interest him at all. On one occasion, when the preacher had far outrun the time limit, Freddie had left off listening to oral instruction, and was interesting himself with scriptural research. Suddenly he gave his brother Alec, who was sitting next him, a tremendous punch in the ribs, and on being asked what was the matter, he replied, in north country fashion, with the question, "Who is this chap, Haggai? I never knew that *he* wrote a book." It was with great pride that Freddie announced his discovery, saying that up till now his father had done all the original research, but that now he could claim his share.

In his reading, Tait formed his opinion about a book, and if it pleased him, he would rather read it over and over again than venture on pastures new, which might possibly turn out not so congenial to his taste.

A Record

Though not by any means a bookworm, he was a fairly wide reader ; the older books rather than the newer he read most frequently. Dumas, Thackeray, and Fielding, he read constantly ; and Scott's " Guy Mannering " was a prime favourite. " The Three Musketeers," " Vanity Fair," " The Book of Snobs," " Rejected Addresses," " The Ingoldsby Legends," " Tom Jones," and Stevenson's " Kidnapped," were books he read and re-read, and he delighted in Herbert's " Defence of Plevna ; " its tale of heroism seemed entirely to appeal to him.

In early years Jules Verne was one of his great favourites, and he read with sustained pleasure " The Mysterious Island," and " The Child of the Cavern." Before entering Sandhurst he had read a good many of the elder Dumas' romances. After leaving Sandhurst he did not for a time devote very much of his leisure to reading, but in the winter of 1894–95, when he was stationed at Edinburgh Castle, he resumed his reading habits. Tait was always ready to talk about books, and possessed a much greater knowledge of them than many probably would have expected. Tales of fighting and adventure, and books that depicted the heroic in life, were naturally dear to him. He delighted in the exposure of humbug and sham which Thackeray made in " The Book of Snobs ; "

and he enjoyed equally the satire of "Vanity Fair," and the irony of "Jonathan Wild."

When Freddie sailed away on his first and last voyage, he left behind him scores of friends and thousands of admirers. He had, indeed, a genius for friendship, and the reason of this is not far to seek. He was possessed of rare tact and sound common sense; he knew how to deal with men and influence them without being aggressive; without showing that he wished to lead, he was able to command. To the gift of tact he added a brightness and openness of character, and a readiness to see men and things in the best light, which made him a source of enjoyment to all who came in contact with him. It was this pleasant, cheery view of life which caused him to be so beloved by the non-commissioned officers and men who were under him. He never disliked anyone, for although he perceived the weak and small points in a man's character, he saw also the better side, which was obscured by petty faults. He never looked out for the possibilities of evil in life, for he was always too much engrossed in trying to discover the probabilities of good.

There was, however, something more than tact, something greater than cheerfulness of disposition, something deeper than mere good nature in Tait, that gave him the extra-

A Record

ordinary magnetic influence over all classes of men which he undoubtedly wielded. It was something deeply rooted in his character, something uncultivated, something absolutely and inseparably part of himself. Whenever we think of him the words seem borne to our ears:—

> " His strength was as the strength of ten,
> Because his heart was pure."

From his father Freddie inherited the firmness and strength of character, and the philosophical disposition which were the groundwork of all his golfing and other successes. From his mother he received a singular sweetness and gentleness of nature which blended well with the more masculine side of his character, and the two influences combined to produce a man whom to know was to love.

A most notable and admirable trait in Tait was his affection for his home circle, and their influence on his every thought and action is most strongly marked. With his mother he was in most perfect sympathy, and every detail of his life was unfolded to her with a very beautiful simplicity.

Wordsworth has written of the " happy warrior " as one who—

> "Is yet a soul whose master-bias leans
> To homefelt pleasure, and to gentle scenes ;
> Sweet images ! which, wheresoe'er he be,
> Are at his heart ; and such fidelity
> It is his darling passion to approve ;
> More brave for this, that he hath much to love."

F. G. Tait

The thought expressed in these lines represents very truly Tait's attitude towards his home. Popular and fêted wherever he went, and mixing, as an honoured guest, with all classes of society, his first thought was ever with his father and mother, his brothers and sisters; and what *they* were thinking of him, not what the public was thinking of him, was always uppermost in his mind. His popularity was founded on love rather than on admiration. Admiration there was, indeed, and to spare, but the root and origin of it all was in the good will that men felt for the man of good will, and the desire to know better one who was so evidently lovable and worth knowing. His character shone forth, quite easily to be seen in his honest face and gallant bearing. One looked into that face and saw that it was good, one looked again and saw that it was honest and brave and true; and looking yet again, one loved. No one who saw him could mistake the meaning of the man, or fail to learn the secret of his popularity. Everything he did was full of love, everything begat love, that was all the secret, that was all the man. He went through life giving joy to the hundreds who knew him as a friend, and pleasure to the thousands who only saw him passing by.

If it be true that there is no better test of worth than the love of one's fellowmen, Tait's

A Record

life was not lived in vain, but was great indeed.

> "He is not lost, though we shall lose his smile,
>   His ringing laugh, his merry harmless jest.
>   Nothing is lost ! for failure cannot be
>   Where wisdom infinite evolves the plan ;
>   'Tis but a part, and not the whole, we see,
>   In worlds unseen revive things dead to man."

F. G. Tait

—◆◇◆—

CHAPTER VII

F. G. TAIT AS A GOLFER.

ABOUT the relative merits of golfers there
will always be controversy and difference of opinion. It must be so in the nature
of things, for one style of play will appeal
more to some than to others ; and probably
there are still many critics who have not yet
arrived at the stage when they " know good
golf when they see it." To know whether a
man is playing well or not, it is often necessary to have some previous knowledge of his
method of play, to know what his shots are,
and to know the likelihood of his success with
these shots. A half-topped approach, which
rolls up to the hole side, may be indeed a
" horrid fluke," or it may be a perfectly
played stroke ; we should have to know something of the player before we could pass a
verdict. Some men are much more obvious
in their methods than others, and as a result
they seem to us more scientific in their play.

F. G. TAIT'S MEDAL CASE.

A Record

It does not take very much understanding of the game, for instance, to see what Mr. Hilton is going to do and how he is going to do it; we cannot do it ourselves, but we can understand his method at once. To show that even in so clear a style a knowledge of a man's play is necessary to a due appreciation of his game, I may note that I have often heard the question asked, "How does Hilton put all that extraordinary cut on his approach shots?" Now those who know his play know that Mr. Hilton does not play his pitching shots with cut at all, but simply lets the club come straight through after the ball, which is the reason that his shots do not break in as it were "from the off." If Mr. Hilton's style is obvious, Tait's was quite the reverse, and I have only mentioned the one in order to contrast it with the other.

I must freely admit that I never wholly understood Tait's style and method of play. It is a significant fact that, though Tait was the most popular and most observed player at St. Andrews for about half-a-dozen years, no one seems to have copied him. At North Berwick Mr. Laidlay has scores of imitators, and the leading players, professional and amateur, leave the impress of their style on the youth of their home greens.

It was not so with Tait, and I take it that the reason for this was that, though many did desire earnestly to imitate him, none were able to do so. The thing looked easy enough until we tried it, but when we attempted to make our analysis, we found that we had failed. There was some ingredient, and that a most essential one, which could not be determined; that ingredient was Tait's secret, and I do not think anyone has found it out. There were many points in his style, such as the slowness of his back swing and the extraordinary control he seemed to exercise over his club, which we could all note. There was also the quick foot action, and the fine follow through of the club, not too soon but just when it was wanted. Then there was the curious grip of the right hand away under the club, the right wrist turned far down towards the ground; and most likely this last was the stumbling block for the would-be imitators. We try this grip; it looks as if it might help us to get some extra force into the stroke, but we cannot hit the ball, and that is essential to our making a start with our new style. When I say we cannot hit the ball, I mean that we cannot hit it straight; our hands seem warring against each other, and there is a great desire to turn in the nose of the club-head, with the result that we pull half-a-dozen balls round to square leg, and finally give up our attempt in vain. Tait, however, did not seem to find any difficulty with this grip, and there

[Photo by W. Dod, Esq.

F. G. TAIT AT THE TOP OF HIS SWING.

[Photo by W. Dod, Esq.

F. G. TAIT PLAYING TO THE SECOND HOLE, PRESTWICK, 1899.

A Record

was no uneasiness about his manner of taking
hold of the club; it must have been natural
to him, else he could not have swung so grace-
fully.

Grace, indeed, and a certain evenness
of style were very noticeable in his game;
noticeable in his driving, especially in later
years, but more evident still in his iron play.
Very unusual was the slowness with which he
took his club back from the ball, drawing it
away rather than swinging it. Tait seemed
to wait patiently until he felt that every factor
which made up the total of his balance was
perfectly adjusted, and then feet, arms, and
hands went forward in a consorted motion of
power and graceful rhythm. Tait neither hit
nor swung; his stroke was rather a combination of the two, a swinging hit. If we had to
draw the line and place him in one class or
another, we should group him with the hitters,
for his driving shot was a hit, but at the same
time a very smooth hit. These last few years
have developed a new idea of golf-ball driving,
and this development has taken the form of
" hitting " instead of " sweeping " the ball
We have all been told that the swing and
sweep of the club are essential to the " true
style," and this of course is so, if we regard
the " true style " as the " swinging and sweeping " style; but perhaps that method is now
ruled out of date. Orthodoxy has no real

F. G. Tait

merit save in the fact that it is the embodiment of the best opinion of the time. We have only to advance the time and change the opinion to make the orthodox become heterodox, and the hitherto received a fallacy. Tait stood in the parting of the ways; he could not be a pure hitter, because the tradition of his youth was too strong to allow of this; he therefore retained the swing, and added to it the additional power of the hit.

When Tait was emerging from boyhood, his driving style had a good deal of a slogging nature in it, and we have seen that in those earlier days he was capable of making prodigious shots. This capacity he always retained, but as years went on he ceased to make a habit of this big stroke, and held it more and more in reserve for great and exceptional occasions. He knew his power, but he realised the danger of giving it free play; he was fearful of its getting the better of him; he held it in check as a good servant who must always be kept in his proper place. Thus he cultivated that habit of "control" which has been so often noticed as the chief characteristic in his driving style. When speaking of Tait's play it is always the extraordinary shots that attract most attention. Tait, however, did not regard them with any pride, but rather as incidents which should have been avoided by more careful previous shots. Still, the fact remains

A Record

that he was not only capable of playing strokes outside the power of ordinary men, but that in the time of his necessity he almost invariably was able to produce them. Perhaps no better example of this can be found than the fact that he was *facile princeps* as a foursome player when in partnership with a weak or erratic golfer.

It was then that those shots, which have been well called "recoveries," were needed once or twice at every hole, instead of once or twice in every two or three rounds. The topped tee shot of his partner had to be made up for by an extra long second, the ball wildly driven had to be snatched from the heather or the whins, and brought back to its proper sphere of influence on the putting green. At such times as these Tait was superb ; the worse the place you put him in, the better pleased did he seem to be ; it was for him but a grand chance of bringing out one of the shots which he had "up his sleeve," but which he required so seldom when playing his own ball. What undoubtedly aided Tait in these recovery shots was the fact that he was invariably "a good trier." He appreciated the value of every shot, and never lost sight of the important fact that it is easier to lose or gain a stroke on the putting green than to lose or gain half a stroke through the green. Everyone knows this, but few act up to their

F. G. Tait

knowledge; Tait was one of these few, and, by the aid of this virtue alone, he gained many of his most famous triumphs.

Tait, in his later golfing years, never hit a ball hard, unless there seemed to be some necessity for doing so. His plan was to play, not for the shot, but for the object of the shot; he never allowed himself to strive to win the regard of the gallery at the risk of losing the hole. He was indeed by nature the player who *did* please the gallery, for the brilliancy of his game made him a first favourite where-ever he went, but there was no striving to show off his strokes, no desire to exhibit his powers. The desire to hit was no doubt his, but he had cultivated a self-control which was more powerful than his physical inclination. The result of this was seen most plainly, as we have already hinted, in the extraordinary control under which he kept his swing. Yet no one knew the value of a long shot better than he, and I can well remember an incident which illustrates this fact. Tait was drawn in a tournament against a player whose game I knew something about. He asked me what manner of man he had to tackle, and when I told him that, when on his game, his anta- gonist was a very long driver, a smile of relief came over Tait's face, and he suggested that he might try one or two big tee shots just to start the game with. I agreed that the plan

THE FINISH OF THE SWING.

[Snapshot taken at Prestwick.

A Record

was sound, and the result proved the value of these extra long shots of Tait's against a player who fancied his own hitting powers.

This "control" of Tait's was seen principally in his back swing, but was to be detected also at the finish of his drive. Though there was a "follow through" far in excess of what would have been expected, judging from the upward motion of his club, yet this follow through had no reckless *abandon* about it, the club at the very end of the stroke was still held by masterful hands.

Even when hitting hard, Tait's head never seemed to move much at the end of his stroke; the body was, in fact, kept under the same restraint as the club. There was, indeed, a transfer of the weight from the right to the left foot at the end of the swing, and a noticeable final rising on to the toe of the right foot, as if the player were about to step forward; but as the finish was often made with the left toe in the air, the heel bearing this transferred weight, no real forward motion was contemplated. The fine leg and foot work which Tait brought to bear on his driving stroke was augmented by a certain amount of knee action, which was sometimes, but not always, present.

St. Andrews is indebted to Tait for the way in which he upheld her honour again

F. G. Tait

and again in the great golfing contests, but
he was indebted to her for that part of his
game which never failed him, namely, his
approach shots. In his full shots there was
the flavour of the St. Andrews style, and that
was all, for his genius was strong enough to
allow him to be unorthodox without fear of
failure, but in his approaching he was most
typically a son of the classic green. There is
no green where the manner of approaching
varies so much with the state of the course
as at St. Andrews. The course on which
Taylor played on in his big match
against Kirkcaldy needed entirely different
play from the green on which he won the
championship so brilliantly shortly afterwards.
When Vardon played the best ball of Mr.
Balfour Melville and Mr. Laidlay, he saw
that it was not a course that could be played
in 85 strokes without some skill, yet in the
Championship of 1900, though the course was
rather longer, he had no difficulty in beating 80. The explanation of this is simple
enough, and it is just this, that the course
to a long straight driver is three or four shots
easier when it is wet than when it is dry.
Now the Spring, and also to a less degree
the Autumn Meetings at St. Andrews,
are held at the time of year when the
greens are impossible to pitch on, and
hard to putt on. Tait realised that if

146

he was to be successful on his home green, he must cultivate a style of approaching which would stand him in good stead, not only when the green was easy, but when the green was hard. He found that the only shot which answered, when the putting greens were hard as paving stones, and the ground resounded when struck, like the ring of a bell, was the short pitch and long run. This shot he played so well, and with so many varieties of pitch and loft, that I cannot help thinking it the most perfect achievement of golfing skill that his genius and science produced. The nature also of the St. Andrews turf when at its hardest in a manner determined the way in which he played these approach shots. No turf was taken, because no turf could be taken, so hard was the lie from which the ball had to be played. This cleanness of hitting the ball, or rather of nipping it up off the hard ground, was noticeable in all Tait's shots, both long and short; it was the lesson which St. Andrews taught him, and he learned it well, and to his advantage, in many a stroke he played.

In " The Book of Golf and Golfers," to which everyone who writes on golfing style must be both consciously and unconsciously indebted, Mr. Horace Hutchinson gives two illustrations of the long approach shot as played by Mr. Frank Fairlie and Mr. J. B.

F. G. Tait

Pease. The pictures are of two quite different sort of shots, but Tait was master of both. The one he used the most—probably the one he liked the best—was the stroke as shown in the admirable photograph of Mr. Fairlie. Mr. Hutchinson speaks of the shot as almost esoteric, and though he pretends to have been unable to understand Mr. Fairlie's method of playing it, he gives a very good description of the manner of so doing only a few lines later in his sketch. Tait played this shot so well, and with so many varieties of pitch and loft, that in my opinion it was the best shot he had in his bag. Ben Sayers plays the shot (and an excellent illustration of it appears in Mr. Hutchinson's book), Jack White can play it, Park can play it, and any St. Andrews caddie will show how it is done, but the reason which made Tait's playing of it so good sprang from a natural rather than a scientific cause. By his great physical strength he was enabled to play the stroke off the wrists and forearm, without any swing, as far as most men's irons would take them with a three-quarter swing. I trust I do not appear to write in any spirit of controversy; such were far from my purpose and intent, and I do not wish to compare Mr. Fairlie's shot unfavourably with Tait's. They were the same in principle but different in degree; Tait's was the stronger shot, Mr. Fairlie's the prettier. What I wish

"RUNNING UP THE LONG PUTT."

[Snapshot taken during "72 round," Feb 1894.

"YOUTH AND OLD AGE."

A Record

to point out is that Tait was able with a short motion of the club to send the ball farther than Mr. Fairlie could ; to get, in fact, the same distance as Mr. Fairlie with what Andrew Kircaldy would call " a push off the wrists " ; and that is where I think Tait had the advantage. When I say a " push," I do not mean that Tait's shot was what is commonly known as "the push shot." It had, indeed, in it more of the push than Mr. Fairlie's, but it was not the real " push " that Mr. Mure Fergusson plays so well ; it was a shot played with the hands and right forearm. When the shot had to be played low or against wind, the right hand came smartly over just as club met ball, and the hands were kept back, not shot forward as in the push shot. The push shot is said to resemble the forward off-drive at cricket ; this shot of Tait's is best perhaps described by reference to the action of the right hand. This action of the hand when the ball is being struck resembles the motion of the hand and wrist when turning a key in a lock from right to left.

All cricketers know the meaning of " leg " break and " off " break, all curlers the meaning of " elbow in " and " elbow out " ; Tait was able to make the ball break both ways, even at long ranges of 120 or 130 yards, and these shots were often very useful to him. Two shots of his I can remember which, if I

F. G. Tait

could only describe them correctly, would
illustrate what I mean, and they were in
themselves so well played as to be deserving
of special mention.   Going to the sixth or
heathery hole at St. Andrews, a mound with
an almost trench-like grassy hollow beyond it
guards the green.   The green itself is a table-
land, and on the occasion of which I write, the
hole was situated on its nearer side.   Tait's
ball lay some 120 yards from the hole.   The
wind was a following one and blew also somewhat from the left.   The hollow was partly
full of casual water, so that a purely running
shot was out of the question.   It was equally
impossible to pitch on to the green and not
run 30 or 40 yards past the hole, as the green
was keen, the hole just over the hollow, and
the wind strong.   To play the push shot
against the bank, which is only about two feet
high, it would have been necessary to have
allowed a good deal for the cross wind from
the left, and the ball would during the latter
part of its course, both before and after it
pitched, have been at the mercy of the golfers'
greatest enemy.   Tait played the shot quite
straight, counteracting the force of the wind
by the upward turn of the right hand, and at
the same time by hitting the ball in the
centre; just as the club was beginning to rise,
he put the forward spin on it which gave it no
chance of refusing to take the hill.   This was

A Record

his leg-break shot, most useful in counter-acting wind or slope of ground. The other shot I have spoken of was played at the fourteenth hole at St. Andrews; it was Tait's third shot. It was played in the course of the Spring Medal Competition of 1899. Tait at the time was leading Mr. Laidlay, his keenest rival, by one stroke. There was a north-westerly wind blowing down and across the course, and Tait had played his second shot well out to the left into one of the grassy hollows which lie to the left of "Hell." He had got so far to the left that the pot bunkers at the foot of the plateau-like green were directly between him and the hole; the green was very keen, and Tait's ball lay on the downward slope of a rather steep hill. The obvious shot to play was the one we have just described. With this shot he could have *pulled* the ball on to the right-hand corner of the green without crossing the bunkers at all. Two things were in Tait's mind against doing this; the first was that the hole was not on right-hand corner but in the middle of the green, and the second was that he knew he could get but little pull on his ball, even with the help of the wind, owing to the hanging lie. To play the ball straight for the hole from such a lie it was necessary for him to cut it, but no amount of cut would have enabled him to pitch the ball on to the narrow tableland and yet stop it from going down the slope beyond. The hole was about 120 yards off, and Tait, taking all risks, picked the ball up almost clean, with but sufficient slice on it to counteract the wind, and drove it hard and low over the bunkers against the face of the green; the ball struck the face and gave one bound into the air, the life was taken out of it, and it lay dead at the side of the hole. One foot lower or higher and the shot must have been a complete failure. The shot was so clearly meant, and the execution so wonderfully carried out, that I shall always regard it as the most skilful stroke I ever saw Freddie play. It is a shot which must rank with Andrew Kirkcaldy's famous approach at the 17th hole in his match with Taylor; the shots were equal in skill. Kirkcaldy, indeed, was playing for his £100, but on the other hand he was compelled to play the shot in the way he did, as it was his only chance of getting on to the green where Taylor already lay in the odd; but Tait played his shot from choice, which showed the extraordinary confidence he had in his own accuracy.

As my poor description of Tait's shot may give but an inadequate idea of its value, I may support my opinion by quoting Kirkcaldy's comment on the shot the moment

A Record

after it had been made. Turning round to a fellow spectator he remarked, " That man's a perfect deevil." Those who know Andrew will know that this meant praise indeed.

Tait was the happy possessor of very strong hands and wrists, and many stories are told illustrative of his powers. This extraordinary wrist strength influenced in no small way his method of playing approach shots. The main result of this power was that he cultivated the wrist shot in all his approach play and made it his motto that the more shots he could bring within its range the better. I use the term wrist stroke in its conventional meaning, for except in putting no shot is played entirely " with the wrists."

Tait played his approach shots almost always with a stiff wrist, hardly ever " swinging " his club, and in this particular his style was in marked contrast to that of his great rival Mr. John Ball. Mr. Ball has a unique power of being able to play a " swinging " shot and to stop the iron at any desired point in the upward circle. This shot Tait never used, his wrist power enabling him to effect the same results without introducing any appearance of " swing " into the stroke. It may therefore be said that Tait hardly ever used the half or three-quarter swing at all; every iron shot was a development of the

F. G. Tait

forearm stroke and his whole approach play a glorification of the so-called " wrist shot."

I remember Tait once telling me that the part of the game in which he was most fearful of " going off " was his putting, and this statement was the more remarkable in that he was always regarded as almost the best putter of his day. So good was his holing-out that days would pass without a putt of under six feet being missed; nor was the holing-out process confined to this radius, it was carried on also from the longer ranges, though not with the same monotony. Tait putted very much as he drove, as to grip of club and the manner in which he took it back from the ball; what difference there was lay mainly in his stance. In putting, he stood almost facing the hole, his body bent forward somewhat, as in the position of one about to start running. He putted with a rather lofted cleek, not a so-called " iron putter," or any of its mongrel relations, but just an old fashioned cleek cut short.

Both in driving and approaching Tait's hands came well through with the club; he brought the club through " on a piece," head, shaft, and hands all going forward together. In putting this system was exaggerated and very noticeable, so that the hands kept not only level with the club head in point of

A Record

advancement, but even after the ball was struck continued to go on, leaving the head behind, as in the manner of cricketers when "playing forward" to the ball. In cricket fashion also was his habit of keeping the body well over the ball, so that when the ball was struck his body was leaning forward, and the left elbow was well advanced. This putting method was a peculiar one, peculiar in two points, viz., the advancement of the hands before the head of the club, and the leaning forward of the body. Both these peculiarities were the natural result of the fact that Tait chose to putt with a lofted club. He did so no doubt because he found that the loft on the club gave him greater control over the ball. When hit with a putter the ball seems to race away to success or failure with a lightheartedness, which, should its destiny be unsatisfactory, is most annoying to the striker. With a lofted cleek on the other hand one seems to be able to control the ball right up to the hole. Tait was a fine player with the putter, and when he was induced to visit the Ladies' Course to take part in some family match, he showed himself the equal of all comers with the old weapon of wood. But he found that in practice he could make the cleek the more useful servant, so he retained the latter in his service on most occasions.

F. G. Tait

In putting, as in all golf, one of the most important things is balance, both mental and physical. The great reason of nearly all bad putting is that the body is thrown forward while the ball is being struck, and the balance of the body, so essential to accuracy of hitting, is lost, just at the very moment when it is most required. At first sight Tait seemed as if he would be apt to fall a victim to this vice, and he did indeed practice it in moderation. It was however but seldom harmful to him, for the very good reason that he had an antidote of his own which counterbalanced the probable evil.

The result of the body movement of which I have spoken is that the ball is pushed outward past the right of the hole ; in fact, " shoving a putt " is nearly always the result of any forward movement of the body or transference of weight from the right leg to the left, in the act of striking. Now Tait played to pull his putts into the hole, and this pulling was accentuated by his peculiar grip with the right hand which we have noted in his driving style. In order to counteract this pull he swayed his body very slightly forward, and the result was that the ball went straight, though it generally fell into the hole from the right hand side. It happened on certain rare days that he moved forward too far, and then the putts were missed, and perhaps half-a-crown lost, but this state of

[Photo by W. & D. Downey.

FINISH OF MEDAL ROUND, September 1899.

A Record

things did not last long, for Tait knew full well
the putting sin which was likely to beset him
There was no false pride about him, and when
off colour on the greens he was quick to ask
for advice, even as he was always ready to
give it, with frankness and courtesy. His
question was never the ordinary one, " What
am I doing wrong ? " It was always " Am I
moving my body, or am I not taking the club
back straight ? " for he knew the game, and
knew that on these two points hang all the
minor laws of putting philosophy.

Tait studied his putts very carefully, going
down on one knee and looking at the line to
the hole from behind the ball, much in the same
fashion as that which Vardon adopts. When
once standing to the ball he putted quickly
and boldly. He did not seem to hit the ball
as hard as one would have expected, judging
from the fact that he played with so lofted a
club, yet he was seldom short, on the contrary,
generally past the hole in his approach putts.
He carried the ball forward with the stroke as
it were, probably by the forward action of the
hands which we have mentioned, and also by
the over-spin he put on the ball by a slight
upward movement of the hands.

Tait had no great love for score play.
Writing in 1898 to his brother in India, he
says : " I can't say I care much for the score
game," and this was indeed the opinion he

F. G. Tait

always expressed. And in truth he was never quite so great as a score player as one would have expected. This variety of the game did not seem to suit his disposition, his particular temperament did not lend itself to this form of golf.

The fun for Tait was in beating his opponent, and this enjoyment is denied to the man who plays for or against a score. The winner of a stroke competition only gets the verdict on points, he lacks the satisfaction of giving the knock-out blow. I remember well, after an argument on the merits of score play, during which Freddie had only been a good listener, his getting up and saying, " Why do you talk about the scoring *game*, there is no more *game* in scoring than in rifle shooting " ; he then left the room. It was generally thus with him—he was not fond of entering into argument, he liked to listen to the views of others, and then, having finally made up his mind on the merits of the case, to give his verdict. As far as he was concerned that was the end ; he was not likely to change his view, so he saw no object in discussing the matter further. It was an honest straightforward method, and one that might with advantage be copied by many. It was moreover quite characteristic of him, characteristic of his manner of dealing with things by means of great *coups*, and of suddenly seeming to determine on some line

A Record

of action and throwing himself into it boldly, not turning back at all.

It is often noticeable that when men have reached the position of being great authorities on any subject, they try to surround their knowledge with a halo of mystery, and place themselves on sacred ground not to be approached save with uncovered feet. This is what the schoolboy calls "side," and it is "side" just the same, whether it be moral or physical, intellectual or athletic. Tait hated "side" in any shape or form, and, in consequence, his popularity was greatly enhanced. He saw the smallness of it, and how common it was in all forms of sport, and he determined not to belittle himself by indulging therein. Tait was approachable to anyone who wished to ask for advice or to receive instruction, no matter what their golfing qualifications were. He never gave a curt reply even to the golfing bore, and would without a smile answer at times the most ridiculous questions put to him after a match by some admiring spectator. Afterwards he might laugh over some particularly crude remark, but at the time there was always that unfailing courtesy to all classes, which is the hall mark of the true sportsman and gentleman. This spirit of courtesy I think he cultivated, for it was more and more pronounced as time went on. He had,

F. G. Tait

indeed, his likes and dislikes, and they were very strong, his disposition being intensely conservative, and his opinions when once formed almost unalterable. On the merits and demerits of golfers and golf courses his views were very pronounced. When once he made up his mind that a certain man was a bad player, no fine score or performance on the part of the unfavoured one would alter Tait's opinion. Freddie would just remark, " He can play none," and this phrase of his became a common expression among his friends. He soon made up his mind as to the qualities of the golfing greens he played on, and having decided that a certain course was good or bad, it made no difference to him whether he played well or badly on it, he stuck to his original opinion. After the Amateur Championship Meeting of 1896, when Tait had been playing perhaps the best golf he ever played, or that has ever been played on any links, I remember asking him if his opinion of Sandwich had altered for the better. " A good one-shot course " was all his answer. He did not think the course a good test of golf, and the fact that he had been successful on it did not alter his opinion one jot. For Tait there was only one first-class course, only one good test of golf; all other links were incapable of being compared with his ideal. Tait was a true and loyal

A Record

son of St. Andrews, and his love for her links was unbounded. He loved them with a constancy which made him almost blind to the charms of other and younger rivals.

At St. Andrews alone he believed true golf was to be found, all other was but a makeshift for "the real thing." He would argue as to the merits of other courses, but if you started a comparison between any of them and St. Andrews, the argument had to cease, for you had ventured on undebatable ground. Tait was brought up on the St. Andrews green, learned all his golf there, knew every inch of ground, and was therefore able to appreciate the difficulties and beauties of the course to the fullest degree.

Next to St. Andrews he considered Hoylake the fairest of greens, and was always of opinion that the Championship should be held alternately on these two. In later years the new course at St. Andrews and New Luffness were also prime favourites.

Tait was intensely Scottish in his golfing ideas and principles, and his keenness for Scottish as opposed to English golf he sometimes carried almost too far. There is a certain irony therefore in the fact, that he won his two great Championship triumphs on the two English Championship courses. His well-known patriotism made him doubly popular with Scottish golfers, who always

F. G. Tait

followed his exploits with the greatest interest, and his victories with the usual national modes of rejoicing. The defeat of Freddie was a subject which could hardly be spoken of, whilst his triumphs caused almost national jubilation. When in 1898 he won the Amateur Championship at Hoylake, who that was there will forget the rejoicing in the North country camp, the cheering and the toasting, and the congratulations from far and near. Nor were the Saxons far behind, for Tait, though "loved at home," was both loved and revered abroad, and Mr. John Ball, that prince of sportsmen, was keenest of all to do honour to the Scot.

From a golfing point of view there was much in his game and manner of playing to account for this extraordinary popularity. Tait's style had about it a wonderful attraction for the onlooker. His grip with the right hand, and the curious piston-like drive he gave with the right forearm would not appear likely to lend grace to his manner of hitting. Nor did they ; and I am inclined to think that he was graceful in spite of, rather than because of, his style. There was, however, an inherent grace of movement, an idea of strength combined with suppleness about his play that delighted the eye altogether apart from the purely golfing qualities of his style. As a boy Freddie's style was not so graceful, because it was more strained, but as he grew up into his full height and strength, he found that he was able to out-drive his rivals without exerting undue power. He abandoned the striving for length, and studied accuracy of hitting, with the result that his six feet of muscle ultimately enabled him to combine the two to a marvellous degree. He was able to hit far, and yet give the impression that he was only exerting about half his real strength. It was this control which he seemed to exercise over himself that perhaps made him so fascinating to watch from the spectator's point of view. There was a feeling that this was not all—that power unused lay behind everything he did ; there was, it may be, even the hope that it might be called into use before the round was over. Yet no mistake could be greater than the common one of supposing that Tait was a player who was constantly getting into difficulties, and making great " recoveries." His extraordinary physical strength and his knowledge of every shot that is possible in golf, combined with a wonderful power of adapting his swing to the nature of his stance and the lie of the ball, made these recovery-shots possible for him. When, therefore, he found himself in a position from which ordinary players could only extricate themselves in fear and trembling, he was often able to get the ball away as

F. G. Tait

far as from a good lie. This power of recovery which I have already mentioned must not be regarded as a necessary part of his game, but rather as an extra and outside factor which he was able to bring to bear in times of need. When playing his best game there were no recovery - shots played, for none were required, and as a rule he was a most accurate player with all his clubs. In his match with Mr. Hilton in the final of the 1896 Championship his driving was as near perfection as it is possible for driving to be; hardly a yard did he leave the line the whole day; there were no recoveries, for none were needed.

Apart from the beauty of his manner of hitting the ball there was something very pleasant to watch about the light - hearted, confident, yet reserved way in which he acted when engaged in a match. A good golfing temperament is as important as a good golfing style, and Tait was blessed beyond most men in this respect. If the true golfing temperament be fitly described as a blending of the qualities of the general and the philosopher, Tait possessed this ideal disposition to perfection. He played the game with his head all the time, and, when misfortune overtook him, his philosophical turn of mind enabled him to make the most of the possibilities of the case.

A Record

If the gallery loved Tait, Tait also delighted in the gallery, and was always seen at his best when playing with a large following. Fear, conceit, and self consciousness are the three things which make a man "funk" before a crowd. It wounds the pride of a man to play badly when people are watching him, and in striving to play too well he does not play his natural game, and fails. The moment a player begins to speculate as to what the spectators are thinking of him, he loses the power of concentrating his attention upon his stroke, which is essential to the proper striking of the ball. The conceited young player may make a good start before a crowd, but he will get a rude awakening before the match is over; the modest man will gain confidence as the round proceeds.

Tait's nature knew nothing of fear, pride, or self consciousness, and for that reason he always played his best when others less gifted would have lost their heads. "Modest" is an epithet which has been applied to Tait's manner in playing so often and by so many writers, that it must undoubtedly express to a great extent a very popular impression. But I do not think that "modest" is a term which really *fully* expresses his conduct when golfing, for there was plenty of light-hearted confidence about his style, and he never went out to play a match with the appearance of

F. G. Tait

one who thought there was any likelihood of defeat. His manner strikes me as being better expressed by the word *natural*. Everything he did was done without any striving after effect; he took his successes as if he expected them and his bad luck as part of the chances of the game.

I have said something of Tait's manner and method of play; it may well be asked from what sources these were derived. The question as regards the former is easily answered. Tait was a true child of the older school of golf, and he never departed from what was best in the traditions of the past. He was an old-fashioned golfer, and took a pride in the fact that he had never been led away from the views and sentiments of his golfing forefathers. He played the game as a Scottish gentleman, with dignity and strictness, tempered with unfailing courtesy. The match was the thing for him, and a congenial foursome gave him the greatest enjoyment of all. One of the oldest members of the Royal and Ancient Club, the Hon. George Lascelles, writing of Tait's golf at York, says—

Lieutenant Tait carried with him the best traditions and customs of the game as played from time immemorial at St. Andrews, and held himself entirely aloof from the pot-hunting fraternity that has sprung up in later days. When quartered at York he could of course, being Champion, have

A Record

easily mopped up all the pots and pans in Yorkshire. The mess table of the Black Watch might have fairly groaned under the amount of plate or plated he could have realised.   He seemed always to prefer a quiet foursome with personal friends, though frequently pressed to take the shine out of the " pro " or to lower the flag of the scratch man of the club.

Tait was always in sympathy with the old things in golf, and hated every form of innovation ; he drew his inspiration from bygone sources, and made even the dry bones of the past live again in himself.

When we come to ask the question, from what player or players did Tait derive his golfing style of play and methods of execution we find the answer more difficult to give. I do not think he copied anyone, but rather built up his own style independently of others.   He was no doubt influenced in his choice of methods by the many good players he played with when a boy, but it cannot be said that he imitated any of them ; nor was it to be expected from Tait's character that he would be easily influenced by the style of other golfers.   He was extremely independent and thought out things for himself, and when he had made up his mind he stuck to his own plan most tenaciously.   I remember, when Vardon's extraordinary play was popularising that manner of holding the club which had for

F. G. Tait

years been familiar to all who had watched Mr. Laidlay play, that someone made the remark to Tait, " Have you tried the ' Vardon grip ' ? " He made no reply, but a look of intense contempt came into his face, which said more plainly than words, " Do you mean to think that, after working out the way that suits *me* best for the last twenty years, I am going to try another plan just because it suits somebody else ? " No, Tait was no imitator, yet all his methods were more or less governed and influenced by the St. Andrews environment in which his style grew.

Writing from India of Freddie's earlier golf, his brother, Mr. J. G. Tait, says :—

The earliest thing I remember about Freddie's golf is the difficulty I had in persuading him to hold a golf club right hand undermost. Some few years ago he told Mrs. Everard that he was deeply indebted to me for licking him till he held his hands the right way. I think this must have been said in jest, however, for I have no recollection of the *licking.* . . . I can never forget one afternoon I took Freddie out to play against a Wimbledon man, P. Strickland, who had come to St. Andrews. I think it was during Freddie's first year at Sedbergh. He was so happy at being taken out to play. He felt no doubt, just as I felt when the Rev. J. G. McPherson took me to play against the Professor one afternoon in 1872 or 1873. . . . In the family foursome one day Willie drove a ball

A Record

to square leg into the middle of the Ladies' Links. The Ladies' Links was crowded at the time, and Freddie, who was just beginning to be proud of his golf, was with difficulty persuaded to go in and play the ball ; you may fancy the shamefaced way he went in and came out. Towards the end of his time at Sedbergh I remember distinctly many foursomes with Mr. Lindsay Bennet and Mr. Frean. Freddie was a wonderful foursome player for a boy. He had a perfectly unruffled temper, and he played a very steady accurate game.

Another reminiscence of that time is the delight he took in manifestations of character. He had been playing as Lindsay Bennet's partner with some fidgety player on the other side. This fidgety gentleman had requested Bennet (who was the pink of propriety in golfing etiquette) to stand further away on the first green, or stand where he could not be seen. For the rest of the round Bennet kept Freddie under his wing at an immense distance away, and relieved his feelings by saying to Freddie, " Look at the fykie body." I remember as if it were yesterday Freddie telling me about it, and asking what " fykie " meant. I was not at St. Andrews after September 1887, and so I have no reminiscences of his golf after that time except a few matches at Wimbledon. I remember how we spent Jubilee Day of 1887 together, and the marvellous quickness with which he inserted his foot and prevented the platform gate being shut at Charing Cross. He was then " cramming " at Blackheath, and he had to catch the last train. It is hardly necessary to say that we sent the porter who was trying to shut the gate, flying, and that Freddie caught his train. Up to 1889, when I last

F. G. Tait

saw him play, he gave no promise of the immense driving power that he soon afterwards showed, but he was very straight, and in approaching and putting very accurate.

These reminiscences, though interesting in themselves, do not indicate directly the origin of Tait's golfing style. We can, however, note in what Mr. J. G. Tait writes the interest and watchful care which the elder brother bestowed on the younger. I have therefore little doubt that Freddie's style was formed originally on that of his elder brother.

Before he went to India, and while Freddie's golf was still in the embryo stage, Mr. Jack Tait was a very fine golfer—good enough indeed to reach the semi-final round in the Amateur Championship at Hoylake in 1887. He was the natural instructor of his younger brothers, and as a golfing hero, not only his methods but also his mannerisms were likely to be copied. After his brother's death he returned from India for a short visit to Scotland.

I cannot remember ever having seen Mr. J. G. Tait before he went to India, but the first shot I saw him make at St. Andrews in the spring of 1900 brought back, almost too realistically, the memory of his brother's golf. Freddie's style was neater, more finished, more polished, than Jack's,

A Record

but under the differences of detail there lay the same *manner of hitting the ball*, the same conception of the game.

To one other golfer alone can I trace any real resemblance of style, and I think that Tait must have probably been unconsciously much influenced by him; I refer to Mr. Leslie Balfour Melville. The finish of the two players in driving was almost identical, the only difference being that Mr. Balfour Melville finished with his hands rather higher; everything else was almost the same. In addressing the ball, notwithstanding the great difference of stance, there was a very marked resemblance in manner. Both addressed the ball with great care, both were excessively particular to have every point in stance and grip and position of club exactly adjusted; nothing seemed left to chance. The whole was moreover carried out very quietly, very smoothly; there was no snapping at the ball. Tait also resembled Mr. Balfour Melville, in contradiction to the usual St. Andrews style, in that he did not play with the very slack wrist that is so characteristic of the Fifeshire players. One has but to contrast the address and finish of Sandy Herd, or Mr. Greig, or Mr. Robb, with the quieter manner of Tait and Mr. Balfour Melville, and it will be seen at once that there is a slackness about the former which is lacking

F. G. Tait

in the latter players. Tait never seemed to let his club "go," but held it and almost guided it right to the end of the stroke. Whether or not I am right as to the influence of Mr. Balfour Melville on Tait's style I cannot dogmatically say, but there were certainly present in their styles many points of similarity.

It is not easy to fix Tait's place among the great golfers of the past and present without using the odious method of comparison. His great personal popularity will, however, I feel sure, disarm any criticism which might be hostile to the opinion that I hold, namely, that he was, taking him all in all, inferior to no player, amateur or professional, of this or any previous generation. He combined extraordinary power with great accuracy, a combination seldom met with. His power was, moreover, unstrained, and therefore not likely to break down, as in the case of so many long drivers who are playing all the time far above concert pitch. And his accuracy was not merely the careful hitting of the ball time after time in exactly the same way, it was rather the fulness of golfing skill applied through many methods to produce the best possible results. There was none of the monotony about his shots that is characteristic of modern professional golf; every shot was played in a different way, each circumstance of lie, wind, or stance overcome with meaning.

A Record

I never saw Tait play a foolish shot, hardly ever a stroke that showed bad judgment. Though his judgment was almost invariably to be relied upon, yet in foursome play he was the most diffident of players. He always followed out the old Scottish custom of consulting with his partner about the way in which each shot should be played, and no one understood better than he the value of playing " to the score " rather than for the shot.

It is difficult to compare Tait as a golfer with professional players, for he was so thoroughly an *amateur*, playing first and foremost for the fun of the thing, that even in the great competitions he took no trouble to train or practice before the events. It was indeed often impossible for him to get practice before starting for a championship, as he sometimes was only able to get leave a day or two before the event. In these latter days, when golf has been brought to such a pitch of perfection, mainly, I think, by the lucrativeness of the golfing profession, continual practice and training are essential if a man is to compete on equal terms with those, whether amateur or professional, who make golf their business.

Tait never won the Open Championship, but neither indeed have Herd or Rolland, and yet they were the acknowledged champions of their great "years." Tait's play was never mechanical enough to suit four rounds

F. G. Tait

of paper and pencil work, and the *match* was the game for him. Who that has ever played with him can forget the feeling that he was fencing with a man who would suddenly deliver a thrust which no skill could parry ?

Who that has ever seen him play will doubt that his genius was unique, his power incapable of being gauged to the full ?

A man may be a fine player but a bad golfer; even as well-born men are not always gentlemen, or great theologians good parsons. A golfer, in the fullest sense of the word, is a man in the first place, and a player in the second; Freddie was this true golfer. If he has done nothing else for modern golf, he has at least shown the true spirit in which the game should be played, he has exemplified the principles of what is best in Scottish sport by his own practice.

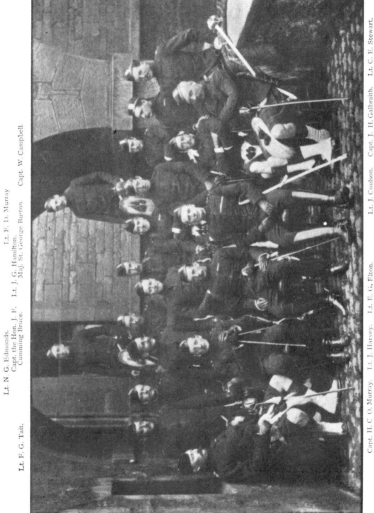

Lt. N. G. Edmonds.
Lt. F. D. Murray
Capt. the Hon. J. F.   Lt. J. G. Hamilton.
Cunning Bruce.   Maj. St. George Burton.   Capt. W. Campbell
Lt. F. G. Tait.

Capt. H. C. O. Murray.   Lt. J. Harvey.   Lt. E. G. Elton.   Lt. J. Coulson.   Capt. J. H. Galbraith.   Lt. C. E. Stewart,
Maj. T. M. Berkeley.   Capt. J. G. Rennie   Maj. A. G. Duff.   Col. A. G. Wauchope.   Lt. A. R. Cameron.   Maj. Hon. H. E. Maxwell.
(Adjutant).

OFFICERS OF THE BLACK WATCH.

A Record

CHAPTER VIII.

----◆◆----

SOUTH AFRICA.

IT is not my purpose in this chapter to attempt to give even a sketch of the events connected with the doings of the Highland Brigade in South Africa, with whom Tait fought and fell. The story of every march and every action has been already told, and will no doubt be told again and again. South African sketches have been drawn from every point of view. No aspect of the war, whether military, political, financial, or racial, has been left undepicted; and though time may have to elapse before the great final picture is painted, there exist already abundance of excellent cartoons. My object is simply to give to his friends such news of Tait, from the time he left this country till his sad death at Koodoosberg, as I have been able to collect from letters sent home from time to time, and from his short Diary, which is fortunately preserved.

F. G. Tait

In order that the reader may follow with
ease Tait's movements, and place his letters
in their proper chronological connection, I
publish his Diary first. It is given just as
he wrote it, as his usual methodical custom
was, from day to day, and never allowing a
day to pass without making an entry.

OCTOBER, 1899.

Wednesday, 18.—Shot with Munro. St. Fillans
to Glasgow. Received wire to rejoin regiment for
service abroad. Travelled to Glasgow.

Thursday, 19.— Glasgow to Edinburgh. Paid a
few calls and said good-bye. Edinburgh to London, 10.50 p.m. Seen off by R. H. J., A. R. P.,
A. G. T., H. J. S., G. H. L., Turnbull, E. S.
B. M.*

Friday, 20.—London to Aldershot. Spent the
whole day in getting kit.

Saturday, 21.—Aldershot. Completed my kit.

Sunday, 22.—Aldershot to Tilbury. 950 men,
29 officers, 2nd Black Watch. Too foggy to start
for South Africa. S.S. *Orient*.

Monday, 23.—Spent whole day in Tilbury Docks;
unable to proceed on account of fog.

Tuesday, 24.—Left Tilbury *en route* for South
Africa about 12.30 p.m. on board S.S. *Orient*.

Wednesday, 25.—Beautiful day on board the
Orient. Drilled officers' squad.

---

* Mr. R. H. Johnston, Mr. A. R. Paterson, Mr. A. G. Tait,
Mr. H. J. Stevenson, Mr. G. H. Law, and Mr E. S. Balfour
Melville, are the friends referred to.

A Record

Thursday, 26.—Another grand day. In the Bay of Biscay; quite smooth. Drilled officers' squad.

Friday, 27.—Splendid day; weather beginning to get hot. Drilled officers' squad.

Saturday, 28.—Another beautiful day. Got inoculated about 10 o'clock a.m. for enteric fever; felt very ill until about 7 a.m. next morning.

Sunday, 29.—Beautiful day. Not very fit.

Monday, 30.—Splendid day. Feeling better. Revolver practice.

Tuesday, 31.—Quite fit. Grand day. Revolver practice and cricket.

NOVEMBER, 1899.

Wednesday, 1.—Arrived at St. Vincent and coaled. Splendid day. Left St. Vincent at 6 p.m. Heard news from Transvaal at St. Vincent. Splendid send off from H.M.S. *Diadem*.

Thursday, 2.—Jolly day; lots of wind.

Friday, 3.—Fine day, with one heavy shower in morning, about 10.15 a.m.

Saturday, 4.—Funeral of a drummer.

Sunday, 5.—Beautiful day. Crossed the Equator.

Monday, 6.—Beautiful day. More wind.

Tuesday, 7.—Beautiful day. Windy. Cricket.

Wednesday, 8.—Beautiful day. Windy. Cricket.

Thursday, 9.—Beautiful day. Less wind. Cricket. Concert and supper given by officers of *Orient*—great success.

Friday, 10.—Strong wind, water washing over bows. Some officers retired from dinner ! ! !

Saturday, 11.—Still rough. F. G. T. very fit.

Sunday, 12.—Sea rough, but splendid day. Passed two steamers a long way off.

F. G. Tait

Monday, 13.—Arrived at Cape Town and anchored outside harbour. Very windy.

Tuesday, 14.—Disembarked and left Cape Town about 10 p.m. for De Aar Junction.

Wednesday, 15.—Breakfast at Worcester, 109 miles from Cape Town; very pretty country and steep gradient all the way. . Lunched at Matjesfontein. Dined at Prince Albert's Road.

Thursday, 16.—Breakfast at Victoria West. Passed detachments of the H.L.I. all the way to Richmond Road. Arrived at De Aar about 3 p.m. Encamped half a mile from railway. Very dusty all night.

Friday, 17.—Pickets out all round. Boers supposed to be near. Beautiful day, jolly hot. On picket from 5.30 p.m. to 6 a.m. No Boers.

Saturday, 18.—Right half Battalion went off to Naauwport; left half remained at De Aar. Bridge blown up by Boers outside Naauwport just after right half got in. Met Heatlie at De Aar and dined with him.

Sunday, 19.—De Aar; awfully hot, 93 in shade. Called on Mr. and Mrs. Heatlie. 91st and 71st arrived. Suffered a good deal from scorched knees. Thunder and dust storm at night, also lots of rain. Stampede of six mules.

Monday, 20.—Quiet day in camp; two parades. 78th arrived.

Tuesday, 21.—De Aar. Warned to hold ourselves in readiness to proceed to Naauwport.

Wednesday, 22.—Reveille at 3 a.m. Left De Aar about 7 a.m., arrived at Naauwport about 12 noon, and joined right half Battalion. Splendid camp and plenty of water. Had some " pop " for dinner ! !

A Record

Thursday, 23.—Mounted Infantry and C Company Black Watch came in touch with enemy at Arundel. Three of our scouts wounded.

Friday, 24.—Went on out-post duty at 4 a.m. Very wet from 8 a.m. to 12 noon; cold night. Saw nothing of enemy.

Saturday, 25.—Relieved at 4 a.m. Splendid day. Arrival of 12th Lancers. 150 Mounted Infantry in touch with Boers at Arundel.

Sunday, 26.—Naauwport; beautiful day. Church parade and short service at 9 a.m.

Monday, 27.—Reveille at 2 a.m.; left Naauwport with left half Battalion and arrived at Orange River about 4 p.m. Met Wolfe Murray and Percy Grant.

Tuesday, 28.—H Company parade at 4.30 a.m. and relieved a company of H.L.I. on Munster Fort, guarding bridge over Orange River. Very hot; on picket from 4.30 p.m. to 5 a.m.

Wednesday, 29. — Very hot again. Bathing parade in morning.

Thursday, 30.—Hot, and very windy; clouds of dust everywhere. Mounted Infantry report Boers in force about ten miles off, towards Hope Town.

DECEMBER 1899.

Friday, 1.—Very hot. Bathed in Orange River in morning. Relieved by company of Seaforths about 10 p.m. Bivouacked for night, tents having been returned to store.

Saturday, 2.—Left half Battalion marched from Orange River to Witteput and on to Fincham Farm, 13 miles. Very hot and dusty. Bivouacked at farm.

F. G. Tait

Sunday, 3.—Very hot. Left half Battalion marched from Fincham Farm to Belmont Farm, starting at 4.30 a.m., rested under trees till 5.30 p.m., then marched to Belmont Station and bivouacked. Very pleasant day at Belmont Farm, ten miles.

Monday, 4.—Left half Battalion marched from Belmont Station to Enslin Station, 13 miles; bad road. Bivouacked there; cold night.

Tuesday, 5.—Hot. Left half Battalion marched from Enslin to Honeynest Kloof Station, five miles; dinner, water, etc. Remained night in bivouac. A Squadron of 12th Lancers arrived. Saw effects of Boer looting.

Wednesday, 6.—Left half Battalion marched to Modder River and one mile beyond, and joined right half Battalion. Jolly day. Bathed in river; 14 miles—whole march, 55 miles.

Thursday, 7.—Enemy attacked Enslin. Whole day at Modder River with 350 men, building redoubts and shelter trenches. Very hot all day; men worked very well. Lightning, thunder, and heavy rain at night; very comfortable.

Friday, 8.—Modder River; outpost duty from 5.30 a.m. to 6 p.m. Saw nothing of enemy. Not nearly so warm.

Saturday, 9.—Naval gun in position, fired a few shots at enemy's outposts with effect. Arrival of more guns and stores.

Sunday, 10.—Forward movement. Highland Brigade, K.O.Y.L.I., 9th Lancers, Howitzer Battery, two Field Batteries, one Battery R.H.A., Balloon Section R.E., 12th Lancers, marched off at 3 p.m., began shelling Boer position at 5 p.m., stopped at 7. Black Watch advanced about one mile. Battle of Magersfontein.

A Record

Monday, 11.—Parade at 12.30 a.m. for night attack. Received tremendous fire in mass of quarter column at 4 a.m.; suffered great loss. Charged to within 200 yards of Boer position. F. G. T. hit in thigh, and remained, being shot at all day, until 7 p.m. at night. Reached hospital at 10 p.m. and got wound dressed. 355 killed and wounded in the Black Watch; seven officers killed and eleven officers wounded.

Tuesday, 12.—Arrived at Modder River, spent day there in hospital. Put on board hospital train *en route* for Wynberg; very comfortable.

Wednesday, 13.—Hospital train all day; passed through Orange River, De Aar, etc.

Thursday, 14.—Arrived at Wynberg, very comfortable hospital; wound redressed.

Friday, 15. — Hospital. Quiet day, writing letters. Poor Berthon died at 8 p.m.

Saturday, 16.—Hospital at Wynberg. Quiet day. Berthon buried.

Sunday, 17.—Quiet day in hospital at Wynberg.

Monday, 18.—Hospital at Wynberg.

Tuesday, 19. — Hospital, Wynberg; received *Scotsman* of 16th and 17th November, also *Golf*, 17th November.

Wednesday, 20.—Moved to Claremont Sanatorium.

Thursday, 21.—Claremont.

Friday, 22.—Claremont.

Saturday, 23.—Claremont.

Sunday, 24.—Claremont. Drove to Wynberg Hospital.

Monday, 25.—Claremont. Visited Rhodes' house and saw the lions.

Tuesday, 26.—Claremont.

F. G. Tait

Wednesday, 27.—Claremont. Arrival of wounded officers from Natal.

Thursday, 28.—Claremont. Visited Rondebosch golf links.

Friday, 29.—Claremont. Went to Cape Town and visited dentist.

Saturday, 30.—Claremont. Visited Wynberg Hospital. Dined with Mr. Michell (manager of Standard Bank).

Sunday, 31.—Train to Simon's Bay; went on board H.M.S. *Niobe*. Lunched, dined, brought in New Year, and stayed the night. Great fun; pipes in great form.

JANUARY, 1900.

Saw the New Year in on board H.M.S. *Niobe*, a very cheery evening. Left Simon's Bay about 8.30 a.m. Cleared for action and dropped a target overboard. The shooting of 6-inch guns was very fine.

Monday, 1.—Arrived in Table Bay about 3.15 p.m. and anchored. Returned to Claremont about 6 p.m.

Tuesday, 2.—Visited Newland's Cricket Ground in afternoon and saw finish of Cape Town *v.* Western Provinces.

Wednesday, 3.—Went into Cape Town with the " Long Un " and spent some happy hours at the dentist's.

Thursday, 4.—Visited dentist and saw some wounded officers on board the transport *Canada* for England. Cricket match, Bar *v.* Navy, at Newlands. Dinner at Sanatorium.

Friday, 5.—Dentist, 10 to 12.30; finished, thank goodness. Entertained a few officers of *Niobe* to dinner at club.

A Record

Saturday, 6.—Dined and slept on board H.M.S. *Niobe*. Very rough sea in Table Bay.

Sunday, 7.—Pleasant day on board *Niobe*.

Monday, 8.—Left *Niobe* at 9.15 a.m. and returned to Claremont. Dined with Innes at Mount Nelson Hotel and stayed night.

Tuesday, 9.—Visited docks, saw the *Majestic*. Wolfe Murray and Innes and Knight dined with me at club. Returned to Claremont in evening.

Wednesday, 10.—Dined at club with Wemyss, and left Cape Town for Modder at 9 p.m. with " Long Un " and Knight of H.L.I.

Thursday, 11.—Day in train. Passed Heatlie on his way South. Played piquet with " Long 'Un." F. G. T.'s birthday.

Friday, 12.—Arrived at Modder River about 7 p.m.

Saturday, 13.—Quiet day at Modder. Visited outposts and Ramsay's grave.

Sunday, 14.—Open-air service. Lord M. present. Visited T. M. B. in outpost line.

Monday, 15.—Quiet day. Visited 75th Field Battery.

Tuesday, 16.—Went on outpost at 3.15 a.m. Very hot all day. Reconnaissance in force on Boer position.

Wednesday, 17.—Arrival of large box full of presents for officers and men. Came off picket at 6 a.m. Reconnaissance in force on Boer position. No casualties on our side.

Thursday, 18.—Went on picket at 6 p.m. Urmston visited my picket. Swarm of locusts.

Friday, 19.—Came off picket at 6 a.m. Went round part of the outposts with Urmston. Saw Boer position very clearly through strong telescope.

F. G. Tait

Saturday, 20.—Very hot in the morning, and two very heavy thunder storms about 12 noon and 5.15 p.m. Frightful dust storm before the rain.

Sunday, 21.—Went on picket at 3.15 a.m., cool up to 11 a.m., after that hot.

Monday, 22.—Came off picket at 6 a.m. Court Martial from 10 a.m. to 4 p.m. Artillery duel.

Tuesday, 23.—Brigade route march. Very hot day. Football match, Black Watch *v.* 12th Lancers. B. W. won by 1 goal. General MacDonald arrived.

Wednesday, 24.—Went on picket at 3.15 a.m. Dust storm all day and rain at night.

Thursday, 25.—Came off picket at 6 a.m. Walk with Wolfe Murray in evening.

Friday, 26.—Went on picket at 6 p.m.

Saturday, 27.—Came off picket at 6 a.m. Walked with Urmston in afternoon.

Sunday, 28.—Morning service at 7 a.m. Visited outpost line and 4·7 guns with Urmston, Yorstoun, and Berkeley. Wolfe Murray and Begbie dined with me.

Monday, 29.—Went on picket at 3.15 a.m. Got very wet about 12 noon. Very heavy rain and strong wind. Dust storm afternoon, and more rain at night.

Tuesday, 30.—Seaforth : Came off picket at 6 a.m. Inspected by MacDonald at 7 a.m. Stewart dined with me.

Wednesday, 31.—Went on picket at 6 p.m.

FEBRUARY, 1900.

Thursday, 1.—Came off picket at 6 a.m. Arrival of more troops. Saw boxing competitions in evening. Begbie, R.A., dined with me.

A Record

Friday, 2.—Saw final and semi-final boxing.

Saturday, 3.—Highland Brigade and one Cavalry Regiment and one Horse Battery moved eight miles down stream from Modder Station. F. G. T. on picket, very hot. Frazer's Drift.

Sunday, 4.—Frazer's Drift to Koodoosberg, 13½ miles. H Company with rear guard, frightfully trying march, very hot, and did not arrive till 3.15 a.m. F. G. T. and most of company rather beat.

Monday, 5.—Changed camp to north side of river. 1,000 Boers made demonstration against H.L.I. picket. H Company on picket from 8.30 p.m.

Tuesday, 6.—Cavalry patrol retired before 500 Boers. Boers made another slight attack.

Wednesday, 7.—Boers made determined attack on outpost line.

The last entry recorded in this Diary was therefore made on the day of his death.

Tait started for South Africa full of hope and good spirits, his one fear indeed seemingly being that his regiment would not arrive in time to see some real hard service. Writing from Aldershot, on the eve of starting for Tilbury, he expresses this fear.

Aldershot,
21 October, 1899.

My dear Mother,

Just a line to let you know that I have got my kit and everything complete. I am afraid there

F. G. Tait

will not be much for us to do when we get out. The Boers learnt a little yesterday. We have got a splendid lot of men, and they will be very useful if they get a chance.

Good-bye and good luck,
Yours affectionately,
F. G. Tait.

After a week of fine weather, Tait writes home again just before reaching St. Vincent, where the *Orient* stopped to coal. He was still evidently taking the light-hearted view of the war which was prevalent before he left home. Little did he know, as he wrote the following letter, that on that very day the disaster at Nicholson's Nek was taking place.

S.S. Orient,
30 October, 1899.

My dear Mother,

We have had a splendid voyage up to now; grand weather all the time. The accommodation and grub are excellent, and we are all in the best of form. We practice daily at a target, slung over the side of the ship from a boom, with revolvers My Mauser pistol is a great success. We will reach St. Vincent to-morrow night (Tuesday) or Wednesday morning. Our next stop after that will be Cape Town. I was inoculated for enteric fever on Saturday, and felt rather sorry for myself on Saturday and Sunday; but now I am all right again. We played a cricket match to-day against the officers of the S.S. *Orient* and the officers of the Mounted Infantry (we have about 300 men and

A Record

about 20 officers of the Mounted Infantry on board), and beat them.

We have a "sweep" every day on the number of miles run by the ship during the 24 hours. Up to now I have not won one.

I instruct the officers every day in physical drill and other gymnastic exercises ; naturally we are all very fit. It is beginning to get a bit hot. We are all anxiously awaiting news from the Transvaal at St. Vincent.

Hope you are all very fit,

Yours affectionately,

F. G. TAIT.

P.S.—I hope the show will not be all over before we get there. The poor Gordons got it fairly hot.

F. G. T.

Just before reaching Cape Town he describes the latter part of his voyage in the two following letters—

S.S. *Orient*,

11 *November*, 1899,

600 miles from Cape Town.

My dear Mother,

We are now having some rough weather, and the sea is coming on board pretty freely. I am still enjoying my grub, which is a good sign. A lot of officers and men have already succumbed to sea sickness. We expect to reach the Cape on Monday the 13th, where we will get our orders. We heard very bad news at St. Vincent from Natal. I hope Sir George White has been able to hold his own.

We expect to go straight up the middle of the Orange Free State with a Division (10,000) on each flank. Our Division consists of a Highland Brigade and a Light Infantry Brigade. The Highland Brigade consists of the Black Watch, Argyle and Sutherland Highlanders, Seaforth Highlanders, and Highland Light Infantry, under Major-General Wauchope. We got a magnificent send off at St. Vincent from H.M.S. *Diadem.* The sailors' cheering was very fine.

I should like to have my Christmas dinner at Pretoria, but I don't expect we shall get there until well on in February at the soonest. I forgot to tell you to spend £15 (fifteen pounds) on some silver thing, and send the account to Harry Hart, Esq., Hon. Secretary, Prestwick Golf Club, Prestwick. Get anything you like, and have "Amateur Championship, 1899," put on.

The officers of the ship gave us a very fine concert and a supper the other night. I shall post this in Cape Town on Monday. I hope you are all very fit.

Give old "Nails" a kidney or two from me.

Best love to all,

Yours affectionately,

F. G. TAIT.

P.S.—Address letters,

The Black Watch,
South African Field Force,
South Africa.

13 *November,* 1899.

We hope to arrive at Cape Town this afternoon about 6 p.m. We have had it very rough last two days. I am still eating a good dinner and a splendid breakfast.

A Record

I enclose programme of concert and menu for book. This letter has to be posted at 1 p.m., and as it is nearly lunch time (12.30 p.m.), I must stop.

All the old lot are with us—Colonel Coode; Majors Duff, Maxwell, Berkeley, Cuthbertson; Captains Bruce, Elton, Eykyn, Macfarlan, Stewart; Lieutenants Cameron, Hamilton, Tait, Harvey (John), Harvey (St. John, 1st Batt.), Ramsay, Edwards, Wauchope, etc.; 29 officers and 950 men.

The young officers that have joined lately are a capital lot.

I have an excellent fellow of the name of Innes in my company.

Yours affectionately,

F. G. Tait.

S.S. *Orient*,
13 *November*, 1899,
About 70 miles N.N.W. of
Cape Town.

Dear Uncle John,

Many thanks for cheque. We have had a most excellent and cheery voyage. The last two days have been rough, but I have enjoyed them immensely.

We expect to get to Cape Town at 6 p.m. to-night. We may have to land there, or we may have to go on to Port Elizabeth. I hope Sir George White has not lost any more regiments. We got a magnificent send off from St. Vincent by the officers and crew of H.M.S. *Diadem*. We heard there that two regiments had capitulated, and that Sir George White had wired to the Queen,

F. G. Tait

and also that he (Sir G. W.) was practically surrounded. * * * * We shall hear everything in five hours or so.

I shall write to you as soon as Kruger has carried my clubs round Pretoria Links.

Yours affectionately,
F. G. Tait.

Tait arrived at Cape Town on November 13th, and left the following evening for De Aar Junction. Writing *en route*, he mentions his first impressions of South Africa.

On the train after leaving
Matjesfontein,
15 *November*, 1899.

My dear Mother,

We arrived at Cape Town on Monday and anchored outside the harbour. On Tuesday we went into harbour and disembarked. We left Cape Town last night about 10 p.m., and we are now about one third of the way to De Aar. The gradients on the railway are very stiff, 1 in 40 is quite common, and in several places as steep as 1 in 30. We have already gone up about 3,000 feet, and our pace has been very slow. We expect to go on from De Aar to relieve Kimberley and Mafeking. The climate here is lovely; a beautiful clear sky and a fairly hot sun. We hope to arrive at De Aar to-morrow, Thursday, about 12 noon.

The railway is patrolled in all the dangerous places by Cape Mounted Police and Volunteers. We have had a very good reception so far, but soon we will get into the disloyal parts, and probably have a shot or two fired into the train. I am

A Record

writing this in the train, which does not run too
smoothly. We have 700 men in this train, and the
remainder come on in a later train. We had a
great reception at Matjesfontein from a large land-
owner (a Scotsman, by name Logan). He is a
member of the Cape Parliament, and one of Rhodes'
lot. A very fine lunch and a most hearty send off.
As far as I can see we have done very little with
the Boers so far in Natal, but I trust that the
reinforcements, which ought to have arrived by
now, will soon put matters right. I think we ought
to be able to cause a diversion on the western
boundary of the Orange Free State, and at the
same time relieve Kimberley and Mafeking. Having
done that, all being well with the Natal force, we
would march straight on Pretoria. That is the
programme at present, but it is quite possible that
we may advance through the centre of the Orange
Free State.

I am very fit. Best of luck to you all.

Yours affectionately.

F. G. Tait.

He arrived at De Aar on November 16,
and his regiment remained at that station for
six days. Writing from there he sent home
the following interesting letter :—

De Aar,

20 *November*, 1899.

My dear Mother,

We arrived here on Thursday last. This is
a most important junction, and our business is to
defend it. The 91st, 78th, and half Battalion of
ourselves are here. We have been expecting an
attack daily, but as yet the Boers have not put in

F. G. Tait

an appearance. Our other half Battalion, under
Major Duff, left here on Saturday to garrison
Naauwport, an important place about 70 miles off.

The Boers blew up the railway bridge close to
Naauwport just after our lot had crossed. We
shall garrison this place here until Lord Methuen
has relieved Kimberley. After that, Methuen's
force will return here, and we will all go towards
the Orange Free State through Colesberg, and from
thence through the middle of Orange Free State to
Pretoria.

We have been supplying the outposts to this
place for the last four or five days, and the work is
very trying and hard. Not a wink of sleep, and
constantly on the alert. I am doing adjutant for
this half Battalion here. Up to now we have been
fairly comfortable, but we always sleep fully dressed,
to be ready at a moment's notice. I was in command of a very important post a few nights ago
with 15 men (200 rounds each), grub and water for
three days, and orders to hold it to the last. I
was in hopes the Boers would arrive, but they
did not. They have made a fatal mistake in not
attacking this place sooner. If they had attacked
a week or so ago they could easily have captured
it, and thereby cut off the large force on the
Orange River from its base, and not only that, but
a large quantity of valuable stores would have
fallen into their hands. At the present moment
they have not much chance unless they bring a
very large force. I met Heatlie here; I dined with
him on Saturday, and met his wife. He enquired
very kindly after you all.

It is very hot here, and our tents are pitched in
a huge bunker, and the dust is something frightful

when it blows. The 71st, with my pal Wolfe Murray, left here this morning to hold the Orange River while Methuen advances on Kimberley. No more time.

Yours affectionately,

F. G. TAIT.

On November 22 Tait moved eastward to Naauwpoort, from which place he writes :—

Naauwport,
25 *November*, 1899.

My dear Mother,

We joined the right half Battalion here last Wednesday. This is a far more pleasant camp than De Aar. Our strength here is one Battery R.H.A., one and a half Battalions Infantry, and a few Mounted Infantry, and an Ammunition Column. I believe we are going to attack Colesberg as soon as we are reinforced. We want a Regiment of Cavalry and another Battalion of Infantry. The Cavalry Regiment is expected to-day, so we ought to be at work soon. We are now in touch with the Boers, about 14 miles from here. On Thursday last we sent out a Company of the Black Watch and some Mounted Infantry in a train in the direction of Colesberg. We had repaired the line the day before to within 15 miles of that place. Our men and the Mounted Infantry found the Boers in a strong position about 16 miles from here. We are about 38 miles from Colesberg. The Mounted Infantry, in reconnoitring the position, got three men hit (one man in four places). We are in a capital position here, but the Boers are too crafty to attack us. General French is in command here. I have just come off 24 hours' outpost duty. It is very tiring work, as you must never sleep, and must be on your feet all the time. Cameron, Innes, and I share a tent. When we advance from here (if we have to leave the railway) we are only going to carry a blanket and a waterproof sheet. A lot of us have started beards; I have managed to shave up to now, but I expect I shall be compelled to give it up. Ramsay and John Harvey look very well in beards. We are all very fit. We have all given up swords and taken to rifles, to be more like the men, and consequently not so conspicuous. I hope Willie and Alec carried my motion. Many thanks for your letters. "South African Field Force" is the correct address.

Hope you are all very fit.

Yours ever,

F. G. TAIT.

The "motion" referred to by Tait was one which he would himself have proposed had he been able to be present at the business meeting of the Royal and Ancient Club. Its object was to give the members of the club, and not the committee, the final appointment of the club secretary. This motion, which was an excellent example of Tait's sound common sense, was unfortunately lost at a small meeting by three votes.

Tait left Naauwport on November 27th, and went by rail North, *via* De Aar, to Orange River Station, and writes from there—

A Record

Orange River,
1 *December*, 1899.

My dear Mother,

I am writing this on the bank of the Orange River. My Company and two others are at present guarding the railway bridge. There are a lot of Boers about nine miles from here, but they won't attack us, worse luck. We ought to have been with Lord Methuen in his last three fights, but as our Battalion was split up into two, just when we were wanted, the 91st were sent instead. We expect to be relieved here by another regiment about Sunday, and then we will follow on and join Lord Methuen, and get up to him in time to relieve Kimberley. Lord Methuen lost a lot of men at the Modder River, about 550 killed and wounded. The 91st suffered the most. Our other half Battalion is at Naauwport, 140 miles from here. We expect them to join us to-morrow or Sunday. We expected an attack last night, from information that we had received from our scouts, but the ruffians did not come. The Boers are awfully keen on blowing up the bridge here, but I don't think they will manage that while we are on the spot. We send a quarter of our Company to bathe at a time, the remaining three-quarters look out for the Boers. We came here from Naauwport last Monday. Two Regiments of our Brigade are already with Lord Methuen; half of our Regiment and the Seaforths are here, so in a few days the Highland Brigade ought to be together at the front. I met Percy Grant, first at De Aar and again here; he is a volunteer doctor during the war. I went round the Boer wounded with him two days ago here. There are about sixty or seventy of them. They are fairly decent-looking chaps, and seemed quite happy. I talked to a good many of them (that is to say to those that spoke English); most of them were jolly glad to be prisoners, and none of them were keen to fight any more. We are wearing khaki aprons over our kilts, as a dark kilt is a splendid thing "to draw a bead on." We are about one and a half miles from camp, on the top of a kopje covering the railway bridge. I have just returned from bathing, with a party of 25 men or so; they enjoy themselves very much in the water. I had a capital swim myself.

The weather is splendid, very hot during the day and quite cool at night. The only thing that bothers us is the dust, which is most unpleasant when there is any wind. Cameron has been promoted Captain. We are only 40 miles from Lord Methuen, and the railway has been repaired right up to Modder River, so we will not take long to reach the front when we start.

Two trains of our wounded came in yesterday. I have not been down to camp to see them yet, but I shall go this afternoon. We get very little news here; in fact, everyone at home must know far more about the war than we do. I hope my motion was carried at St. Andrews. General Andrew Wauchope is looking very fit and well. We have just been warned to be ready to go off to-morrow (Saturday), so my next letter will be from somewhere near Kimberley, I hope.

Merry Christmas and Happy New Year to all at 38, George Square, 8, Belgrave Crescent, 51, George Square, etc., etc.

Yours affectionately,

F. G. TAIT.

A Record

Owing to congestion on the line, the left Battalion, in which Tait was, proceeded northward on foot, the right Battalion having previously gone forward by train.

Writing to his brother Alec from Honey Nest Kloof, Tait describes the journey towards Modder River, and, as usual, does not forget to send a kindly message with regard to " Nails' " welfare, which no doubt the dog duly appreciated—

> Honey Nest Kloof,
> South Africa,
> 5 *December*, 1899.

My dear Alec,

I thought you might like to hear a little about this show out here, so as I have a little time to spare I write you a few lines. We join Lord Methuen to-morrow at the Modder River, 12 miles from here. Our right-half Battalion is already there. They went by train ; we are marching, as the line, which is only a single one, is much congested with traffic. Stores, ammunition, troops, and supplies of all kinds go up, and empty trains and trains with sick and wounded come down. We have to march 55 miles from the Orange River, over very bad, sandy tracks, with very little water (water is very scarce in this part of the country). It is very hot during the day, and sometimes very cold at night, especially about 2 a.m. There is absolutely no shade, and the dust is very bad ; under the circumstances, you will see that 12 miles a day is quite good going. Each officer and man carries upwards of 35 lbs., without counting clothes.

F. G. Tait

We all carry rifles and 100 rounds of ammunition, a large coat, a large water bottle (holding two quarts), field glasses, and a haversack. People think nothing of a 15 or 20 mile walk in England when dressed in a shooting suit and carrying nothing but a stick or a gun ; personally, I would sooner walk 35 miles like that in England than 14 miles here at this time of year, dressed as we are. We carry rifles and the same equipment as the men, in order to make it more difficult for the Boers to pick out the officers. The transport, which consists of mules and bullock waggons, carries a blanket and a waterproof-sheet for each of us (inside the blanket we carry a spare shirt, a pair of socks, a sponge, and a few articles of that sort). That comprises my whole wardrobe at present. I have managed to shave up till now, but nearly all the rest have got beards, as water is so scarce, and sometimes you don't get an opportunity of shaving for two or three days at a time.

We expect to have a big fight at Spitfontein at the end of this week or the beginning of next. Lord Methuen's last fight at the Modder River was by no means a success, but by Thursday this week he will be reinforced by the Highland Brigade, another Battery of Artillery, and the 12th Lancers. The Boers are in a very strong position at Spitfontein, and will take some shifting. I expect we will get our share of the fighting. We join Lord Methuen to-morrow, and the Seaforths, the last to arrive of the Brigade, on Thursday. I am writing this under a shelter made from galvanised iron and wooden props, the remains of a store looted by the Boers some time ago. It is well over 90° in the shade now. When we have cleared the Boers out of their

A Record

position at Spitfontein, then Kimberley will be relieved; after that I expect we will march on Bloemfontein. I have been very fit so far, but it is rather too hot for my taste.

Remember me to Sandy Morton, the Smiths, Maclean, etc.

No more time.

I hope you carried my motion. Give "Nails" a good Christmas and New Year dinner from me. I hope he is very fit.

Yours ever,

F. G. TAIT.

Tait arrived at Modder River on December 6th, and joined the other half of his Battalion.

A few hours before the fatal attack on the kopje at Magersfontein he writes to Mrs. Tait—

Modder River,

10 *December*, 1899.

My dear Mother,

I have only time to write a short note, as we are off on a night march to-night and will attack enemy at dawn to-morrow. We shall probably be away for five or six days from here. The enemy is in a very strong position, but we hope to turn him out to-morrow. Our force consists of the Highland Brigade and Yorkshire Light Infantry, four Batteries, and 9th Lancers. Your last letter must have gone astray, as I have received nothing for a fortnight. We expected the last mail to-day, but it has been delayed, so we shall probably not get any letters for a week.

F. G. Tait

I wrote to Alec last mail; this will be a week after his letter. The Black Watch lead the advanced guard, so we may get it fairly hot. Best of luck to you all, not forgetting " Nails."

Yours affectionately,
F. G. TAIT.

At 12.30 on the morning of the 11th December, Tait started with the Highland Brigade on their ill-fated attempt to carry the Boer position at Magersfontein. How, having failed properly to locate the Boer position, they were surprised, when marching in mass of quarter column and on the point of defiling, by a terrific rifle fire from the advanced Boer trenches, is now a matter of history.

Something akin to panic seized the advancing brigade, and it was at this crisis, and in an environment which made his action the more characteristic, that Tait rallied his company—" all that was left of them "—and continued the attack. In the work he did—the work of a moment—Tait showed that he had not mistaken his vocation.*

There was no time for deliberation, for what was to be done had to be done without a moment's pause for thought. Tait's action, therefore, in unhesitatingly rallying his men

---

* Sergeant Dyke of the Seaforth Highlanders, who carried Tait off the field, describes his conduct as being conspicuously gallant.

A Record

and advancing in the face of the deadly
fire which confronted him, can hardly be
altogether ascribed to his great presence of
mind and his undoubted faculty for grasping
quickly the circumstances of a situation.
When there is no time for thought, the
natural impulses of the man, not his reason-
ing faculties, dominate his actions. The
supreme moment of Tait's life came to him
amid the darkness and disorder at Magersfontein, and without an instant's hesitation,
he instinctively chose the course that was
natural to him.

On the following day, December 12th,
Tait started in the hospital train *en route*
for Wynberg, and arrived at the hospital on
the 14th. A fellow officer, wounded at
Magersfontein, writes as follows of his
journey with Tait to Wynberg—

I remember being among the first into the
ambulance train which brought us wounded to
Wynberg after Magersfontein, and keeping the
berth next me for Freddie, who, both in the train
and afterwards in hospital, seemed much more concerned for my comfort than ever he was for his own.
One of the last letters he ever wrote was one he
sent to me just before they started for Koodoosberg,
full of details about our losses at Magersfontein,
which he knew I was anxious to have, but which
must have been most troublesome to obtain in the
hurry before starting—but that was just like him,
he always had time to help a pal.

F. G. Tait

On reaching Wynberg Hospital, Tait wrote his first impressions of Magersfontein to his mother.

Wynberg Hospital,
Near Cape Town,
15 *December* 1899.

My dear Mother,

We started a night march on the enemy's position at 12.30 a.m. on Monday morning last. The Black Watch in front, then the Seaforths, Argylls, and H.L.I. The night was pitch dark, and the country we had to go over was covered with small boulders and low, thick, prickly bushes. We got nothing to eat before starting, and very few of the men had time to fill their water bottles. The march went all right until about 2 a.m., when a tremendous thunderstorm broke over us, and lasted for more than an hour. We were absolutely soaked to the skin. With the rain the night got still darker, consequently we got along at a painfully slow rate. A night march is bad enough on a fairly clear night, but on a really dark night it is hopeless. About 4 a.m. we could dimly see the kopje that the enemy were holding. At that moment we were in *mass* of quarter column facing the kopje, and, as far as I could judge, about 600 yards from it. We were just going to deploy when the most terrific fire suddenly started about 300 yards off (that is to say, midway between us and the kopje). It was still too dark to see anything clearly. Our orders were to lie down, fix bayonets, and charge. Not wanting to miss anything, I got in front of the front company and charged. We got along a 100 yards or so when we got into the dreadful flanking as well as frontal

A Record

fire, and lost very heavily. I could now see that the enemy were in trenches about 200 to 250 yards off. We managed to get 50 yards nearer, losing heavily all the time, and there we lay down (what was left of the lot with me) and began firing. I was about 15 or 20 yards in front, and had just got up to get back in line when I got a bullet through my left thigh. I was knocked clean over, but two of my men got up and pulled me back into the line. It was still not quite light. I was able to turn over on my stomach and fire at the Boers. A quarter of an hour later it was quite light, and then we began to get it properly. The men on each side of me were hit straight away, and in a few minutes very few were left unhit. It was quite impossible for any ambulance or doctor to advance, so all our wounded lay within 200 yards or so of the Boer trenches all day in a broiling sun, being shot at whenever they moved until 7 o'clock at night, most of them without a drop of water.

When our artillery fire was very hot, and the Boer fire in consequence slacker, I managed to get some badly-wounded fellows back to some bushes and shade about 100 yards in rear. I lay all day from about 4 a.m. to 7 p.m. being shot at. I got a shot through my haversack and another grazed my heel, and the rest hit all round. I smoked some cigarettes, munched a little bit of biscuit, and would have been fairly comfortable but for my wound (which hurt a good deal), and for the heat, which was excessive. I knew the bullet had not hit a bone or an artery, so I felt fairly cheerful under the circumstances. I got back to hospital about 10 p.m. and got dressed, and then had two big bowls of tea and some biscuits, and since then

F. G. Tait

I have been all right. The wounded have had a very comfortable journey down here in hospital trains, and this is a capital shady spot, very unlike the Modder River. I expect to go north again in a week. We lost the Colonel, and, worst of all, poor old Macfarlan and Ramsay, also Bruce and Elton. Twelve officers wounded, and total in the regiment 355 killed and wounded. Young Wauchope is hit in four places, but he is getting on well. All I hope is that next time we get a chance of giving back a bit of what we have received. How is poor old " Nails " ? Give him plenty of bones from me.

I hope you are all very well.

With best love,
Yours affectionately,
F. G. TAIT.

Tait remained at Wynberg Hospital for a week, after which he was removed to Claremont Sanitorium. On leaving Wynberg, where he was evidently comfortable, he sends another pleasant message to " Nails."

Wynberg Hospital,
Near Cape Town,
19 December, 1899.

My dear Mother,

I have nothing further to write except that I am getting on first rate, and hope soon to be back at the front. I enclose telegram,* which you might put into the book. The hospital here is very comfortable, and all the wounded are doing well. One of our officers died here of blood poisoning, very

---

* This telegram was from the representatives of 40 Golf Clubs in Manchester and district, wishing Tait a speedy recovery.

A Record

suddenly ; he was wounded in the leg. That makes seven killed and eleven wounded. Things seem to be going very badly for us just now   *   *   *   *
Our brigade was simply thrown away ; hundreds of splendid fellows were killed and wounded, and nothing gained in the end. You will get this letter along with my last, which I wrote last Friday or Saturday. The mail goes to-morrow morning.

Hope you are all very well,

Yours affectionately,

F. G. Tait.

P.S.--How is " Nails " ? Give him plenty of food.

F. G. T.

P.S.S.--We miss the mails regularly ; as we get to one place they go on to another, and so on. I have not had a letter for over three weeks.

F. G. T.

Tait was convalescent by this time, and writing from Claremont, on December 26th, gives further particulars of Magersfontein—

Claremont,

Near Cape Town,

26 *December*, 1899.

My dear Mother,

I came here last Wednesday, and I appear to be getting on first rate. I hope you got my telegram all right. This is a rum sort of establishment ; it seems to be a home for all sorts of broken-down people. The Government have taken part of it for wounded officers. I thought at first that the bullet that hit me had gone clean through my thigh

F. G. Tait

without hitting anything, but it now appears to have gone through the thigh bone. I don't feel any ill effects; my appetite is excellent, and I feel really very fit; of course, I am very stiff, and my leg feels weak. I enclose a telegram for the book. I got your December letter before the November one. A lot of our wounded officers will have to come home; Major Duff, young Wauchope, Drummond, and possibly Cameron, and a Harvey that you don't know. It is awfully sad about poor Macfarlan and Ramsay; I am awfully sorry for Mrs. Macfarlan. I was with Macfarlan and Ramsay when we first charged, but they both went off with a lot of men to try and work round the flank of the Boers. I never saw them again, as I went on with the frontal attack. General Wauchope and our Colonel, and Captain Bruce and young Edmonds, were all killed with the lot of men that I accompanied. General Wauchope is in no way responsible for the fearful loss of life amongst the Highland Brigade; he got his orders, and had to carry them out, and he was killed in front of his brigade. I feel certain that if we had been led up in line we should have rushed the position with probably a quarter of the loss that we actually suffered. As it was, we arrived rather late and in mass of quarter column. I will explain that formation to you: There are eight companies in a battalion, and four battalions in a brigade; quarter column means a column of companies with six paces between companies; mass of quarter column, in our case, meant thirty-two companies one behind the other at six paces interval, with a slightly longer interval between battalions. Our front was about 50 yards and our depth about 300 yards; a pretty formation to arrive within

206

[*Snapshot.*

ON BOARD H.M.S. "NIOBE," January 1st, 1900.

(*Last photograph of F. G. Tait.*)

A Record

350 yards of the Boer position. You may imagine the effect of a tremendously hot rifle fire into that compact body. Our men behaved magnificently, and a cooler lot of officers and men I never want to see. Some of our men on my right actually got into the trenches, and were then shelled out by our own guns and forced to retire. ✳ ✳ ✳ ✳ I am glad Roberts is coming out, as the troops have great confidence in him. Your present of socks and tobacco will be very welcome when it arrives.

I hope you all had a very pleasant Christmas; I cannot say I enjoyed mine much. I had a drive to Rhodes' house yesterday.

The last mail has arrived at Cape Town, and ought to be delivered this afternoon here.

I hope you are all very well. Give my love to Aunt Jane and Uncle Crum, and a bone with plenty of meat on it to " Nails."

Yours affectionately,
F. G. TAIT.

Being now well enough to get about, Tait went down to Simon's Bay and spent a couple of happy days cruising on H.M.S. *Niobe*. He joined the cruiser on the 31st December, and so was able to show them the true Scottish method of bringing in the New Year. He refers to his cruise in the following short note—

Claremont Sanatorium,
2 January, 1900.

My dear Mother,

I start next week for the front again. Nothing of importance to tell you. I had a little

F. G. Tait

trip on board H.M.S. *Niobe* (first-class cruiser) from Simon's Bay to Cape Town, and enjoyed it very much. I am practically all right now. If I have time to-night I will write a little more. Love to all.

Yours affectionately,

F. G. TAIT.

He returned to Claremont on January 8th, and on the 10th started again for the front, his last birthday (11th January) being spent in the train.

In the following letter he mentions having taken some photographs, which are, unfortunately, not sufficiently distinct for reproduction in these pages.

Civil Service Club,

Cape Town,

9 *January*, 1900.

My dear Mother,

I got two of your letters yesterday. I go to the front again to-morrow (Wednesday). I spent a few days on board the *Niobe*, and I am now quite well again. I have no news at all. I shall let you know about the tobacco and the other presents you sent to the men by the next mail. All my letters go to Modder River and then come back, so I always get them a week late. Please thank Aunt Jane for her kind present. I hope to get it when I arrive at Modder again. Wolfe Murray and I are going up to-morrow night together. I send you a few photographs, taken by myself, which may interest you. I have written on the back of each one

Yours affectionately,

F. G TAIT

A Record

When Tait arrived at Modder River he spent several uneventful days, during which he wrote the following letters to Mr. Herbert Johnstone and myself, which refer mainly to his experiences at Magersfontein.

Modder River,
14 January, 1900.

My dear Herbert,

You are a " ripper " writing to me, you have no idea how much I enjoy a letter from home. I arrived here yesterday again, after being away down near Cape Town for a little over four weeks. I am quite fit again, and ready for another go. I got shot through the thigh early in the morning, and while it was still fairly dark. (Beastly fluke ! !). I was only about 250 yards off the trenches all the time, trying to organise another rush. The shot felt very much like a terrific kick without any pain ; it knocked me clean off my legs, and two fellows hauled me back into the line. I was beastly uncomfortable all day, as I was lying on a sort of small ant heap, and the brutes crawled up my legs and amused themselves round about the two holes in my leg. I plugged away with my rifle, and I can almost swear to two Boers, which was not so bad, but when I get them on the open, or attacking us, I will have a much bigger bag. ✻ ✻ ✻ ✻ Their position was by nature very strong, but was made trebly so by the trenches and entanglements that they had made. To have attacked their position with any prospect of success we should not have had less than 5,000. ✻ ✻ ✻ ✻ We were all led to understand that the enemy's position was a large kopje,

F. G. Tait

and when we were about 600 yards off it, as far as we could judge in the darkness, we were just beginning to deploy, when we got a terrific fire from the front and flanks. We then found out that their first position was a line of trenches more than 200 yards in front of the kopje.

We got the order to lie down, fix bayonets, and charge. Our front three companies charged straight on, and the other five went off to the right to try and turn the Boers' right flank. The front three companies (I was in that lot) got to within about 200 yards, but we could not get any nearer; the remnant of the three companies lay down at this point, and held their ground until 7 p.m. in a hot sun, without water and food, and being plugged at all the time. I think only six men of this lot got away unhurt after fifteen hours' fighting. The Boers never hit me again, although I got any number most unpleasantly close; two through my haversack, the rest hitting the ground in front, or whizzing past my ears. General Wauchope, Colonel Coode, Bruce, and young Edmonds, were all killed within fifty yards or so on my left. Many of the men were hit three or four times, and some more. Poor young Wauchope got hit four times, and lay out all the night, and was not brought in till 11 o'clock the next day. He is an awful plucky fellow. I never expected to get away, so I made the best of a bad job and smoked cigarettes. We were never supported all day. The Gordons advanced about 10 o'clock, but never got very close.

My two best friends are killed—poor old Anak Macfarlan and Ramsay, two splendid fellows. Old Anak bagged four Boers before they got him.

A Record

I hope you are very fit. I should like to be playing matches with you this winter. If I get back we shall have lots; but if we have another Magersfontein, I have my doubts. The whole thing is absolute luck; one man is hit four or five times and recovers, and another man gets hit once and is killed, and some don't get hit at all. From my experience of fifteen hours' fighting, it is not to be compared to the excitement or interest of a good finish at golf. After you have been shot at by people you cannot see to shoot at, it becomes deadly dull. Possibly when one does all the shooting it may be more interesting. Please give Mrs. Herbert my kindest regards. John Harvey is all right; we expect him here to-day.

Please remember me most kindly to Archie Pat, Leslie, Harry Stevenson, John Menzies, Tom Clark, and with many thanks.

Yours ever,
F. G. Tait.

Modder River,
19 January, 1900.

My dear Johnnie,

Many thanks for your kind letter. It was awfully good of you to write. I am all right again now, and back at the front. I should have had my leg badly broken if the bullet which hit me had not had an awful "slice" on. The "slice" made it go round the bone. We had a jolly hot time of it I can tell you, but it was a very one-sided show, as the Boers were behind trenches, and we were in the open. I got plugged about 4 a.m., about 250 yards from the trenches in our front line, and lay there till 7 p.m. at night, getting

F. G. Tait

plugged at all the time ; only about six of this front line got away without being hit. The papers say the Highland Brigade retired and re-formed. The Black Watch never did ; and, furthermore, we held our ground all day.   *   *   *   *

I hear excellent news from Colenso to-day. Buller has got his whole force across the Tugela. I don't think we will take more than three or four months now. Poor Macfarlan, Ramsay, Elton, and Edmonds, are an awful loss to us.

I am afraid I cannot get back in time to play the May Medal with you. I should like to see you pull it off; you have not had any luck lately in the important events.

Many thanks, old man, for your letter. My kindest regards and love to Stuart Paton and other friends at Woking.

Yours ever,

F. G. TAIT.

In a letter written on January 17th, Tait describes a reconnaissance on Magersfontein, and on the following day in a letter to his mother, gives his views on the future prospects of the campaign. The letter written to his brother Alec on the same day is of peculiar interest. Tait had come through the extremities of war at Magersfontein, and he here gives expression to a thought which he must purposely have concealed from his mother, and only lightly hints at to his brother in the now pathetic words, "in case of accidents."

A Record

Modder River,
17 *January*, 1900.

My dear Mother,

I got back here last Friday. Your box arrived here to-day, and was much appreciated. Tobacco, socks, shirts, pipes, and anything of that sort are always useful.

I don't know whether you ever received my wire or not. I sent one from Wynberg about a week after I got hit, but you do not mention having received it. Please let me know if it arrived. We are just off on a reconnaissance in force on Magersfontein again. Two regiments and a battery or two. The heat here is rather too much, and it is generally accompanied by a dust storm. We start in about three quarters of an hour, so I must now close. I will add some more later.

Yours affectionately,

F. G. Tait.

Modder River,
18 *January*, 1900.

My dear Mother,

Our reconnaissance yesterday ended without any casualties to us, although the Boers put a few shells fairly close to us every now and then. The officers are very much pleased with the box, which, as I said, arrived yesterday. They all send their best thanks. The shortbread is excellent; a large number of clay pipes were broken. The work now is very hard. Each Company is on picket three nights out of five, and the duty lasts 27 hours. The men get a chance of a little sleep on picket, but the officers have to be on the alert all the night.

F G. Tait

We go on at 3 a.m. and come off at 6 a.m. the following morning. If it was cooler during the day one could put in a few hours' sleep, but it is far too hot for that. I could not write last week as I was travelling up from Cape Town, and I missed the mail at Modder River. I have had a lot of very kind letters from people all over the country. One enjoys a letter very much out here. I am awfully sorry for all the people at home having all their dances and fun stopped on account of the war. I think it is a great mistake, as it gives too much time for thought, and goodness knows there is plenty to think about. I think everything ought to go on all right as soon as Ladysmith is relieved. The great difficulty that we have in carrying on the war is due to spies. The whole of Cape Colony is just bristling with disloyal people who give excellent information to the Boers.

Our information about the Boers is generally very bad, and often most misleading. I believe that a good many of our scouts are in the Boers' pay. I shall write to Alec this mail if I have time. Please tell the Governor to pay some money into Cox & Co. for me. I had a good look at the Magersfontein position yesterday when we were out. * * * * I believe Kimberley would have been relieved six weeks ago if we had left a small force to hold Modder River and moved out with the remainder round the Boer flank through the Free State and on to Kimberley.

The Boers then would either have had to come out and fight us in the open or remain in Magersfontein and see Kimberley relieved. In any case, the relief of Kimberley was a great error. An advance up the middle of the Free State from Orange

A Record

River would have been far better, as the Free State is absolutely level, and the Boers would not then have had the great advantage of taking up a series of splendid positions in front of us and forcing us to fight whenever they felt inclined. Another thing, the mere fact of a strong force of 20,000 men moving up the Free State would have relieved Kimberley, as the force investing Kimberley would have had to withdraw to defend Bloemfontein. I miss poor old Anak and Ramsay very much. I wish they were here to enjoy the shortbread. Give poor old " Nails " some kidneys for his kind present.

No more time.

Kindest regards and love, etc., to all,

Yours affectionately,

F. G. TAIT.

P.S.—I hope the Governor is better.

F. G. T.

Modder River,
18 *January*, 1900.

My dear Alec,

I have not much time, but I can manage a few lines. Thanks for your letter. I got up here a few days ago, and am quite well again. I had a jolly lucky recovery, half an inch more and I should have had my thigh-bone smashed. I hope you are very fit. I am sorry we lost our motion at St. Andrews, but we did very well, as we never canvassed at all. It is too hot out here for my taste. I hope you got my letter from Honey Nest Kloof. We will never be able to replace MacFarlan and Ramsay, they were two splendid fellows. We have lost over one-third of the Regiment, and I have lost one-third of my Company.

F. G. Tait

The work here is very heavy just now, three days out of five on picket for 27 hours at a time without sleep. I think we ought to finish the show in four months if Ladysmith is relieved soon. John Harvey, Berkeley, and I are the only three officers back as yet. We will get two more almost at once, making five out of eleven wounded, but we shan't see the other six for many months, I am afraid. Poor young Edmonds, Colonel Coode, General Wauchope, and Bruce, were all killed close to me. I had some desperate near shaves. Two bullets through my haversack, etc. I have received many kind letters, but it is awful work writing in this heat. Remember me to all my Glasgow friends, and, in case of accidents, I want George Law to get my putter, and old Ponkie Kerr something too. Arty Wolfe Murray said it was lucky my bullet had a "slice" on !! Have you got your partnership yet?

Good luck.

Yours ever,

F. G. TAIT.

Writing to his old friend, Ian McIntyre, a week later, Tait gives another interesting description of the battle of the 11th December, and pays a high tribute to the men of the Black Watch—

Modder River,
24 *January*, 1900.

Dear old Ian,

Many thanks for your letter. You have no idea how much I enjoy a letter from the old country, especially when it is from a "Fettesian." Isn't that

A Record

what you call yourself? I remember some club coming over from Edinburgh to play golf at St. Andrews last September with a name something like that. The members were a funny lot. They blocked the green, crowded out the Club-House, cooked their scores, and forgot to (or couldn't) pay their caddies. Now that I have put the Turkish bath question all right I shall proceed.

I am back again at the front, and quite recovered, and ready for another go. I hope the Boers will attack us just for a change. We have been ordered not to advance at present. I suppose that means waiting until one of our columns is level with us in the Free State. I think things are beginning to improve a bit. I think the war will be over in four months. Our fight was very much worse than a rough football match in this way; if you get scragged or kicked in a football match you can generally give as good as you get, but at Magersfontein we never had a chance, we were led into a place something like this—*

You will see that we were led into a re-entering part of the kopje, and were fired at on three sides in the dark. We were not extended at the time. The extreme darkness of the night was mainly responsible for the failure of the attack. I got plugged at for 15 hours at about 250 yards, after being hit in the dark in our last rush. The position was very strong by nature, and their trenches were cleverly planned, and they made use of wire fences, which are dreadful obstacles in the dark. Our men behaved magnificently, and I have the greatest confidence in

---

* Tait here gives a sketch showing the three-sided position of the Boer trenches.

F. G. Tait

them. Everything is very quiet here just now, except that the picket work is very hard; we are on for 24 hours three days out of every four. That does not leave much time for sleep. Hope you give England and Wales a proper hammering.*

With many thanks, old man.

Yours ever,

F. G. TAIT.

P.S.—Kind regards to Mrs. Ian, also to Mr. and Mrs. McIntyre, senior.

F. G. T.

In a letter to his uncle, Mr. John Porter, dated February 2nd, Tait throws some fresh light on the Magersfontein disaster, and on the same day, writing to his mother, he makes special mention of the death of Private Macgregor, well known to all frequenters of St. Andrews, as the painstaking and courteous Caddie Superintendent, who was a Reservist.

Modder River,

2 February, 1900.

My dear Uncle John,

Many thanks for your letter and enclosure about J. B. * * * * I don't know who was responsible for the close formation. The formation was all right if we had deployed sooner;

---

* This refers to John Ball's departure for South Africa with the Cheshire Yeomanry.

that is where the mistake occurred. Mass of quarter column was the only possible formation to march in that night. It was very dark, but at the same time we had plenty of light to deploy at least ten minutes before we were fired into.

General Wauchope never made any remark about its not being his fault. His A.D.C. and galloper have both told me so; and, if they had not, I should never have believed that he made the remark—it is not the least like him. * * * * Many thanks for the Cox & Co. arrangement. We expect to move from here soon; in which direction I don't know, but I hope on Bloemfontein. We receive reinforcements every day. We have a very strong force of guns here now. I must send this off to catch the mail. Hope Mrs. P. is very well.

Yours affectionately,

F. G. Tait.

P.S.—The Black Watch never retired at Magersfontein. What other regiments did I only know from hearsay.

F. G. T.

Modder River,
2 February, 1900.

My dear Mother,

Thanks for your letter. * * * * I have inquired about Stewart and MacDonald, and I am afraid they were killed; they are at present reported missing. The Boers buried about 70 of the Highland Brigade, mostly our men, I am afraid, and there was no record kept of their names. Shoes, socks, etc., arrived all right; many thanks. We expect to move

F. G. Tait

from here shortly ; large reinforcements arrive daily. I hope we are going to march on Bloemfontein, as I am tired of fighting in our own country. I am afraid Ladysmith is in a bad way ; Sir George will have to cut his way out, I expect, and leave his wounded and sick. I am very glad to hear that the governor is better. It is still very hot here. I want some shirts badly. I am afraid MacGregor, the Caddie Superintendent, is dead. Hain, my old servant, is missing or killed ; also Scullin, the one I had at Glasgow.

Love to all,

Yours affectionately,

F. G. TAIT.

On February 3rd Tait's brigade moved westward down the Riet River, some eight miles, to Frazer's Drift, and on the following day arrived at Koodoosberg Drift. From here, on the morning of his death, he wrote a short note to his mother, which is reproduced on the opposite page.

Tait was killed during the reconnaissance which took place at Koodoosberg Drift, under General Macdonald. A description of the engagement would be both out of place here and foreign to my purpose. The circumstances of his death have been fortunately preserved for us in the following letter from Private Scott, who, writing to his mother, after describing the preliminary skirmishing at Koodoosberg, tells of the rush that was

Hoodersburg
23 miles West of Modder
River Station
7th February

My dear Mother
We arrived
here last Monday after
a two days march
what we are supposed to
be doing I don't know
Our force consists of
Highland Brigade, 1 Battery
+ 1 Cavalry Regt. + some
Engineers the Boers
seem to be in considerable
force here as they have
attacked us the last
three days To-day
they are making a
more determined attack.
but they have not
attacked our section
of the Outpost line
yet. We expect to be
sent off to reinforce
at any moment—
No more time. I have
to post this to-day to
catch next Tuesdays
mail. Love to all
Yours affec
J G Tait

TAIT'S LAST LETTER.

A Record

made by Tait's Company in order to check the Boer advance. He says:—

I got down beside our officer, Lieutenant Tait, on his right hand. He said, " Now, men, we will fight them at their own game." That meant that each man was to get behind a rock and just pop up to fire and then down again. And we found it a good way, for we were just as good as they were at it, and we did not forget to let them know it either, for, whenever one showed himself, down he went with half-a-dozen bullets through him. After firing for about half-an-hour, the Boers stopped firing, and the order was given not to waste our shot. Lieutenant Tait's servant came up with his dinner, and he asked me if I would like a bit of dinner, and I said I would, and thanked him very much. He gave me and another man half of his dinner between us. Little did I think, when we were joking with one another, that we were helping him to eat his last dinner. Just as we finished, he said, " I think we will advance another fifty yards, and perhaps we will see them better, and be able to give it them hot." We all got ready again, and Lieutenant Tait shouted, " Now, boys! " We were after him like hares. The Boers had seen us, and they gave us a hot time of it. But on we went. Just as our officer shouted to get down, he was shot. I was just two yards behind him. He cried out, " Oh ! they have done for me this time." I cried up to him, " Where are you shot, sir?" and he said, " I don't know." He had been shot through the heart, and never spoke again. Just a minute afterwards I was shot through the leg, and dropped. All this

221

F. G. Tait

time the sun had been burning down on us, and to make things worse, we had no water. But our men stuck to it, and about six o'clock the Boers began to retire. I suppose they thought they had enough, but we thought otherwise, and pumped it hard into them when they were retiring. I was glad when it was over, for I had suffered very much. I crawled for about fifty yards to one of my comrades, and he dressed my legs. After it was dark they started to carry down the dead and wounded. To give you an idea of the hill I was on, it took them three hours to carry me down to the foot.

The kindly action which is so simply recorded in this letter forms a fitting termination to a life that had been all kindness and goodwill towards men.*

Tait, with his natural pluck and keenness, had evidently been pushing on to gain a more advantageous position when he was struck down. His party must have been subjected to a very hot fire, as Private Scott seems to have been hit almost at the same moment as his officer.

Private Scott's account is supplemented by four other letters from men of the Black Watch, which give the same story, with slight but natural variations. There is no need to

---

* Lieutenant Blair, of the Seaforth Highlanders, who was also killed during the engagement at Koodoosberg, was a schoolfellow of Tait's, and it is a strange coincidence that Dr. Fell who examined their bodies was also a contemporary at Sedbergh.

comment on the feeling of affection and sorrow which runs through all three letters.

" He always had a smile on his face. Our Company would have followed him anywhere."

No words could more eloquently express the relationship in which Tait stood to his men.

From Pioneer Sergeant Howden, 2nd Battalion Black Watch—

It was in the afternoon that poor Lieutenant Tait was killed. He was in command of H Company. He had just made a rush forward with the company, about 50 yards, so as to get closer to the Boer position. He was in the act of lying down to get under cover when he was shot, pretty high up on the breast. He exclaimed, " I am afraid I am badly hit," and dropped down and died in about a minute. He was carried back to camp, and was buried the next day on the bank of the Riet River ; a very pretty place close to the drift, surrounded by South African plants and trees.

The men put a small wooden cross, with his name on it, on the grave.

Koodoosberg is about 28 miles from Modder River Station.

Lieutenant Tait was thought an awful lot of by both officers and men ; he treated men as men, and not as dogs. He will be greatly missed in the regiment.

From Private Hacker, Bandsman, 2nd Battalion Black Watch—

27 *February*, 1900.

By the time that this reaches you, no doubt you will have heard that we have lost poor Lieutenant

F. G. Tait

Tait, one of the best of fellows. Just the day after I came back from hospital he came up and shook hands with me, and said, "No more lying in bed now, lad, till we get back to Old England. We must make it hot for the Boers."

5 March, 1900.

Since I wrote to you last we have buried poor Lieutenant Tait. It is a nice spot where he is buried; but, poor chap, he is a long way off home and friends. All the chaps miss him, he was so cheery.

14 March.

I was not there when Lieutenant Tait was killed, but carried him into hospital.

30 March.

All the chaps seem to miss Lieutenant Tait; he was one of our best officers, and was always so bright and cheery, and made you feel as if you was the same as himself.

From Private David Rowat, 2nd Battalion Black Watch—

We lost in our regiment two officers and one man; eight wounded. One of the officers was Mr. Tait, as you speak of; he was shot through the chest. We buried him before we left, and decorated his grave with plants and stones the best way we could. You will see it in the papers before you get this letter.

In a letter received from a private of the Black Watch by his parents in Pittenweem, giving an account of the part taken by the

A Record

Highland Brigade in the engagement on Koodoosberg Hill, he says—

Out of my company (H) we had six wounded and one of our officers was killed. I think you will know him—Lieutenant Tait, the great golfer. He was well liked by the company, and I tell you he adored it as well. When we carried him over the rocks at night there were a good many tears shed. He was buried at Koodoosberg Drift, and we made a little cross for his head. He was a good officer, and always had a smile on his face. Our company would have followed him anywhere.

On Monday, February 12th, the first rumour of Tait's death reached London, in a telegram from the correspondent of the *Morning Post*. Throughout the whole day eager enquirers visited the War Office, trying to elicit information from the authorities; but no news had been officially received. Never throughout the course of the war had so many enquiries been made about any officer.

Although the authorities telegraphed for information, no news was received, the War Office replying to all enquiries that, as Tait's death had not been reported to them, they saw no reason to credit the rumour. As the days passed and still no confirmation came, the hope arose and began to grow almost into a certainty that some mistake had been made by the *Morning Post* correspondent. Though no news was even yet received at the War Office, all hope was gone when, on February 14th, Professor Tait received an unsigned telegram from Wynberg Hospital saying :

" Freddie killed instantaneously."

It afterwards transpired that the telegram had been sent by Tait's old friend, Lieutenant Wauchope, who had been severely wounded at Magersfontein.*

It is impossible to describe the universal feeling of sorrow which the intimation of Tait's death brought to the whole of Scotland, and to many who knew him elsewhere. But one name was on everyone's lips, but one thought in the hearts of all who knew him. It would be impossible to attempt to chronicle the feeling of universal sympathy for his family, and the deep sense of personal loss which was felt by all. No word of sympathy was more appreciated by Tait's family than the simple note from Freddie's old friend Mr. W. Greig, of the St. Andrews Golf Club, while the letter from the secretary of that club is so pregnant with the thoughts which filled the hearts of a thousand golfers, that I venture to reproduce it here.

---

* A Memorial Fund was at once started, and the sum of £1,500 was soon raised. This will be mainly devoted to building a new wing for the Cottage Hospital at St. Andrews.

A Record

St. Andrews Golf Club,
February 19.

Dear Professor Tait,

The Members of the St. Andrews Golf Club desire, through me, to respectfully tender yourself, Mrs. Tait, and family, their sincere sympathy in this your time of sorrow. We are but humble working men of dear old St. Andrews to whom Freddie Tait was something apart from all other men. Not alone by his golfing abilities was he so, for of no other golfer of this generation could it ever be said that they possessed the love and hero-worship which was so readily given to your soldier son.

Yours most respectfully,
ALEXANDER MILNE,
Hon. Sec.

The following letters, written shortly afterwards, express the love and admiration which Tait's brother-officers felt for him.

Wynberg Hospital,
February 13.

Dear Mrs. Tait,

Just a line to say how we all feel poor Freddie's death, and how deeply we all sympathize with you.

He was, as you know, my Subaltern, and, I suppose, was commanding my Company on that fatal day. It may be a small consolation to you to know he was killed instantaneously and suffered no pain. Wauchope sent you a wire to that effect from here yesterday.

I think I may number myself amongst the greatest friends he had in the Regiment—we always got on splendidly together, and the Battalion will never be the same without him; in fact, the poor Regiment will be hardly recognizable after this horrible war is over; it is heartbreaking to think about it.

With the deepest sympathy for yourself and the Professor,

I remain,

Yours sincerely,

ARCHIBALD R. CAMERON.

Wegdraii,
15 *February*, 1900.

My dear Professor,

It was with the greatest sorrow that I forwarded to you from Modder River on February 12, registered, a small box, containing dear old Freddie's watch, cap-badge, skene dhu, diary, notebook, whistle, three keys, two little charms, garters, sleeve links, cheque book, packet of letters, pipe and tobacco pouch, purse, hackle, pair of scissors, and Mauser cartridge. These articles were all on his person when he was killed. His valise, and any kit which he had stored in Cape Town, I have ordered to be sent home to you, and will, I hope, arrive safely. I thought you would prefer to have them. His claymore, revolver, and Sam Browne belt are stored at De Aar with all of ours, as we carry rifles, and are dressed the same as the men. They will be sent to you some day, but I cannot promise you when. It is impossible to get at them at present. I cannot find words to express the very great sympathy which I feel for you and your family in your terrible bereavement, and in saying this, I only express the feeling of every officer and man

Dear Father I
am sure you
will be glad
to hear from
me I see
me
my little
paw. I
am very well & they
are giving me lots
to eat. I was away
for 7 hours on Tuesday
& the family were in
great state Yoursaffect a

LETTER FROM "NAILS" FOUND IN TAIT'S POCKET
AT KOODOOSBERGH.

A Record

in the Battalion. We all loved your son; his was such a bright, cheery nature. Through all the hard work of this arduous campaign he was always the same—so keen, so light-hearted. I tell you, his loss to us we shall not get over. We all mourn with you in your great sorrow. He was such a very dear fellow. I think I knew him specially well, and I could not possibly feel his death more acutely had he been my own brother. He died nobly, doing his duty, leading his Company up that awful kopje. It is some sort of comfort to know that his death was instantaneous. He was shot in the right breast, and exclaimed, " They have got me at last," and was gone. He is buried on the banks of the Riet River, close to where he and I bathed together the previous day, when he was just like a school boy, larking in the water, and so thoroughly enjoying it. One of our fellows took a photograph of the grave, which I shall forward to you some day, when we can get it printed.

My dear Professor, I grieve for you and yours from the bottom of my heart. To us, dear old Freddie's loss is quite irreparable.

Very sincerely yours,

T. MOWBRAY BERKELEY.

Paardeberg Drift,
23 *February*, 1900.

My dear Tait,

I cannot express to you how grieved we all are at the loss of your brother who was killed at Koodoosberg, and how we sympathise with you and your family in your great loss. Freddie was shot in the right breast, and it must have remained in his back as there was only one bullet mark.

229

F. G. Tait

He was mercifully killed at once, without any pain. I saw his body when it was brought in, and his face had its usual expression, and he looked almost as if he were smiling. He was buried at Koodoosberg, and I hope later that we will be able to give you a photo of his grave. I would have written sooner, but we have been on the march and fighting ever since, and even now I see no chance of getting this letter away for the present.

I have to thank you for your letter about the two boxes, both of which have arrived and have been distributed to the N.C.O.'s and men according to instructions from Mr. Wauchope. Your brother personally saw to the distribution of both boxes, as he knew more about them than anybody else here.

Please convey the thanks of the Regiment to all those who so kindly contributed and collected the goods for us, and I can assure you their kindness was much appreciated.

With my deepest sympathy to you and all your family in your terrible loss,

Believe me, my dear Tait,
Yours very sincerely,
JOHN E. H. HAMILTON.

Letters of condolence and sympathy to his parents came in hundreds from all ranks and conditions of men and women, all breathing the same thought, expressed in different ways. It would be out of place to produce many of them here, and unnecessary, for everyone must know the message they contained. I will therefore close this last chapter of Tait's life-story with a letter just received

A Record

from Major Archibald Urmston, of the Marines, who tells me some incidents of no small interest about his old friend and comrade-in-arms.

I only saw Freddie once or twice before Magersfontein, one occasion being the very evening before the attack. Amongst others present were Wolfe-Murray (71st), poor Macfarlan and Colonel Coode. We were talking about the impending fight, and the chances of getting hit, and Freddie, amongst other remarks said, it would just be a golfer's luck to be hit somewhere bad in the arm, and so finish his golfing career. Well, next day two out of that party (poor Colonel Coode and Macfarlan) were no more. Wolfe-Murray got hit in the wrist, and Freddie in the leg; but as he said afterwards it wasn't so bad, as he and Wolfe-Murray were sent back to the hospital at Wynberg, and, when convalescent, had some good times before rejoining, amongst which was a visit to Commander Erskine Wemyss on board H.M.S. *Niobe.* Here they made the Christmas evening hideous to all but stout-hearted (or eared) Scotsmen, by giving a skirl on the pipes, Freddie being the chief culprit. His account of being struck by the bullet, was that it felt as if someone had mistaken that particular spot for a football, and had duly administered a good drop kick. Not being able to do much else he managed to get into a kind of hollow some 300 yards off the Boer trenches, and, like Micawber, just waited for " something to turn up." His patience was rewarded after some seven hours of the doubtful pleasure of being made a target of at intervals by some of the more enterprising of the enemy, but it is only fair to state that Master Freddie rather brought

231

it on himself, as he had his gun handy, and let fly at
the top of the trenches whenever he saw even the
shadow of a hat. He never got a right shot at a
fairly exposed target, which he didn't seem to think
was quite " cricket." His logic was, " I gave them
a fair shot (or rather, many shots) at me, and I fancy
I ought to have one at least in return." Anyhow he
gave this sort of amusement up after an hour or two,
as the only result of his firing, as far as he could
reckon, was to draw several shots all round him.
The final decision to " quit sniping " was made,
when one of these most unpolite of enemies landed a
bullet pretty near where his tail would have grown
had he been a monkey. Fortunately, not having
one, he couldn't lose it, but he had no less than
27 holes drilled through the plaits of his kilt instead;
so, as I said before, he " quit sniping," and got to
smoking cigarettes as a diversion, and pondering
over events in general, and his somewhat undesirable
situation in particular. If my memory does not play
me false, I think he passed the odd intervals between
" smokes " in sundry forty winks.

Anyhow, after a fortnight or three weeks, he
returned once more to Modder River, and rejoined
his Regiment (which had suffered terribly severe loss
at Magersfontein). His first jump was a desire to
see the position the Highland Brigade attacked.
I had various detachments with guns on the ground
overlooking Magersfontein, and being so constantly
there, I knew a good deal about the Boers and their
position, which was about 5,000 yards distant. So
we went up one day—Freddie, Harvey (Black
Watch), and myself, to take a look at Magersfontein.

Even then it took them much consultation and

A Record

scratching of heads as to whether the Highland Brigade had attacked on the side of the spur nearest to our position, or "just round the corner." However, after much thought as to "this, that, or something else," they concluded it must have been "just round the corner," in which decision I have no doubt they were right. It must be remembered it was dark during their advance to the attack, and kopjes all look much the same.

Another time, Freddie told me his colonel (Carthew-Yorstoun) would like very much to go round the batteries and see the various points of interest. We arranged a day, and on picking them up, found Frederick was perched up on horseback, though he confided to me going out that he hardly reckoned riding as one of his strongest points. Anyhow, if he hadn't said so, one would not have noticed anything wrong, as man and beast stuck together in quite a friendly way; and it wasn't for want of pace, as, being short of time, we went up to the Naval 4·7 Battery at a good sharp gallop. But Freddie was there all the time, and apparently enjoyed himself A 1. I never saw him outside a horse again.

It was almost an afternoon custom to go out somewhere or other to escape sand storms, flies, etc., if possible. Up the river was the best and most pleasant place, but it was hard to get Freddie away from the batteries; and he was fairly tickled when he was allowed to pull the lanyard of the R.M.A. 4·7 gun, and send a lyddite into the Boer trenches, always hoping it was a "good putt" (certainly a good long one). He was always trying to egg Major Nichols, of the R.A. Siege Battery, to "give it them." Nichols used to ask him if he could see anything worth firing at. By Freddie's showing, there must have been whole armies of Boers marching and counter-marching behind their works, not to speak of whole convoys of waggons, etc. No doubt they were there, as Freddie made out, only the most powerful telescopes failed to locate these hordes sufficiently accurately to warrant Nichols in distributing his ammunition over a few square miles of country on the "off chance," besides which, Nichols, to use the vulgar boy's phrase, "had been there before." On our homeward journeys, Freddie would own to having seen, perhaps, some half-a-dozen Boer warriors at most, or, anyhow, he thought they might have been Boers.

The Highland Brigade left Modder about break of day on February 3rd, to hold the drift at Koodoosberg. It was the last time I ever saw the poor old boy. I was up to see off my brother (A. and S. Highlanders), who was then Brigade Major to General Hector Macdonald, commanding the Highland Brigade, so I saw both him and Freddie, and walked a bit of the way with the latter, who was, of course, marching with his Company on foot. He was full of go and keenness to "have at" his friends again. He was carrying a service carbine, on which he placed great reliance and value, saying, he intended to be level with the men who beat him at Magersfontein, or some of their fellows. The poor old boy, he no doubt did his best, and most likely succeeded, but at far too great a cost, as he never returned from Koodoosberg, where his grave now lies, and will no doubt be held in reverent memory by every man, woman, and child who knew him. Always cheery, always the same genial and happy disposition, taking such

A Record

keen interest in everything, and one of the most charming of companions.

Tait was buried in a quiet and beautiful spot hard by the Riet River, with comrades who had fallen with him—comrades in rest as in work. A small cross marks the spot, the left-hand one of a group of three, and behind and around are trees, and greenness, and freshness, all rendered more pleasant by contrast with the sandy barrenness of the surrounding country. At the grave side stood his Highland company, hardly a man with eye undimmed. In death, as in life, a singular sweetness of expression was noticed on his face, for there had been no pain, no parting, no sorrow of regret for friends left behind; in a moment the passing had taken place, and left his outward form unchanged. "Rest is good after the work is done," and Tait seemed to be tasting a little of its sweets before entering into the greater sphere of work which lay before him.

> "How sleep the brave, who sink to rest
> By all their country's wishes blest!
> When Spring, with dewy fingers cold,
> Returns to deck their hallowed mould,
> She there shall dress a sweeter sod
> Than Fancy's feet have ever trod.
>
> By fairy hands their knell is rung,
> By forms unseen their dirge is sung:
> There Honour comes, a pilgrim gray,
> To bless the turf that wraps their clay;
> And Freedom shall awhile repair
> To dwell a weeping hermit there!"

F. G. Tait

Thus we leave what was mortal of the brave and lovable soldier, far out in the rolling veldt, simply resting—resting after his short life's work was done. *Himself*, his real life, the soul we knew, with its cheery brightness, its honour and its love shining through the keen, kind eyes—*that* lives on in the hearts of a thousand friends—a great inheritance, a possession indestructible.

The life cut short, its military side almost undeveloped, its future unknown—these must be sad thoughts; for Tait had not yet come to his fulness, and there were much greater things which he would have done had he been allowed; but that was not to be. But there is a brighter side—he died the death he would have chosen, he went quickly to rejoin his old friends, a goodly company—who had fallen at Magersfontein. He died the true soldier's death—too soon, indeed—his work not yet done, but still the true soldier's death.

If all life be not a gigantic anticlimax, Freddie has gone forward with many a trusty comrade to that unknown land where there is no seeming failure, and no incompleteness, to the land of all fulness. He will enrich it with his presence.

THE END.

236

APPENDIX I.

---◆◆---

RECORDS OF CHAMPIONSHIP MATCHES,
ETC.

I HAVE deemed it inexpedient in the story of Tait's life to burden the pages with accounts of the great matches he played in the Amateur Championship. That golfers in the future should be able to find some account of his historic tussles, collected for sake of reference, I append the following descriptions of games which are likely to be of more than passing interest. Though I saw most of the matches which are detailed in this Appendix, I have not thought it necessary to describe them anew, considering that the accounts, written at the time, would, for the purposes of reference, be more satisfactory than fresh descriptions re-written from memory after the lapse of several years. The records are taken mainly from the reports in the *Field*, the *Scotsman*, *Golf*, and the *Times*. They do not claim to be more than scrapbook cuttings, but have the advantage of being the *first impressions* of the writers.

I have omitted descriptions of stroke play, as this variation of the game of golf has little interest when detailed. Two accounts will, however, be found of Tait's record scores at St. Andrews; the one of his medal record, the other of his famous record of 72 made in 1894; the last-named being taken from Mr. Everard's description in *Golf*.

AMATEUR CHAMPIONSHIP, 1892, PLAYED AT
SANDWICH.

1st round.—F. G. TAIT, a bye.
2nd round.—F. A. FAIRLIE beat F. G. TAIT by 1 hole.

MR. TAIT v MR. FAIRLIE.

The second round was decided in the afternoon, and the best matches were those between Mr. F. G. Tait and Mr. F. A. Fairlie,

F. G. Tait

Mr. A. D. Blyth and Mr. W. E. Fairlie, and Mr. H. G. Hutchinson and Mr. N. R. Foster. Mr. F. G. Tait won the first and second holes, halved the third, Mr. Fairlie won the fourth and fifth, the sixth was halved in three, the seventh was won by Mr. Tait, and the eighth was halved, the ninth Mr. Fairlie won. At the thirteenth hole Mr. Tait was three up, but Mr. Fairlie, by excellent putting, took the next three holes, making them all square at the sixteenth. At the seventeenth Mr. Fairlie was nearly stimied, but he holed. Going to the eighteenth Mr. Tait was away to the left, but Mr. Fairlie was dead straight in his drive. Mr. Fairlie played a beautiful second just over the bunker, and it ran dead, a "three" hole winning him the tie by the narrow majority of one hole.

AMATEUR CHAMPIONSHIP, 1893, PLAYED AT PRESTWICK.

1st round.—F. G. TAIT, a bye.
2nd round.—F. G. TAIT beat H. H. HILTON by 3 and 2.
3rd round.—F. G. TAIT beat L. M. BALFOUR by 2 and 1.
4th round.—F. G. TAIT beat W. GREIG by 2 and 1.
Semi-final.—J. E. LAIDLAY beat F. G. TAIT by 1 after a tie.

Writing at the time, Mr. John Kerr thus comments ont he play—*Golf*, May 1893 :—

Next to the actual Champion the most remarkable figure in the Championship was that of another young player, Mr. F. G. Tait. Had he vanquished Mr. Laidlay, as he was within an ace of doing, he and not Mr. Anderson might have been Champion. In our opinion the Champion has Mr. Tait in part to thank for his victory, for the keen contest which Mr. Laidlay had to come through with that dashing young soldier-golfer before he reached the final, gave the divinity student a better chance of beating him. Mr. Laidlay did not seem wearied, but the great effort required of him at the close of the final seemed slightly to suffer, because a similar effort had been required in his contest with Mr. Tait.

Over the field Mr. Tait's driving could only be described by Dominie Sampson's word "prodigious." So sweetly the ball left the club, and so far and sure did it soar, it was indeed "a sicht for sair een," and if even a Blackwell beats it we shall be surprised. Certainly it was not beaten or equalled by any at Prestwick. Mr. Tait generally started his round by allowing his opponent to get three ahead. Whether this was due to nervousness, which he gradually got rid of by the copious incense of his briar-root, or whether by parting company with the tobacco pipe, he might, if he had chosen, have avoided being three down, and thus become

A Record

Champion we cannot judge ; but that he has the Championship in him no one who saw him play at Prestwick can have the slightest doubt. There is a dash and daring about his golf, and, if he only carries the same with him as a soldier, he will certainly win renown for himself in the army. Of all the players at Prestwick, we should say, from what we saw of him, that he was the most genial and goodhearted.

His victory would certainly have been a popular one. The hearty shake of the hand he gave to Mr. Greig, a workman-player, who fought well against him in one round, and his kindly way with the wee " hirplin " caddie who carried for him, were to us very inning touches. That such a fine young player should have come so well forward was one of the most pleasing features of this Championship meeting.

MR. TAIT v MR. HILTON.

While there were a number of matches in the second stage which gave promise of some close play, unquestionably most interest centred in the meeting between Mr. F. G. Tait—who has made a mark for himself before now by the form he has shown at St. Andrews—and Mr. Hilton, whose high position among amateur players was so fully established in the Open Championship Tournament last year. A large crowd followed the match, and in their expectation of seeing a fine exposition of the game they were not disappointed, for although, undoubtedly, both players made mistakes, the play was well worth following. Mr. Tait began magnificently. He had a very pretty approach to the Cemetery—the first hole—and he excelled himself on the green. Giving his long putt every chance, he kept the line all the way, and was down in three. Mr. Hilton, good as his approach was, could not equal this, and the lead went to his opponent ; but the advantage was shortlived. The second hole is short, and an easy loft brings the player to the green. It was while on the green that Mr. Tait failed. To begin with, Mr. Hilton had laid a long putt dead, and it was apparent that the hole at best could be nothing but a half for the other player. When matters stood in this position, Mr. Tait played with bad judgment. He took the wrong side of the hole, laid himself a " stimie," and to get a half in three was beyond his powers. Crossing the Cardinal, Mr. Hilton had the better second, and he was well up in three, while in that figure Mr. Tait was short of the green. The advantage which the champion thus gained he took care to keep. He was down in five, while Mr. Tait took six, and he led by a hole. This lead he further improved at the Black Bridge. Mr. Tait did not play the hole altogether as it ought to have been played ; but in order to win it Mr. Hilton had something like a " stimie " to negotiate. It did not prove very troublesome, and he got down in four, and now stood two up. The "Himalayas" to players of this calibre is a quite possible three, and in three it would have been halved, had not Mr. Tait missed an easy putt when a half was almost in his hands. Playing the approach from the Elysian Fields, Mr. Hilton kept too much to the left, and he was not on the green in his second. Mr. Tait took a better line, and though his opponent played the next—a nasty stroke—well, the advantage was still on his side ; but he gave it away by being short in his long putt, and Mr. Hilton got a lucky half in five. For this however the Royal and Ancient representative made ample amends at the railway. He had the hole in a perfect three, and deservedly won it, reducing the lead against him to two holes. Monkton was characterised by indifferent putting on both sides, and Mr. Hilton was again far from deadly on the green at the turn. So badly, indeed, did he hole out that he threw away his chance of a half, and Mr. Tait had the satisfaction of beginning the homeward journey only a hole down. With a strong long game the first hole "in" should be done in five. A five it was for Mr. Tait ; but his opponent left himself too much to do on the green, and taking six, he had the mortification of seeing the last of his lead knocked off. From this point the match assumed an altogether different face to what it had borne. Instead of the Hoylake player being the aggressor, the running was taken up by his opponent. Both carried the "Himalayas" in fine style, but the advantage in the approach lay altogether with Mr. Tait. Handling the iron magnificently, he lay within possible holing distance in two, and Mr. Hilton had the long odds to play on the green. Knowing the necessity of being up, he gave the putt "plenty" and a little faulty in line, it overran the hole. He had to play two more, and got down in four. It now remained for Mr. Tait to play one of two. He did it to such purpose that he got down, and for the second time in the match led by a hole. The hazard at the next—the twelfth hole—is the wall in front of the green. This is a difficulty which can only be negotiated by a deft use of the iron. At this point, Mr. Hilton did what for him is a most unusual thing—he altogether miscalculated the distance. The ball hit the top of the wall, and fell back into sand. He tried again to get across, but without success, and his case becoming more hopeless still, he elected to give up the hole without playing it out, because Mr. Tait lay very nicely on the green in three. The next hole however was probably the turning point of the match. It is a good five at any time, and it seemed when both players went forward to the green, that it would be halved in that figure ; but Mr. Tait came away in great style. He holed a magnificent long putt, got down in four, and stood three up with five to play. A half in five followed, and amid increasing excitement on the part of the crowd, the players approached the fourth last hole. Mr. Hilton lost ground considerably by "duffing" his approach, but he made a fine recovery, and when each had played three there was little to draw between them. The hole was played out without incident. It was a half in five, and Mr. Tait stood in the comfortable position of "dormie" three. The end came at the third last hole, for although Mr. Tait gave his opponent a distinct chance by failing in the first instance with his approach, Mr. Hilton on his part missed a putt which would have given him the hole in four. It was halved, and the match was Mr. Tait's by three up with two to play.

Mr. Tait played a remarkably powerful long game. "Far and sure" though the Hoylake player drove, he found himself often outdistanced by ten or fifteen yards. Perhaps however it was on the putting greens that the Open Champion towards the close of the match failed most. He was not playing with the confidence which was so characteristic of his game at Muirfield last autumn, and indeed all round he was under his game. Still, a golfer of his class is never an easy nut to crack, and great credit belongs to Mr. Tait for so distinguishing himself to-day. The scores in the match, giving Mr. Hilton a nine for the twelfth hole, are :—

Mr. Tait : Out—3 4 6 5 4 5 3 5 5 = 40.
In—5 3 5 4 5 5 5.
Mr. Hilton : Out—4 3 5 4 3 5 4 5 6 = 39.
In—6 4 9 5 5 5 5.

MR. LAIDLAY v MR. TAIT.

Circumstances combined to invest the match between Messrs. Laidlay and Tait with special interest, for the former is a player who has proved his prowess on many fields, and Mr. Tait's brilliant appearance has been one of the features of the meeting. A large crowd, eager and critical, followed the play. Up to the turn, although Mr. Laidlay had the best of the game, there was not a great deal in the match. Mr. Tait, two down there, succeeded in squaring matters at the "Dyke," the twelfth hole, and the game assumed an interesting phase, for the next two holes being halved, there were but four holes remaining. On the fourth last green, Mr. Laidlay once more forged ahead. It was only a momentary advantage, for a great putt gave Mr. Tait the next hole in three. The excitement among the spectators was now great, and it was rendered more intense when the last two holes were splendidly halved in four, and the match resulted in a tie. There was nothing for it but to play on till one or other of the players won a hole. The result was not long in doubt. A hole decided matters.

F. G. Tait

Mr. Tait's long putt at the Cemetery was on the strong side, and as his opponent's odds had laid him three feet from the hole, Mr. Tait had this—a four-foot putt—for a half. He did not get it, and Mr. Laidlay had only to hole out in four, to win the closest of matches. The scores, approximating where the holes were not played out were :—

Mr. Laidlay : Out, 5 2 6 5 5 4 3 4 6=40.
In, 6 5 6 5 4 4 4 4 4=42 ; total, 82.

Mr. Tait : Out, 4 5 7 6 4 4 4 5 5=44.
In, 6 4 5 5 4 5 3 4 4=40 ; total, 84.

AMATEUR CHAMPIONSHIP, 1894, PLAYED AT HOYLAKE.

1st round—F. G. TAIT beat J. G. Gibson by 7 and 6.

2nd round.—F. G. TAIT beat H. G. HUTCHINSON by 1 after a tie.

3rd round.—F. G. TAIT beat R. B. SHARP by 5 and 3.

Semi-final round.—S. MURE FERGUSSON beat F. G. TAIT by 4 and 3.

MR. TAIT v MR. HORACE HUTCHINSON.

The chief interest of the second round centred in the fight between Mr. Tait and Mr. Horace Hutchinson. The former lost the first two holes, according to his custom throughout the tournament, but playing the third and fourth very strongly through a hailstorm, made matters square. At the seventh hole faulty putting on the part of Mr. Hutchinson had put Mr. Tait two ahead, but his own faulty driving lost him them again at the turn. On the way home the fight was keen, Mr. Hutchinson playing steadily, and Mr. Tait after occasional aberrations, making brilliant recoveries, until at the end of the round they were all even and had to go out for an extra hole. This hole Mr. Hutchinson looked like winning after the second stroke, but Mr. Tait laid a long approach near, Mr. Hutchinson overran, and after his opponent had holed out, failed to do likewise, and lost a well-fought match by one at the nineteenth hole.

MR. TAIT v MR. HILTON.

On the morning of Thursday Mr. R. B. Sharp held Mr. Tait for a while, but in the end the latter went away and beat him easily. In the afternoon the great attraction was the match between Mr. Tait and Mr. Hilton. Mr. Tait, of course, lost the first two holes, but thereafter played with his usual pluck. His driving, moreover, was better than in his match with Mr. Hutchinson, but his putting and approaching were not quite so remarkable ; indeed, his steadier driving left him less heroic efforts to make by way of recovery. A poor second shot of Mr. Hilton's to the fifteenth hole went far to decide the match. At this point the players were all even, but Mr. Hilton's worse-than-indifferent record went to ground in a rabbit scrape. Mr. Tait won the hole, and never lost the advantage, finishing 1 up on a finely-played match.

MR. TAIT ᴠ MR. MURE FERGUSSON.

The first round of the final day—a perfect day for golf, though rain fell nearly without interruption during the afternoon—saw Mr. Ball pitted against Mr. Laidlay, and Mr. Tait against Mr. Mure Fergusson. The former seemed to promise a very good fight ; the latter was generally thought to be a comparatively easy matter for Mr. Tait. Mr. Tait at once, as usual, fell two behind, but recaptured the lost holes quickly and took the lead, only, however, to have it worried away from him by Mr. Mure Fergusson's persistency. Until near the finish the play was not good, but after Mr. Fergusson, striking the top of the bunker going to the short hole, had won this hole somewhat luckily, and so put himself two up, he played the next hole brilliantly, and finished the match at the fifteenth hole, four up and three to play. There is no doubt that Mr. Tait was a little broken in nerve by the severity of his previous matches. He had fallen into a tough place in the draw and was suffering from the effects of his hard work.

AMATEUR CHAMPIONSHIP, 1895, PLAYED AT ST. ANDREWS.

1st round.—F. G. TAIT, a bye.
2nd round.—F. G. TAIT beat J. E. LAIDLAY by 5 and 3.
3rd round.—F. G. TAIT beat A. STUART by 6 and 4.
Semi-final round. —J. BALL, junr., beat F. G. TAIT by 5 and 3.

MR. TAIT ᴠ MR. LAIDLAY.

In this match the play at times was brilliant. Mr. Laidlay however was a bit off his driving, and was not nearly so straight as usual, while his putting was very often faulty. Mr. Tait, on the other hand, played with his accustomed dash, the feature of his game being the extraordinary accuracy with which he approached the hole. At least 500 spectators watched the game with great interest. The first hole was played to perfection. A drive and an iron shot found both golfers over the burn on the green, and a half in four was the natural result. Mr. Tait kept the line better than his opponent from the tee to the second hole, but both got home in two. The St. Andrews man made the better approach to the hole and had an easy four, Mr. Laidlay leaving himself with too much to do to get a half. Mr. Tait approached the third hole in fine

F. G. Tait

style, and was only two yards to the left of the hole in two, while Mr. Laidlay was fifteen yards over. The latter's third stroke was weak, while Mr. Tait touched the lip of the hole. The Honourable Company representative made a bad putt, and Mr. Tait had no difficulty in placing himself two up—the first three holes costing him only four each. The fourth hole was halved in five after equal play, and the Long Hole was divided in six, the play on the green being faulty, more particularly as regards Mr. Tait. Mr. Laidlay lost a shot by getting bunkered with his tee shot going to the sixth hole, and Mr. Tait playing it in par—four—stood three up, his opponent requiring five. Although Mr. Tait was bunkered at the Ginger Beer hole by drawing his drive, he got well out, and, aided by a missed putt on the part of the ex-champion, he was able to claim a half in five. The Short Hole was an unfortunate one for the St. Andrews player. Taking his cleek, he got too much curl on the ball, and dropped into a nasty bunker. After making two ineffectual attempts to get out, he lifted his ball, Mr. Laidlay having had an easy three on. The out hole was remarkable for the very fine performance of Mr. Laidlay. Driving from the tee, he toed his ball, and landed among rough ground. He got a fair distance with his second shot, but still was unable to get clear of the bents. With his third, however, he landed on the green from ten to fifteen yards over the hole; Mr. Tait being comfortably situated some six yards from the hole in two, Mr. Laidlay had to play two more, and, approaching the hole with a beautiful putt, the ball found its way to the bottom, leaving Mr. Tait a nasty putt to win the hole in three. The St. Andrews man was unable for the task, and accordingly he turned two up. Mr. Laidlay's drive to the tenth hole was off the line, while Mr. Tait had one of his long, straight swipes. Mr. Laidlay was past the hole with his second, and Mr. Tait landed his on the green. Mr. Laidlay's third was short, and Mr. Tait, holing out a long putt, won the hole in three to his opponent's five. The eleventh hole should in ordinary circumstances have gone to Mr. Tait, for his partner found himself in a bunker. Mr. Tait, however, putted very weakly, and allowed his opponent to secure a half in four. Mr. Laidlay had again the misfortune to make the acquaintance of sand from the tee, but Mr. Tait foozled his second shot, and each player approached the hole on an equal footing. Mr. Laidlay, however, failed to get up the ridge before the hole, while Mr. Tait succeeded, and eventually ran down a long putt, adding another point to his lead. Mr. Tait was now four up and six to play. The green play at the thirteenth and fourteenth holes was faulty, Mr. Laidlay missing a short putt at the former, and Mr. Tait following his example at the latter. Halves in six were declared, and Mr. Tait stood dormie four. The

A Record

match finished at the fifteenth hole. Both were on the green in three, and, while Mr. Laidlay had a chance of winning the hole, he should at least have got a half. He, however, failed to hole out an easy shot, and Mr. Tait finished five up and three to play. Mr. Tait's victory was a highly popular one.

MR. TAIT v MR. BALL.

The following account is taken from the *Field* :—

This now left as survivors Ball, Tait, Leslie Balfour Melville, Auchterlonie, to play the semi-final, which was entered upon at two o'clock. Ball had Tait as his opponent. Those who had been looking forward to the probable meeting of the two men prophesied a brilliant struggle, but it was a very disappointing and one-sided contest. By the time the match started the crowd had gathered thousands strong, and although a rope was stretched across the course, and policemen and committeemen endeavoured to keep order, their efforts were unavailing, and for the first few holes it was just a rush to secure a vantage place at the next green. Ball was accustomed to this sort of work, but Tait, although he had previously played with a crowd at his back, was evidently put out. He was, as usual, particularly strong in his driving, but was deficient in his approaches, and especially in his putting. Ball carried the first three holes right off. A stoppage to this victorious career took place at the fourth green, but Tait all the way out was only able to secure halves, and at the turn, after six holes had been divided, Ball was still leading by three holes. The scores out were 43 and 46 respectively. Another half followed at the first homeward green. Ball carried the high hole in three, and was now four up and seven to play. Three other halves after this followed, and Tait saw his chance become smaller and smaller as the match neared home. The match ended at the fourth last green, Ball getting down a long putt by five and three to play. Ball had played, despite the crowd who were pressing at his heels, as a machine, and if he did make a mistake, and was punished, he never failed to recover himself with his accustomed adroitness. Tait, it should be mentioned, had a lot of bad luck to contend against.

AMATEUR CHAMPIONSHIP, 1896, PLAYED AT SANDWICH.

1st round.—F. G. TAIT beat C. G. BROADWOOD by 7 and 6.

2nd round.—F. G. TAIT beat C. HUTCHINGS by 4 and 3.

3rd round.—F. G. TAIT beat J. E. LAIDLAY by 3 and 1.

4th round.—F. G. TAIT beat J. BALL, Jun., by 5 and 4.

5th round.—F. G. TAIT beat H. G. HUTCHINSON by 3 and 2.

6th round.—F. G. TAIT beat H. H. HILTON by 8 and 7.

F. G. Tait

The following descriptions are taken from the *Scotsman* :—

MR. TAIT ᵥ MR. HUTCHINGS.

The match between Mr. Tait and Mr. Hutchings, which was also of an international character, was scarcely so well contested, but at the same time the latter did not accept defeat without making a good fight. In the first instance it seemed that Mr. Tait's extraordinary strong driving game might get him into trouble when the wind was with him ; for at the very start he got a tremendous ball away, and was trapped by a bunker which is not usually reached from the tee. With a splendid recovery he had a four, and drew first blood. He had another raking drive to the second hole, which, however, carried into the rough. Though he did not make much of the heavy lie, he won the hole, but Mr. Hutchings' approach was far too strong. The hole over the " Sahara " was halved in four, and Mr. Hutchings won the fourth in four, Mr. Tait playing it indifferently. Faultless play saw the fifth halved in three, and " The Maiden " was faced with the Scottish amateur one up. He carried the hazard in the teeth of the wind in grand style, and he practically won the hole from the tee as his opponent drove slap into the face of the hazard. A perfect four gave Mr. Hutchings the seventh, and the Royal Liverpool player had the satisfaction of squaring the match at the next hole, where Mr. Tait lost himself in " Hades." A glaring mistake at the tee where Mr. Hutchings topped his ball enabled his opponent to again secure the lead, and after the tenth had been halved Mr. Tait gradually drew away. At the long sea hole, where the force of the gale was most felt, he had his opponent completely in hand. Out of the next four holes he won three, and dormie four, he finished the match with a half at the fourth last. Mr. Tait's score was :—

Out, 4 5 4 6 3 3 5 5 5 = 40.
In, 5 4 6 5 7 5.

Omitting the sixth hole, Mr. Hutchings' figures were :—

5 6 4 5 3 0 4 4 6 5 5 6 6 8 5.

Mr. F. G. TAIT (Black Watch) beat Mr. JOHN BALL (Royal Liverpool) by five up and four to play.

Keen interest was taken in the encounter between Mr. Ball and Mr. Tait, and the contest between them was the more interesting because it was a pitched battle between two of the best-known English and Scottish amateurs. The meeting gave Mr. Tait an opportunity of wiping out the defeat which he suffered at the hands of Mr. Ball a year ago at St. Andrews, when he was beaten by five

A Record

up and three to play in the semi-final, and he did not fail to avail himself of it. He came away with a brilliant game, and from the very start held the lead, playing at the very top of his game. He early secured an advantage, which he gradually increased, until it was apparent that nothing but a complete breakdown on his part could lose him the match. In approaching and on the greens, he was especially brilliant, his putting indeed being faultless. It was really on the greens and in his mashie play that he won the match, for in the matter of driving there was nothing to draw between the couple. A magnificent start was made with a half in four, Mr. Ball playing a perfect wrist approach, after being a little wide in his second, played from the rough. From the second tee Mr. Tait kept well to the right to avoid the bunkers, and had a long approach. Playing it admirably he was on the green in his second, and Mr. Ball, who had placed his drive very prettily with the "like," heeled badly, and was among bents to the right of the green. He had still a four-foot putt for a half in four, but he failed to get it down, and Mr. Tait, dead with a finely-played long putt, holed the like, and assumed the lead. After crossing the "Sahara," Mr. Tait had a fine chance offered him, for Mr. Ball was a bit wide and short in his mashie approach. At the moment it seemed that he was not to profit by the opportunity. He was desperately short with his second, but he retrieved himself by holing out very prettily in four, and was two up. Both were home with their seconds to the fourth hole, and Mr. Ball had a nasty lie behind the green. He made the most of it, and might have halved the hole in four, had he not completely duffed his putt of five feet. Mr. Tait down in four won the hole, and he played the next faultlessly in three, and faced "The Maiden" four holes to the good, Mr. Ball having sliced his drive into bad country in this case. Both carried the hazard at the sixth hole, though not with too much to spare, and giving the odds the Scotsman ran down a four-yard putt. Not to be beaten, Mr. Ball holed the like from much the same distance— an excellently pretty piece of putting on the part of both. Both were bunkered immediately before the seventh green, and both got out without trouble. Mr. Ball's recovery was especially good, a brilliant stroke in fact, and he secured the hole in five, as Mr. Tait was somewhat feeble in giving the odds. With an eight-foot putt the Scotsman just managed to halve "Hades," and at the ninth green the same player again secured a half by very pretty holing out, and turned three up. A foozled pitch on the part of Mr. Ball, who did not appear to such advantage as usual in approaching, cost him dearly at the first hole in. He was bunkered and again in sand. In trying to get clear too finely he had to give two more on the green. Mr. Tait, though there were weaknesses in his play at this hole, was down in five, and again led by four. Superb holing out on the Scotsman's part was the feature of the play at the eleventh green. Mr. Ball lay quite safe with the odds for a five ; but a half was denied him, as Mr. Tait gave the like (a fifteen-yard putt) in splendid fashion, and holed. The Scotsman could now breathe quite freely. He had a lead of five, with only seven to play, which meant that unless he utterly broke down, victory was assured to him. Mr. Ball had a very hard struggle indeed to get even a half at the twelfth in five, and this brought the match to the far hole. Mr. Tait played his second to carry the dangerous hazard which guards the green, and, as it seemed, was fortunate in not getting it clean. He lay short of the bunker, and quite safe for a pitch ; while Mr. Ball, having now to risk everything, adopted bold tactics, and fell foul of the trap. A wonderfully fine recovery extricated Mr. Ball from his difficulties ; but still he had to be content with a half in six, which meant that Mr. Tait was dormie five. Again, at the "Suez Canal," the water hazard at the fifth last, Mr. Ball played the dashing game. He drove the water with his second, and Mr. Tait, recognising that a half was all he required, played short from a rough lie. Both were home in three, and a half in five saw Mr. Tait in possession of the field. The scores were :—

Mr. Tait : Out, 4 4 4 4 3 3 6 3 5 = 36.

In, 5 4 5 6 5.

Mr. Ball : Out, 4 5 5 5 4 3 5 3 5 = 39.

In, 8 5 5 6 5.

SEMI-FINAL.

Mr. F. G. Tait beat Mr. H. G. Hutchinson by three up and two to play.

The match between Mr. Tait and Mr. Hutchinson almost monopolised the attention of the onlookers in the afternoon. They came out in the expectation of seeing a battle royal, and they were not disappointed. There was of course, much speculation as to the result of the encounter, and the respective merits of the players were keenly discussed. On the one hand, there were those who thought that Mr. Hutchinson's undoubted powers and his great experience as a match player would carry him through. On the other hand the young Scotsman had made troops of friends by the superb form he had shown in his earlier encounters, and his supporters were fairly confident that he would emerge successfully from the ordeal. Mr. Tait scarcely played with his usual judgment at the first hole. Taking a line to the right to avoid the bunkers, he lay with an open course to the green, when Mr.

A Record

Hutchinson was in sand, the result of trying to carry the trap with a driving iron for his second stroke. Forgetting the lie of the ground, the Scotsman pitched instead of running his approach, and the stroke was killed by the rising face. Mr. Hutchinson with the like played splendidly from the bunker, and he was able to secure the hole in five. The second was halved in four, Mr. Hutchinson all but getting a three, and the third and fourth were also halved, without any particular incident. On the next green, to which the Scotsman had the better approach, the Westward Ho! player holed a six-yard putt—the odds—very prettily for a three, and as Mr. Tait did not give his like a chance, the match stood Mr. Hutchinson two up. A raking ball from the tee carried Mr. Tait clear of " The Maiden." Mr. Hutchinson took the wrong line, and while over the hazard was in a sandy pot to the right of the green. He got out of the difficulty, but was wild in his third, so that he had to give the two more. The hole was Mr. Tait's practically without its being played out, and the lead against him was down to one. When both had reached the green at the seventh hole, the advantage lay with Mr. Hutchinson. With the odds however Mr. Tait got down in deadly fashion, and as his opponent was beaten by a four-foot putt for a half, the match was all square. Over " Hades " Mr. Hutchinson had a perfect drive. Mr. Tait's tee shot was short a little, and he was lamentably weak in his long putt, which he might well have played strong, considering the lie of the ground. He paid the penalty of his mistake by losing a half, and with a wretchedly bad lie from his drive to the ninth hole, he was no more than up to the ninth green in three. A powerful long game through the green gave Mr. Hutchinson a great putt at this point, and playing one off two he holed in four, and turned two up. Approaching the tenth green, which is a nasty pitch, Mr. Hutchinson duffed his stroke badly and was bunkered. In his effort to recover he failed, was caught in another trap, and Mr. Tait had the hole in hand. Now only one down, Mr. Tait put himself on equal terms with his opponent. At the next hole both were on the green in two, and Mr. Hutchinson was strong in his long putt. Mr. Tait laid the like safe for holing, and Mr. Hutchinson failed with his chance, which however depended on an eight-foot putt. Two grand drives brought the Scotsman, who was now playing a splendid game, to the twelfth green. The Westward Ho! player had rather a nasty stand from which to play his second. He failed to get a hold of it, and was wide with his |next. A perfect four gave Mr. Tait the hole, and he had his head well above water for the first time since the start. A tremendously powerful long game enabled the Scotsman to

F. G. Tait

cross the hazard and be on the next green in three with the mashie, and though Mr. Hutchinson had a great recovery from the bunker, he was unable to get a half. A mistake on the green however cost Mr. Tait the fifth last; but the battle again went in the Scotsman's favour at the next, where both were lucky in not being trapped, for there he had the better of the holing out, Mr. Hutchinson's three-yard putt for a half jumping out of the hole after being in it. Mr. Tait's position was at this stage very comfortable. He was two up with three to play, and he finished the match by holing a long putt for a three on the next green. The scores were :—

Mr. Tait : Out, 6 4 4 5 4 4 5 4 5 = 41.
In, 5 4 4 5 6 4 3.
Mr. Hutchinson : Out, 5 4 4 5 3 5 6 3 4 = 39.
In, 6 5 5 6 5 5 4.

From *Golf* I take the following general review of the tournament and description of the Final :—

The first words I heard on arriving at Sandwich were that "Freddie Tait is playing a great game." Well, we all knew by past experience that Mr. F. G. Tait could play what is termed "a great game"; but in past championships he had always failed, at one time or another in the competition, to quite reproduce that marvellous form which we well knew he was capable of, and the failure, in the past two years, at least, had rather unfortunately occurred at the moment when he was called upon to meet opponents against whom it was necessary that he should be in his very best form in order to avert defeat. Hence his failure to claim to his credit the high-sounding title of "Amateur Champion Golfer of Great Britain"—a distinction which his many admirers and friends had predicted would be his in the very near future. The past week, however, has done a great deal to enlighten the sceptical as to how Mr. Tait could play when in his best form, not only for one individual round, but through a series of matches against the leading lights of the amateur golfing world. His play culminated in a succession of victories which have probably never been equalled in the history of the Amateur Championship. Mr. Tait had no easy work on hand in the second round, Mr. Hutchings, the St. Andrews medallist, having to be disposed of. The St. Andrews crack proved equal to the task, however, and after the Hoylake player had held his own fairly well in the early stages of the game, he had to acknowledge defeat by four up and three to play.

In the third round the match between those old opponents, Messrs. Laidlay and Tait caused a great deal of interest. Neither

A Record

played quite up to their best form, the result being a confirmation of last year's form, Mr. Tait proving too much for the ex-champion.

The fourth round saw Messrs. Tait and Ball face to face. So easily had Mr. Ball defeated Mr. Tait in the penultimate round last year at St. Andrews, that many came to the conclusion that it was probable that Mr. Tait would not show his best form against the ex-champion; but the result proved that they were wofully wrong in arriving at this conclusion, as nothing could have been finer than Mr. Tait's play. After a half at the first hole, Mr. Tait ran clean away from his opponent, finally winning by five up with four to play. The winner holed out with great accuracy, and this must have been somewhat demoralising to his opponent.

The semi-final stage found Messrs. Hutchinson and Tait in antagonism. Mr. Hutchinson commenced well by securing a lead of two early in the round, but his opponent brought the match all even at the seventh, only to be again two down at the turn. The tenth hole was probably the turning-point in the match, as from an indifferent lie Mr. Hutchinson made a sad mess of his approach, and although Mr. Tait also made a poor approach, he eventually secured the hole in five to six, and from this point never looked back, finally winning by three up and two to play.

The final round resolved itself, as in the past two years, into a struggle between the representatives of St. Andrews and Hoylake golf, and if it proved disappointing in the fact that the game did not produce a close struggle, on the other hand it gave the spectators an opportunity of witnessing as fine an exhibition of the game of golf, on the winner's part, as one could wish to see. At the very first hole Mr. Tait got down a three-yard putt for the hole, and this proved a precursor of what might be expected. Holding an advantage in the long game, Mr. Tait followed this up with some marvellously accurate putting, and to cut a long story short, his opponent never had a look in. Completing the outward half in 35, Mr. Tait reached the twelfth hole in 42, or two under fours, and it certainly appeared as if he would complete the round in a marvellously low total, but towards the conclusion his putting fell somewhat off from its previous high standard of excellence, and 76 was the final result. The scores for the round were (giving Mr. Tait credit for an almost certain putt, which he did not hole out) : —

Mr. Tait : Out, 4 4 4 5 4 2 4 4 4 = 35
In, 4 3 4 5 6 5 5 4 5 = 41 ; total 76.
Mr. Hilton : Out, 5 4 5 5 3 4 6 4 4 = 40
In, 5 4 5 6 6 5 4 4 5 = 44 ; total, 84.

Mr. Tait's score is a new record for the green. Holding an advantage of six holes on the round, the result was left almost

F. G. Tait

beyond doubt, and although Mr. Hilton raised slight hopes by securing the first hole in the second round, Mr. Tait soon asserted his supremacy, finally winning by eight up and seven to play.

There is no getting away from the wonderful merit of Mr. Tait's victory. Drawn badly in the first instance, he had anything but an easy task in order to qualify for the semi-final stage, as on his way there he had to overcome Messrs. Chas. Hutchings, J. E. Laidlay, and John Ball, junior, all in successive heats. All these three he overcame with comparative ease, whilst if Mr. Hutchinson did cause him a little inconvenience at first, the Champion came away in fine style on the homeward half. In the final round nothing could have been finer than the form he displayed. His driving was marvellously accurate, and not once during the whole of the first round could any stroke from the tee be called at all off the line. His tee shot to the " Maiden " and the three strokes up to the long fourteenth hole in particular were exceptionally fine, in fact he may be said to have played faultless golf, which could not have been excelled by Taylor, Herd, or any other of the leading professional players. With a continuance of his present form, Mr. Tait will surely have to be reckoned with at Muirfield next week.

AMATEUR CHAMPIONSHIP, 1897, PLAYED AT MUIRFIELD.

1st round.—F. G. TAIT, a bye.

2nd round.—F. G. TAIT beat C. L. DALZIEL by 3 and 2.

3rd round.—W. GREIG beat F. G. TAIT by 1 hole.

MR. TAIT v MR. GREIG.

The great event of the third round is the defeat of the Champion, Mr. F. G. Tait, who has been beaten by Mr. W. Greig by one hole, after a splendid match. When six holes had been played Mr. Greig led by a hole. Both balls lay within putting distance on the seventh green, but Mr. Tait failed with the odds, and Mr. Greig pocketed the hole and again led by two. Playing to the eighth hole, Mr. Greig experienced very hard luck. He landed in the bunker with his second, but as Mr. Tait made the same mistake, the consequences did not seem very serious. Mr. Tait got his ball well out, and it rebounded from the wall on to the green. Mr. Greig's was a clear stroke, too clear in fact, for the ball disappeared over the wall. He paid the penalty of losing the distance, dropped another ball into the bunker, and played the odds. Though he got out, he was short, and the hole went to his opponent. The ninth hole was halved in four, and the home

A Record

journey was begun with the St. Andrews representative leading by one hole. The details of the half round were—

Mr. Tait, 3 5 5 4 5 5 4 6 4 = 41.
Mr. Greig, 3 6 4 5 6 4 5 5 4 = 42.

The tenth hole was halved. A sliced ball landed Mr. Tait among the rough to the right of the network of bunkers which guard the approach to the eleventh hole. He played his second short, and lay on the edge of one of the hazards, and his third skirted the bank of another, but lay clear. Mr. Greig pulled his third, and through indifferent putting was only able to secure a half, when it appeared almost certain that he would add another to his credit. Trapped from his drive, Mr. Greig recovered in great style, and obtained a hard half at the twelfth hole. The next was also halved, and with five to play the St. Andrews man was leading by one hole. Mr. Tait was off line, and strong in his putt at the short hole, which however was halved in three, though the leader just missed the hole with his second at the sixteenth, where Mr. Greig had missed a long putt for three. Mr. Tait had a nasty downhill putt to win the hole. He played it carefully but missed, and thus the seventh half in succession came about. The long hole was brought to the green before it was decided. Indeed, had it not been that Mr. Tait's fourth lay on the edge of the hole, and more than half stimied his opponent, it also would have been halved. As it was, the hole was won by the Champion, and the match was all even with two holes to play. Mr. Tait cut his drive slightly, but both balls lay on the green in two. Playing the odds, Mr. Tait was weak. Mr. Greig made no mistake, and lay dead. Mr. Tait missed his fourth, and this gave his opponent the hole, and he was in the happy position of being dormie. Mr. Tait had the advantage in the long game to the last hole. He lay on the green with his second, whilst Mr. Greig had to play the odds from behind the bunkers. His approach was short, but so was Mr. Tait's, and the hole was halved in five. Mr. Greig's victory was received with loud applause by the large crowd of spectators, who evidently appreciated the sturdy fight which he had made against his redoubtable opponent. The in-coming scores were—

Mr. Tait, 4 6 5 4 3 4 5 5 5 = 41.
Mr. Greig, 4 6 5 4 3 4 6 4 5 = 41.

AMATEUR CHAMPIONSHIP, 1898, PLAYED AT HOYLAKE.

1st round.—F. G. TAIT, a bye.
2nd round.—F. G. TAIT beat J. WILSON by 4 and 2.
3rd round.—F. G. TAIT beat C. HUTCHINGS by 1 after a tie.

253

F. G. Tait

4th round.—F. G. TAIT beat H. H. HILTON by 6 and 5.
5th round.—F. G. TAIT beat J. GRAHAM by 1.
Semi-final round.—F. G. TAIT beat J. L. LOW at 22nd hole after
   a tie.
Final round.—F. G. TAIT beat S. MURE FERGUSSON by 7 and 5.

Mr. F. G. TAIT beat Mr. C. HUTCHINGS at the 19th hole
after a tie.

Against Mr. Tait was Mr. Charles Hutchings, a well-known
and an experienced match player. This encounter promised
to produce the first sensation of the championship. It ended
in a neck-and-neck race, exciting at the close to a degree, and
trying the staying powers of the players to the utmost. The
run of the game shows how close the contest was. With a couple
of fours Mr. Hutchings, who is a player probably double Mr. Tait
in years, secured the advantage. A lovely iron stroke came to
the Scotsman's relief at the long hole, and a pretty three at the
"Cop." The fourth enabled Mr. Tait to square matters. With
a fine second the same player secured the fifth in four, and with
a long putt he won the "Briars" in the same figure and was two
up. At the eighth he had still this lead, but he lost the ninth
by duffing his approach, and he gave a half at the tenth to
his opponent by deplorably weak play on the green. The "Alps,"
where the Scotsman had an indifferent drive, fell to Mr. Hutchings
in three, so that with seven to play the game was even. A long
putt on the twelfth green, which gave him a three, enabled Mr. Tait
to again forge ahead, but Mr. Hutchings paid him back in his
own coin at the next, the "Rushes," by holing a twenty-yard putt
for a two. Thus the game was kept going merrily on. Slicing
with his brassey at the "Field," Mr. Hutchings got a wretched
lie, and after endeavouring without success to extricate himself
he gave up the hole, so that Mr. Tait was one up with four to
play. Amid growing excitement on the part of the large gallery
the "Lake" was halved, Mr. Hutchings just failing with a ten-
foot putt for the hole, but the Royal Liverpool player after being
very lucky in scrambling through the bunker in front of the third
last green, ran down the like, an eight or nine-yard putt and won
the hole. This bit of good fortune—for that it certainly was—
enabled him to square the game, and sent him off in good spirits
for the second last hole. Every stroke was now eagerly watched,
and the excitement ran very high. By faultless golf, especially
in running up to the hole, the second last was halved in four, so
that everything depended on the home hole. There it fell to
Mr. Hutchings, who was thirty yards behind Mr. Tait in the

A Record

drive, to give the odd for the second. He tried to carry the bunker but was trapped. Mr. Tait's opportunity now seemed to have come. He had a beautiful approach. Mr. Hutchings lay badly in the sand, and appearances seemed against him getting clear. He was equal to the occasion however. On the green with the niblick he laid his odds dead, and a halved hole in five meant a halved match. The couple at once went out to decide matters. A hole was sufficient. Mr. Tait had a grand second to the green, whereas Mr. Hutchings, lying heavily, duffed his. This gave Mr. Tait a considerable advantage, and down in four, he won the hole and the match.

FOURTH ROUND.

MR. TAIT beat MR. HILTON by 6 up and 5 to play.

A large gathering of spectators turned out to witness the match between Mr. Tait and Mr. Hilton, the prospect of which had been eagerly looked forward to from the start of the tournament. Mr. Tait and Mr. Hilton are old opponents in the Championship. A half in five opened their round ; then Mr. Tait stepped to the front. He had the better approach to the second green, but it was not this piece of play, good as it was, which gave him the lead ; it was a lamentable weakness on his opponent's part, for he had a half in hand. All he had to do was to run down an easy enough putt. He was weak at the crucial moment, and home in five. Mr. Tait took the lead. There were weaknesses on both sides in the putting at the third—a long hole—which was halved in six ; and again in this part of the game Mr. Hilton failed at the " Cop," and gave away his chance of a half with a putt of little more than a yard, after Mr. Tait had holed the odds for three. The " Telegraph " hole was splendidly halved in four, but Mr. Tait introduced the sensational element at the " Briars," where he ran down a forty yards putt for a three—a great effort, which gave him a lead of three. In pretty style the seventh was halved in four. If there was no incident, there was some variety in the play to the eighth. In his second to it, Mr. Hilton carried into a treacherous bunker. Mr. Tait gave the hazard a wide berth, and after his opponent had taken two to get clear, he had the hole in hand, for the Englishman was giving the three more on the green. Disaster again overtook the Open Champion at the ninth. He got his second heavily, and was severely punished. With great dexterity he extricated himself and reached the green, where he made a desperate but unsuccessful effort to hole the long odds. Down in the like Mr. Tait was now five up, and it was apparent that unless Mr. Hilton pulled himself together the end was only a matter of time. The Englishman had a distinct advantage on the tenth green, which, to the dismay of his supporters, he allowed to

F. G. Tait

slip. The hole was halved, as also were the next two, and the Englishman's discomfiture was complete at the " Rushes," where, too strong in the long putt he failed even to get a half. Mr. Tait was thus left a winner by six up and five to play. It is noteworthy that Mr. Hilton never won a hole. Scores:—

Mr. Tait : 5 5 6 3 4 3 4 6 4 5 3 5 3

Mr. Hilton : 5 6 6 4 4 4 4 8 5 5 3 5 4

FIFTH ROUND.

Mr. F. G. Tait (Black Watch) beat Mr. J. Graham (Royal Liverpool) by one hole.

From the outset it had been anticipated that in the event of Mr. Tait disposing of Mr. Hilton, he would have to deal with Mr. Graham, the young Liverpool amateur, who deservedly enjoys more than a local reputation. Mr. Tait entered into the contest with every confidence, not only because of his own great powers, but because of the magnificent victory which he gained over Mr. Hilton yesterday afternoon. Mr. Graham, on the other hand, must have felt that he had a very heavy task before him, and if in the end the fortunes of war went against him, he at least carried the game to the home green. In some respects the match was disappointing, for neither player was at the top of his game. Mr. Tait ought to have secured an early advantage, but he was weak in his short game. On both the first and second greens the holes were halved, but Mr. Tait lost the long hole, where he duffed his second and was lucky in jumping the bunker. Profiting by a mistake of Mr. Graham at the "Cop," Mr. Tait had the match squared there, but the same player gave away a distinct chance of assuming the lead at the " Briars," where a four-foot putt would have given him the hole. He showed however to better advantage at the eighth, where he holed out in good style with the odd, leaving Mr. Graham a putt of little more than a yard for a half, which he failed to get down. Having now the lead, Mr. Tait ought to have kept it at the ninth, for he had the better drive and the better lie off it. He unaccountably foozled his second, and was bunkered, and finally gave up the hole, so that the match was all even when the couple entered upon the latter half. Indifferent putting on Mr. Tait's part gave Mr. Graham the lead at the tenth, but on the next three greens the latter was decidedly weak, and Mr. Tait, winning each hole, stood two up with five to play. A long putt beautifully judged gave Mr. Tait the " Field," and with him three up and four to play few expected to see the game go to the home hole as it did. There was not much between them on the fourth last green, and the hole might well have been halved. Mr. Tait however was not equal to a putt of about a club length. The lead

A Record

was thus reduced to two, and the next, where Mr. Tait was in rough country off the line, and Mr. Graham was bunkered at the green, was halved in six, leaving the former dormie two. Having the best of the short game at the second last, Mr. Graham, down in four, won the hole, and an exciting match ended in Mr. Tait's favour on the home green, where Mr. Graham failed to hole a putt of about two feet, which would have made it a halved game. The scores (approximately stated) were—

Mr. Tait : Out, 5 5 6 3 4 5 3 5 7 ; total 43.
In, 5 4 4 3 4 6 6 5 5 ; total 42.
Mr. Graham : Out, 5 5 5 4 4 5 3 6 4 ; total 41.
In, 4 5 5 4 5 5 6 4 5 ; total 43.

FINAL ROUND.
Mr. F. G. TAIT v Mr. MURE FERGUSSON.

The first round opened at half-past 10 o'clock. Mr. Mure Fergusson had the better drive, but Mr. Tait beat Mr. Mure Fergusson with his pitch and gave him a good deal to do to secure a half in five. Both reached the second green nicely in a couple, but in this instance it fell to Mr. Tait to play the odd. He did so to some advantage, and gained a half in four. In driving to the long hole Mr. Fergusson heeled his ball amongst the crowd, striking a lady on the shoulder ; the ball lay on a putting green, and under the local rule it had to be lifted and dropped without penalty clear of the green. Mr. Charles Hutchings, who was referee, proceeded to do this, with the result that the ball landed in a hole. Mr. Tait refused to take advantage of his opponent's misfortune, and promptly went forward and teed the ball. This sportsmanlike act was greeted with a round of applause. Both were on the green in three, and the hole was halved in six. At the turn Mr. Tait was one up. Mr. Mure Fergusson had played the two previous holes in superior form to that displayed by Mr. Tait ; but he went off his driving at the short "Alps." The result was that he made acquaintance with sand and lost a stroke. Mr. Tait holing out splendidly in four gave his opponent no chance, and now held a lead of two. Mr. Tait continued to play the more consistent golf, and he finished the round three holes up. The approximate scores were :—

Mr. Tait : Out, 5 4 6 3 5 6 3 4 4 = 40
In, 4 4 4 4 5 6 5 5 4 = 41

Total, 81

Mr. Mure Fergusson : Out, 5 4 6 4 5 4 4 4 4 = 40
In, 5 4 5 4 5 6 6 4 4 - 43

Total, 83

R

F. G. Tait

In the afternoon the second round was followed by an even larger gathering of spectators, who behaved wonderfully well. The feature of the first hole was that Mr. Mure Fergusson with his approach sliced out of bounds ; he however had a splendid third, and as Mr. Tait ran into rough country a half in five resulted. At the second Mr. Mure Fergusson sliced his tee shot, and the ball landed on the top of the " Cop." Handicapped by an awkward stand he overran the green into the ditch. On the other hand, Mr. Tait by a splendid approach got down in three, and easily won the hole. This increased his lead to four. The long hole was capitally halved in five. After Mr. Tait had half topped a brassey shot, Mr. Mure Fergusson lipped the " Cop " hole for a two, and gave a half in three. A half in four resulted from the play to the " Telegraph " hole. Being out of bounds Mr. Mure Fergusson handicapped himself at the " Briars " but he gave an exhibition of splendid approaching which enabled him to reach the green in three. Mr. Tait, instead of taking advantage of his opportunity, foozled his second, with the result that he ran into the sand behind the " Cop." It was an awkward position to get out of, and he lost the hole in six to five. Mr. Fergusson was four down at the turn. Crossing the " Alps " Mr. Tait pulled his tee shot, and Mr. Mure Fergusson followed by slicing his. The putting was weak, particularly on Mr. Mure Fergusson's part, so that Mr. Tait won in four to five. Now five up and six to play, Mr. Tait became almost a certain winner of the championship. The certainty was even more emphasized at the twelfth hole, where Mr. Mure Fergusson overran the green into the water hazard. Mr. Tait played the hole perfectly in four to Mr. Mure Fergusson's five, and stood "dormie" six. The end came at the " Rushes " which Mr. Tait secured in a capital three to a four by Mr. Mure Fergusson, who exhibited weakness in his putting. Mr. Tait, who was cordially cheered and congratulated, won the championship by seven up and five to play.

AMATEUR CHAMPIONSHIP, 1899, PLAYED AT PRESTWICK.

1st round.—F. G. TAIT beat A. R. AITKEN by 4 and 2.

2nd round.—F. G. TAIT beat H. M. BALINGALL by 3 and 2.

3rd round.—F. G. TAIT beat S. H. FRY by 2 and 1.

4th round.—F. G. TAIT beat G. F. SMITH by 5 and 4.

5th round.—F. G. TAIT beat H. H. HILTON by 1.

6th round.— F. G. TAIT beat J. M. WILLIAMSON by 3 and 1.

7th round.—J. BALL, Junr., beat F. G. TAIT by 1 hole after a tie.

A Record

Mr. F. G. Tait (Black Watch) beat Mr. H. H. Hilton (Royal Liverpool) by 1 hole.

A large crowd of spectators followed this match, as it was undoubtedly the *piece de resistance* of the present meeting, and speculation was rife regarding the result, for it is acknowledged on all hands that as a golfer Mr. Hilton has few equals, which is proved by his double victory in the Open Championship, though he has hitherto failed to win the Amateur Championship, Mr. Tait having four or five times been the cause of his failure. At the first green, which both reached in two, Mr. Hilton by a good pitch and putt, won in four against five. A perfect two for Mr. Tait at the second squared matters, but Mr. Hilton again took the lead at the "Cardinal," having laid his approach dead, while Mr. Tait was out of holing distance. The "Bridge" hole was halved in four, Mr. Tait making up for a defective pitch by laying his long putt dead. The greens being evidently keener than in the morning, both overran the hole considerably in their second stroke on the "Himalayas" green; but Mr. Tait won by a long putt, and again squared the match. Perfect play on both sides gave a half at the "Redan," and imperfect approaches at the seventh were responsible for four on each side. On this green Mr. Tait in his putt gave himself a half stimie, but he managed to get down. The eighth hole was badly played by both. Mr. Tait topped his drive, and his ball was within a foot of the bunker, about eighty yards from the tee; then he pulled his second into rough ground to the left, and his approach was only on the edge of the green. Again however he laid the ball dead, and Mr. Hilton failing both in his approach and long putt, allowed him to get off with a half in five. Each had two good strokes toward the end hole, but on the green, though Mr. Hilton had the advantage of putting uphill, he was twice miserably short, and taking three strokes to get down to his opponent's two, Mr. Tait turned one up. The tenth hole was halved in five, both being on the green in three, and both lipping the hole in putting for four. The eleventh saw another half in four, and at the Dyke hole Mr. Tait had a putt of ten feet for four, but did not manage to get down, and another half in five was called. Driving to the right at the thirteenth, both were in rough ground and recovered well. Mr. Hilton laid his pitch on the green within putting distance; but Mr. Tait's pitch carried to the rough grass beyond, and here he played one of the most dexterous downhill putts ever witnessed, making the ball screw round off the grass almost at a right angle and curve round to within two feet of the hole, and so securing a half in five, Mr. Hilton not getting down. For the fourteenth both drove well, and Mr. Hilton's second was within twelve feet of the

F. G. Tait

hole; but Mr. Tait from the edge of the green lay dead, and Mr. Hilton taking three strokes to get down, his putting being lamentably weak, the Champion stood two up with four to play. A very fine putt at the fifteenth green secured a half for Mr. Tait, for after three strokes Mr. Hilton lay stony, while Mr. Tait was six feet away, and a downhill putt to play. The sixteenth was also halved in four, through perfect play on both sides. In going to the "Alps" Mr. Tait was in the rough to the right, and attempting to carry with a wooden club, he only went fifty yards. Mr. Hilton played short in two, and Mr. Tait in three, and excitement was great when after neat pitches on both sides, the former holed in five, and the latter failed to get down. The match was thus carried to the last hole, when Mr. Tait ended matters by laying his opponent a stimie. Scores:—

> Mr. Tait: Out, 5 2 5 4 3 4 4 5 5 = 37
> In,   5 4 5 5 4 4 4 6 4 = 41
>
> Total, 78
> Mr. Hilton: Out, 4 3 4 4 4 4 4 5 6 = 38
> In,   5 4 5 5 5 4 4 5 5 = 42
>
> Total, 80

FINAL ROUND (From the *Scotsman*).

MR. F. G. TAIT ʏ MR. J. BALL.

The tussle between Mr. F. G. Tait and Mr. John Ball became interesting from the very outset; for after Mr. Ball had started nicely from the first tee, those whose sympathies lay towards Mr. Tait had an anxious time from the moment the latter's drive left the club until it landed. It looked as if his ball was going on to the railway, but fortunately for him it struck the dyke and rebounded on to the course. Both had good seconds on to the green, and Mr. Ball, who played the odd, lipped the hole with his third. Mr. Tait's like left his opponent a stimie to negotiate, and as Mr. Ball failed to get past, Mr. Tait won the first hole in 4 to 5. This was a good beginning for the Scotsman, and when Mr. Ball spared his cleek going to the "Tunnel," and fell into the bunker in consequence, Mr. Tait's prospects became exceedingly bright; for he was lying nicely on the green with his drive. Mr. Ball made a good recovery with his second, but he had to play two more on the green, and as Mr. Tait ran down a four-foot putt, the Englishman never really had a chance, the hole going to Mr. Tait in three to four. Two up on the first two holes was of course a lead which could not have been improved upon, but for some time after this the Englishman kept a hold on his opponent, though it was not until the sixth hole was reached that Mr. Ball won his first hole. The third,

A Record

fourth, and fifth were each halved in four. Both got over the dreaded "Cardinal," the difficulties of which have spoiled so many good scores, with their seconds. With his next Mr. Tait was rather strong, while his opponent lay within three yards of the hole. A magnificent putt however secured Mr. Tait a four, and Mr. Ball followed suit, his rival's deadly putting having apparently no effect upon his nerve. The "Burn" was prettily played, and at this hole Mr. Tait had a fine approach to within eight feet of the hole. He did not manage to get down the long putt, however, and the Englishman did well to secure a half. Both drives crossed the "Himalayas" and lay on the far side of the green, and while Mr. Tait was short with his second, Mr. Ball was too strong, and each required four where three ought to have been the figure. At the "Elysian Fields" the crowd had an object-lesson in regard to Mr. Tait's long-driving abilities; for off the tee here last year's Champion, though going slightly off the line, out-drove his opponent by nearly 40 yards. This advantage however was made little use of, as Mr. Tait was not on the green with his next, while Mr. Ball was within fifteen yards of the hole. Mr. Tait had a nasty run up to play, and Mr. Ball, always having the best of the short game at this green, got a four to Mr. Tait's five, and thus won his first hole. Going to the railway, Mr. Tait had a fine drive to within five yards of the hole, while Mr. Ball lay to the left. The latter played the odd and was short, Mr. Tait, by getting a perfect three, winning the hole, and standing two up on the match. "Monkton" allowed Mr. Tait to increase his lead to three. Two long balls were sent off from the tee, and Mr. Ball's approach was a beauty, while Mr. Tait lay to the left. The Englishman was in much better position. Playing the odd Mr. Tait was by no means dead, but he got down his putt, and Mr. Ball, though lying only fourteen inches from the disc, missed his easy chance of a half, and Mr. Tait was thus three up with a four to his opponent's five. Both played a safe game at the end hole, and after approaching much to the left Mr. Ball again threw away his chance of a half by weakness on the green, though all the same a little luck might have given him a five instead of a six. Mr. Tait thus turned four up.

Going to the tenth hole, Mr. Tait got into trouble. He sliced his ball into the rough, and he had to use a mashie to get on to the course again. Taking a brassie for his third stroke however he recovered splendidly, and lay within twelve feet of the hole. Mr. Ball with a fine run up to the hole side, secured a half. The eleventh hole was halved without incident in an orthodox four, but the "Dyke" was interesting. It fell to Mr. Ball. Mr. Tait pulled his drive very badly, and nearly found the burn, but had a better second than his opponent, and both lay in front of the wall with equal chances. The Englishman's pitch was excellently judged,

F. G. Tait

and laid him eighteen inches from the pin, his finely played stroke eliciting loud cheers from the immense crowd. Mr. Tait's like was watched with great interest, but it was poor in comparison with that of his opponent, and lay fifteen yards on the far side of the hole. The Scotsman made a plucky bid for a half, but the putt was too much for him, and Mr. Ball won the hole, as he deserved to do, and again reduced his opponent's lead to three. Mr. Tait however took the first opportunity of getting four up once more. His approach to the thirteenth was as accurate as it well could be, and he was lying within easy holing distance. Mr. Ball on the other hand duffed his like, ran past the hole with his fourth, and missed his fifth. His opponent had thus two for it, but he only required one, and holed in four. Neither got a good drive at the fourteenth, but both were over the bunker and on the green in two. The Scotsman got down his fourth— a four-foot putt—and Mr. Ball, failing with a putt only half that distance, once more lost a hole through indifferent putting. At the next hole Mr. Tait was in difficulties. He lay in rough ground to the left with his second, but he recovered nicely though a little too strong. He played two more, and failing to get up with his fifth, gave up the hole. Mr. Ball was almost dead with his second, and though he did not hole out, a three was a fair approximate score for him. This made Mr. Tait four up with three to play. The "Cardinal's Back" was halved in five, after Mr. Tait had pulled his tee shot. Mr. Ball however duffed his approach and narrowly missed the bunker, Mr. Tait's effort for a four running round the lip of the hole. Both carried the height at the "Alps," but only to land in the bunker by the hole side. Each got out with his third, but too strongly, and both balls overran the hole. The fourth strokes were hardly up, and while Mr. Ball got down a four-yard putt amid cheers, Mr. Tait just missed a half, and again his lead was down to three. Both drives were off the line going to the home hole, Mr. Ball's being sliced, while Mr. Tait's was pulled. The former's approach was a very fine one, but the Scotsman was short with his. It ought to have been Mr. Ball's hole, but again he missed an easy putt of about two feet, and he allowed his opponent to get a half in four after an indifferently played hole. Approximating where the players did not play out, the details of the first round are as follows :—

Mr. Tait : Out, 4 3 4 4 4 5 3 4 5=36
In,   5 4 5 4 4 6 5 6 4=43

Total, 79

Mr. Ball : Out, 5 4 4 4 4 4 4 5 6=40
In,   5 4 4 6 5 3 5 5 4=41

Total, 81

A Record

The afternoon was fine, and once more an immense crowd followed the players. Mr. Tait, with his substantial lead of three holes, was generally looked upon as a comparatively easy winner, and few in the crowd could have been prepared for what was afterwards to take place. As was the case in the former round, Mr. Tait got close up to the wall from the first tee, and he had a difficult stroke to play for his second. This time, unfortunately for him, he got over the wall and on to the railway, thereby losing a stroke, and these misfortunes lost him the hole; for his opponent was down in a perfectly-played four. Mr. Tait looked like making good his previous mistakes at the short hole. He had a beautiful pitch from the tee to within three yards of the hole. Mr. Ball however was dead with his second, and Mr. Tait, failing to get down in the like, had to be content with a half in three. As far as the long game was concerned, the " Cardinal " could not have been better played; for both were within thirty yards of the green with their seconds. After that however Mr. Ball had a fine loft to about two yards of the hole, and Mr. Tait, being very short with his approach, had to play the long odds. Mr. Ball failed in his effort for a four, but as matters turned out he did not require to hole out in that figure even for a half; for Mr. Tait failed to take his chance, and Mr. Ball was thus only one down on the match. Play now became more interesting than ever. Going to the burn, Mr. Tait took a dangerous line, but getting away a cleanly-hit ball he kept out of trouble, and as Mr. Ball sliced his second into the bank at the waterside, it looked as if the Scotsman was again to forge ahead. Mr. Ball had a very bad lie, and as he had very little chance of getting out of his difficulties, it would have been better for him to have gone into the Pow burn, for in that case he would simply have lost a stroke. He made one attempt to get clear, but was no better off than before, and with Mr. Tait on the green in two he gave up the hole. This made Mr. Tait two up again, but the " Himalayas " was perfectly played by the Hoylake Club representative, and Mr. Tait being very short with his run up, the Scotsman's lead was once more reduced to one, Mr. Ball holing out in three, while his opponent required one stroke more. Matters had now been taken from the interesting to the exciting stage, and the tension became very severe when Mr. Ball, by winning the " Elysian Fields " in a nice four, was able to square the match for the first time since the start. The " Railway " was halved in four—one too many. Mr. Ball was too strong from the tee, and found the burn,

263

F. G. Tait

thereby losing a stroke. His third was very short, but so was Mr. Tait's, who made a poor show in trying to take advantage of his opponent's troubles. Mr. Ball made ample amends by holing a long putt on the sloping green, and his nicely-judged effort was greeted with a hearty cheer. Mr. Tait tried hard to take the hole, but his putt wanted strength, and he had to be content with a half in four. Still another half followed, "Monkton" being divided in five. Mr. Ball had the better approach, but he never gave his long putt a chance, and Mr. Tait also showed a weakness on the green. The struggle for supremacy still continued, and those who were desirous of a victory for the Scotsman began to have grave misgivings about the result; for Mr. Tait was playing far below his true form, while Mr. Ball kept the course much better, and was as a rule more steady all round. The end hole gave no idea as to how the match would ultimately go, for it also was halved in five, which is par play.

The tenth hole saw Mr. Tait still off his game, and it was lucky for him that Mr. Ball's putt for a four did not get down, as probably it deserved to do. If Mr. Tait had putted in the same way as he did in the morning, the hole might have been his; but he no only missed his opportunity of again taking the lead, but he just managed with nothing to spare, to get a half. Driving against the wind at the eleventh, both were in rough ground. The green however was safely reached in two, and by missing a two-yard putt, Mr. Ball lost the hole, and stood one down on the match. The hopes of Scotsmen were just beginning to rise again; but at the tee to the "Dyke" they were again dashed to the ground. Mr. Tait pulled so badly that he lay on the other bank of the Pow burn, and according to rule he had to lift to the near side and count a stroke. His opponent was over the wall in one less—viz., three to Mr. Tait's four—and after playing two more, and then overrunning the hole, Mr. Tait gave up, neither player holing out. Again matters were all square, and with only six holes to go, and after playing thirty holes, the Championship was in reality as near decision as when play started in the morning. But from a Scottish point of view, affairs became rather gloomy when Mr. Ball, amid intense excitement, won the thirteenth, and for the first time during the match took the lead. Mr. Tait pulled both his first and second strokes, and again got into difficulties with his third. Mr. Ball was on the green with his like, and ultimately won the hole in four to six. The fourteenth was halved in four, Mr. Tait striking the back of the disc in his effort for a three. Mr. Tait however was not to be beaten without making a plucky effort to pull off the match, which at one time seemed so safe for him. He won the fifteenth, and once

A Record

more there was nothing between him and his opponent. His approach play and putting were perfect, and he was down in four. Mr. Ball tried well to get a half, but he was not successful. Thus with only three holes to play it was even yet a very open question as to who would be Champion. The winning of the " Cardinal's Back " by Mr. Ball however seemed to point to his ultimate success, especially as the hole over the " Alps " was halved. The " Alps " however were not crossed without incident. Mr. Tait's second dropped into the water in the bunker, while Mr. Ball's like, striking the bank and rolling back, also found a sandy bed. His ball fortunately escaped the water, but only by an inch or two. There was of course nothing for it but that Mr. Tait should wade in and get out of his troubles as best he could, for another lost hole meant to him the loss of the Championship. Much therefore depended on his recovery, and amid cheering and excitement, which the crowd made no effort to suppress, he got well out. Mr. Ball also extricated himself nicely from a bad lie, and he too got a round of cheers. A half in five was the result, but at the " Home " hole Mr. Ball pulled his drive, and as Mr. Tait had the better approach, he won the hole, cheer after cheer being raised in acknowledgment of his pluck in saving the match at this stage. With the thirty-six holes played the match was thus a tie, and a wild rush was now made by the excited crowd from the " Home " to the first green, Amid a breathless silence the competitors took their stand at the first teeing ground. Mr. Ball outdrove his opponent by about twenty yards, and Mr. Tait's approach overran the green, while his opponent's lay within holing distance. Mr. Ball, down in three to Mr. Tait's four, won the hole, and thus became Amateur Champion for 1899, after the most exciting tussle that has ever taken place. His victory, though it must have caused disappointment to the majority of the crowd, was hailed with great cheering, and some of the new Champion's more enthusiastic supporters carried him off shoulder-high towards the club-house. The approximate details in the second round were as follows :—

Mr. Ball : Out, 4 3 5 7 3 4 4 5 5 = 40
In, 5 5 4 4 4 5 4 5 4 = 40

Total, 80

Mr. Tait : Out, 5 3 6 4 4 5 4 5 5 = 41
In, 5 4 7 6 4 4 5 5 3 = 43

Total, 84

F. G. Tait

The following is a short account of Tait's record medal round of 78, St. Andrews, September, 1894.

ST. ANDREWS MEDAL, Sept. 1894.

Two players who were also strong favourites were Mr. F. G. Tait and Mr. C. Hutchings. During the past year Mr. Tait has occupied a most prominent position in the amateur golfing world. Last September he carried off the club's gold medal with a score of 80, taking second place to Mr. Mure Fergusson. At Hoylake at the Amateur Championship he was first favourite until he fell before Mr. Mure Fergusson, and at the open meeting at Sandwich he not only occupied the highest position amongst the amateurs in the championship competition, but also showed his undoubted superiority by holding the field until the semi-final of the amateur v. professional golf tournament when the rest of his compeers had succumbed. At the spring meeting of the Royal and Ancient Club, Mr. Tait carried off the chief award, and proving in the best form yesterday he repeated his May victory. He opened a grand round with a capital four, but threatened to spoil his score with a six at the second hole. Having a bad lie from his drive, a cleek shot for his second landed him in the road, with the result as stated. At the fourth hole Mr. Tait finished off a splendid hole by getting down a long putt of twenty yards for a three. This excellent play was rather discounted at the long hole, where, after being on the edge of the green in a couple, he required half-a-dozen to hole out. At the high hole again, Mr. Tait, in approaching the hole, made acquaintance with the bunker and registered another six. With a forty out, Mr. Tait started the journey in, in splendid fashion, and continuing to display the best of form, he accomplished the inward journey with the splendid score of seventy-eight—a record for medal play on the green. His details were:—

$$\text{Out, } 4\ 6\ 4\ 3\ 6\ 4\ 6\ 3\ 4 = 40$$
$$\text{In, }\ \ 4\ 3\ 4\ 4\ 5\ 5\ 4\ 5\ 4 = 38$$

$$\text{Total, } 78$$

As none of the remaining players came near this score, Mr. Tait won the King William IV. Medal, and also gained the Glennie Aggregate Medal for the year.

Record score of 72 (from *Golf*, Feb. 16, 1894).

On the morning of February 5th Mr. Tait again broke 80, with 38 and 41 = 79; and in the afternoon with 72, 36 each way. In view of this latter feat, it may be that golfers, especially those abroad, will not find it wearisome if we describe the round some-

A Record

what minutely. First, as to the position of the holes: the first was on the medal green to the right, the tee some 70 to 80 yards from the railings; the second, on a newly-made green to the right (the putting here being rough), rather farther on than the medal hole; the tee to the third hole is 30 yards further forward than on medal days, and a good deal to the right, among the rough grass. From that point every hole and tee was much about the same as on medal days, as far as distance is concerned, until the end hole, which was only some ten yards past the small bunker, and just to the right of it. Turning homewards, though the tee is a little more forward, the balance is about restored by the hole being placed about the same distance further back—the eleventh hole was far to the left, close to the Eden, on a small table with steep sides, and immediately behind the bunker; it could not have been reached from the tee save by a driver of exceptional power, such as Rolland or Mr. Tait himself. Thus it will be seen that the next hole was considerably shorter; in fact, Mr. Tait, with a terrifically long ball, could, and actually did, reach the green. From this point the only alterations to be noted are—from the "Hole o' Cross" to the "Ginger-beer"; a much longer hole than on medal days, by reason of the tee being put very far back; and at the eighteenth hole, where the same remark applies. Any exceptionally fine play is invariably met by the criticism that "it was not the medal round"; this in Mr. Tait's case is certainly true; but, had he played the same game on the exact medal round as he did on this occasion, his score probably would have been as good. For a player of his power there is little to choose between the difficulties of the two courses; if the ninth and twelfth holes were easier, the difference was quite made up by the extra length of the long hole home, and of the last. Here then is the actual score:—

$$\text{Out,} \quad 5\ 4\ 4\ 3\ 5\ 4\ 5\ 3\ 3 = 36$$
$$\text{Home,} \quad 3\ 3\ 3\ 5\ 5\ 4\ 4\ 5\ 4 = 36$$
$$\text{Total,} \quad 72$$

Details as thus:—

1. Two long drives over the Burn to left; short loft; two putts.

2. Two, rather to right; short pitch; putt (two yards).

3. Drive; pitch; two putts (almost a three).

4. Very long shot; driving mashie; putt (10 to 12 yards).

5. Two drives on to narrow table fronting green; approach; two putts (nearly a four).

6. Very long drive; approach a little past; two putts.

7. Drive drawn into second bunker; niblick; approach; two putts.

8. First very wide to the right; approach putt two yards past; third, in (good recovery).

9. Very long drive; nearly home; two putts.

10. Drive to foot of green; approach 10 or 12 yards past; third, holed out.

11. Long shot to left of teeing-ground; putted up; holed out from 10 yards.

12. Very long drive which just reached green on the left; two putts.

13. Carried all the bunkers; indifferent iron shot, heeled; three putts.

14. Two very long drives; an iron shot quite straight; two putts (almost a four).

15. Long drive; cleek shot to foot of green (too heavily taken); approach dead; one putt.

16. Drive; wrist approach; two putts (almost a three).

17. Drive somewhat drawn to left; second to right of bunker; running loft on to green; two putts.

18. Long drive; cleek shot past hole; two putts; the first of which hit the hole for 71, and ran about a yard past.

The crucial putt was well holed by Mr. Tait amidst loud plaudits.

TABLE OF VARIOUS RECORDS.

ST. ANDREWS—MEDALS.

Sept. 1890.—Unplaced 95.

Sept. 1891.—Unplaced 93.

Sept. 1892.—Unplaced 91.

May 1893.—Under 90 for first time [85 score].

Sept. 1893.—Round in 80. 2nd Medal (Mr. S. M. Fergusson wins 1st Medal in 79.)

May 1894.—Won in 83. 1st Medal.

Sept. 1894.—Won in 78. 1st Medal. New Record.

Out—4 6 4 3 6 4 6 3 4=40
In—4 3 4 4 5 5 4 5 4=38

78

Won Glennie Medal as well [161 *strokes*.]

May 1895.—Second Medal at 85 strokes after a tie.

Sept. 1895.—83, but unplaced.

May 1896.—86, but unplaced.

Sept. 1896.—(Residing at Ballater) did not compete.

May 1897.—84, won after a double tie with L. M. B. M.

Sept. 1897.—81, 2nd Medal, finishing with three sixes.

Won Glennie Medal for second time [165 *strokes*.]

A Record

May 1898.—86, unplaced.

Sept. 1898.—82, 2nd Medal, after a tie with Mr. Leslie Balfour.

May 1899.—80. Won 1st Medal.

Sept. 1899.—83. Won 1st Medal.

Won Glennie for third time [163 *strokes*].

CALCUTTA CUP.

Aug. 1890.—Score beaten in Semi-Final by Mr. Nimmo.

Aug. 1894.—Owe 2. Won.

Aug. 1899.—Owe 4.—Won (New Course.)

JUBILEE VASE.

Sept. 1890.—Score beaten in Final by Mr. H. A. Bethune.

Sept. 1895.—Owe 3. Won.

Sept. 1899.—Owe 5. Beaten 5th round by Mr. C. A. W. Cameron.

ST. ANDREWS AMATEUR RECORD.

5th Feb., 1894.

Out, 5 4 4 3 5 4 5 3 3 = 36
In, 3 3 3 5 5 4 4 5 4 = 36

Total, 72

ST. ANDREWS FOURSOME RECORD.

26th Sept., 1898. Partnered by Mr. A. G. Tait.

Out, 4 6 4 4 6 4 4 3 3 = 38
In, 3 2 4 5 6 5 4 4 3 = 36

Total, 74

ST. ANDREWS "BEST OF BALLS" RECORD.

30 Nov., 1897. Partnered by Mr. Edward Blackwell **v** W. Auchterlonie and Andrew Kirkcaldy.

Out, 5 4 3 4 4 4 4 1 4 = 33
In, 3 4 3 5 5 4 4 4 4 = 36

Total, 69

CARNOUSTIE RECORD.

July, 1894.

Out, 4 3 4 4 4 3 4 3 4 = 33
In, 4 5 4 3 5 4 5 5 4 = 39

Total, 72

269

F. G. Tait

NORTH BERWICK RECORD.

11th May, 1896.

Out, 4 5 4 3 4 4 4 5 3 = 36
In, 4 4 4 4 4 3 5 6 4 = 38

Total, 74

NEW LUFFNESS GOLF CLUB.

LECONFIELD MEDAL (Spring).   HOPE GOLD MEDAL (Autumn).

April,   1895.—Won First Medal (score 76. Record).
Oct.,   1895.—Won First Medal (score 86).
March, 1896.—Second to Mr. T. T. Gray (82 to 81).
Oct.,   1896.—Absent.
May,   1897.—Won First Medal (score 78).
Oct.,   1897.—Absent.
April,   1898.—Absent.
Oct.,   1898.—Won Hope Medal (score 79).
April,   1899.—Second, score 78 (Mr. A. W. Robertson Durham 77).

ST. GEORGE'S CUP (SANDWICH).

THREE WINS.

May, 1896.—Score 84 + 81 = 165
June, 1898.—Score 84 + 79 = 163.
June, 1899.—Score 76 + 79 = 155 (Record).

TANTALLON GOLF CLUB.

8th April, 1899.—Medal Competition. Score 94 (unplaced).
9th Sept., 1899.—Medal Competition.   Score 89 (unplaced).
Mr. Laidlay won with 87.

EDINBURGH CONSERVATIVE CLUB.

5th May, 1899.—Medal Competition. Won, score 87.

ARCHERFIELD RECORD.

15th July, 1899.

Out, 4 4 3 3 3 4 3 4 3 = 31
In, 3 4 3 4 3 4 4 3 4 = 32

Total, 63

A Record

GANTON RECORDS (AMATEUR).

20th March, 1897.

Out, 35
In, 33

Total, 68

The course was on this occasion about 3 shots easier than usual.

21st July, 1899.

Out, 5 3 4 4 3 3 5 5 5 = 37
In, 3 2 5 4 5 3 5 3 3 = 33

Total, 70

This score is accepted as the amateur record.

MUIRFIELD RECORD (AMATEUR).

21st March, 1896.

Out, 3 5 4 4 5 4 4 5 4 = 38
In, 4 4 4 4 4 3 4 3 5 = 35

Total, 73

[Tait was elected a member of the Honourable Company of Edinburgh Golfers in October, 1899, but never played for any Medal.]

MORTON HALL.

On 25th June, 1896, Tait went round in 72, making a fresh record for the medal round, the previous best being 75.

BARNTON.

Tait was elected a honorary member of the Burgess Golf Club in May, 1896, and in a match with Mr. W. T. Armour and Mr. T. T. Gray holed out in 76.

OPEN CHAMPIONSHIPS.

1891, at St. Andrews.—30th ; score 182.
1892, at Muirfield.—20th ; score 326.
1893, at Prestwick.—Absent.
1894, at Sandwich.—9th [1st Amateur]; score 340.
1895, at St. Andrews.—14th ; score 341.
1896, at Muirfield.—3rd [1st Amateur]; score 319.
1897, at Hoylake.—3rd ; score 317.
1898, at Prestwick.—5th ; score 315.
1899, at Sandwich.—7th [1st Amateur]; score 324.

271

APPENDIX II.

EXTRACTS FROM F. G. TAIT'S MATCH BOOK,
1896—1899.

I AM permitted, through the kindness of Lieutenant Tait's family, to publish the following portions of his Golfing Diary. The years 1896—1899 embrace most of his greater matches. No match of real importance has been left out, and no comment of Tait's has been deleted or altered in any way.

Date	Links	Match	Odds	Won	Lost	Remarks	Score
1896 Jan. 30	St. Andrews	F. G. T. & W. Mac-Farlan **v** J. Blackwell & Capt. W. Burn.	—	4	–	Self and W. MacF. very good; round in 82.	82
,, ,,	,, ,,	,, ,, ,,	—	5	–	Both partner and I played a very fine game after 5th hole, and a magnificent game in on a very long course (right-hand course); in 34, out 44, 4 4 3 4 4 4 3 4 4 = 34.	78
,, 31	,, ,,	F. G. T. & W. Mac-Farlan **v** A. F. Macfie & J. Blackwell.	—	6	–	MacF. and I again in great form with exception of 17th hole = 8. Macfie off his game.	85
,, ,,	,, ,,	F. G. T. **v** J. Blackwell & W. Mac Farlan (3 balls).	—	3 2	–	All three played fairly well. MacFarlan beat J. B. by 2. This was a fine match for long driving.	—
Feb. 1	,, ,,	F. G. T. **v** W. Mac-Farlan.	—	7	–	Played very well until match was over. MacF. completely off his game. F. G. T. out in 40 and 4 4 3 first 3 holes in.	—
,, 4	,, ,,	F. G. T. **v** John Oswald	Giving 4 strokes.	4	–	Both played indifferently -	—

Golfing Diary

Date	Links	MATCH	Odds	Won	Lost	REMARKS.	Score
1896 Feb. 4	St. Andrews	F. G. T. **v** D. I. Lamb & J. Oswald (best of balls).	—	7	–	Played very well; round in 77, left-hand course. Out, 5 5 4 4 5 5 4 3 4 = 39. In, 4 4 3 4 7 3 5 3 5 = 38. D. I. L. and J. O. both off their game.	77
,, 5	,, ,,	F. G. T. **v** D. I. Lamb -	+ 3 holes	2	–	Played very well with exception of a few holes.	—
,, ,,	,, ,,	,, ,, ,,	,, ,,	–	5	Played badly going out, but well in. 39. Won 3 byes. David Lamb much better. Self 44 and 39 = 83.	83
,, 6	,, ,,	F. G. T. **v** J. Blackwell & C. H. P. Carter (3-ball match).	+ $\frac{1}{3}$	5 3	–	Played very well; round in 80. Carter good. J. B. rather off his game.	80
,, ,,	St. Andrews New Links	,, ,, ,,	+ 2 holes + $\frac{1}{3}$	2	1	Played badly to start with. J. B. got 4 up. Coming in I played well with exception of last hole. J. B. and Carter good.	—
,, 7	St. Andrews Old Links	F. G. T. **v** A. F. Macfie	—	6	–	Played very well, strong cross wind. Macfie rather off his game. Self, round in 80. Out, 5 5 4 5 5 **6** 4 4 4 = 42. In, 5 3 4 4 **6** 4 4 4 4 = 38. Also 2 byes.	80
,, ,,	St. Andrews New Links	F. G. T. & C. H. P. Carter **v** A. F. Macfie & J. Blackwell.	—	3	–	Carter and self in very good form. Carter holed out very well. Macfie and Blackwell fair. F. G. T. and C. H. P. C., 85.	85
,, 8	,, ,,	F. G. T. **v** W. Auchterlonie (ex-Champion).	36-hole match.	3	–	Played very well; round in 82, first round with two 7's and one **6**. Not quite so good, second round 85. Auchterlonie very good second round.	82 85
,, ,,	St. Andrews Old Links	F. G. T. **v** L. M. Balfour-Melville & C. H. P. Carter (3-ball match).	10 holes Carter 3 up.	5 1	–	Played very well. Carter also good. The Champion missed some short putts. Out, 6 5 4 4 4. In, 5 4 3 5 5. Five holes out and in.	—
,, 10	,, ,,	F. G. T. **v** D. I. Lamb & C. H. P. Carter (best of balls).	—	4	–	Played very well; round in 78. Strong cross wind. Out, 4 5 5 4 5 4 5 3 3 = 38. In, 4 3 4 4 7 4 5 5 4 = 40. Carter and Lamb fair.	78
,, ,,	,, ,,	,, ,, ,,	—	–	1	Did not play quite so well. Carter and Lamb rather better. Wind rather stronger. Played well in with exception of 17th hole. Out 44, in 41.	85
,, 11	,, ,,	F. G. T. **v** W. Auchterlonie.	36-hole match.	2	–	Played very well first round, and badly second. Lonie bad first, good second. Self 82 in morning; 83 in afternoon. Strong cross wind.	82
,, 13	,, ,,	F. G. T. **v** H. Boyd & A. H. Cochran.	Best of balls.	Halved		Played well, with exception of last two holes. Boyd and Cochran good. Self 84. Last two holes 7 and 6 ! ! ! !	84
,, ,,	,, ,,	,, ,, ,,	,, ,,	Halved		Played well out, with exception of 5th hole 7 !! Out 42, in 40. Cochran and Boyd good, with exception of last hole. Splendid day.	82
,, 14	,, ,,	F. G. T. **v** W. Gordon -	$\frac{1}{2}$	2	–	Played well, 82. Gordon also very fair. F. G. T. one or two bad holes. Strong wind.	82

273   S

F. G. Tait

Date	Links	MATCH	Odds	Won	Lost	REMARKS	Score
1896 Feb.14	St. Andrews New Links	F. G. T. **v** W. Gordon -	½	4	–	Played well, 82. Rather bad luck coming in. Strong wind. Gordon not quite so good.	82
,, 15	St. Andrews Old Links	F. G. T. **v** H. Boyd & A. H. Cochran.	Best of balls.	Halved		Splendid match all through; all played well. Self had last 5 holes. Out 38, in 45.	83
,, ,,	,, ,,	,, ,, ,,	,, ,,	2	–	Another splendid match. F.G.T. 79. Out, 5 4 5 4 6 4 4 4 4=40. In, 4 3 4 5 6 3 5 5 4 = 39. Boyd and Cochran both good.	79
,, 25	,, ,,	F. G. T. **v** D. I. Lamb -	+ 3 holes	4	–	Played fairly well. D. I. L. off his game entirely. F. G. T. driving very well. Very cold and windy.	86
,, 26	,, ,,	F. G. T. **v** D. I. Lamb & A. H. Cochran.	Best of balls.	2	–	Played well, with exception of one or two holes. D. I. L. and A. H. C. not on their best game. D. I. L. pressing. Very windy.	83
,, ,,	,, ,,	Same Match - - -	,, ,,	3	–	Played well on the whole. Some indifferent holes. D.I.L. and A. H. C. fair. Two bad holes.	83
,, 27	,, ,,	F. G. T. **v** A. H. Cochran.	+ ⅓	7	–	Played well. Strong cross wind. 40 and 40. Cochran completely off his game. Also 5 byes.	80
,, ,,	,, ,,	Same Match - - -	+ ⅓	Halved		Cochran much better, self most indifferent, very little under 90. Wind much lighter.	
,, 28	St. Andrews New Links	F. G. T. **v** J. H. Blackwell.	+ 2 holes	–	2	Played badly going out, very well in. J. H. B. good all through and putting very well. Self in in 38, J. H. B. 39.	
,, ,,	St. Andrews Old Links	Same Match - - -	,, ,,	–	2	J. H. B. very good last 5 holes on medal course in 20, 4 5 4 4 3 = 20, and twice bunkered. Self very fair. Some bad holes going out.	
,, 29	,, ,,	F. G. T. **v** D. I. Lamb -	+ 3 holes	2	–	Played well, with exception of 3rd hole out, and well back except long hole 8! D. I. L. good until last 3 holes.	
,, ,,	,, ,,	F. G. T. & D. I. Lamb **v** Andrew Kirkcaldy & A. H. Cochran.	—	–	4	Andrew and Cochran good. D. I. L. very much off his game. Self very fair.	—
Mar. 3	St. Andrews	F. G. T. **v** J. H. Blackwell & W. Gordon.	2 strokes 9 ,,	2 4	– –	Played well. Jim also good. Gordon off his game. Jim's two strokes both told. F.G.T. 85 with 8 to 2nd hole and two other bad holes.	85
,, ,,	,, ,,	Same Match - - -	2 ,, 9 ,,	– –	– –	Stopped by snow 5 holes from home. 1 up with Jim, 3 down with Gordon.	—
,, 4	,, ,,	F. G. T. **v** W. Gordon -	9 ,,	3	–	Played very well, with exception of 2nd and 3rd holes, 6 and 7. Out in 43, in 37. Out, 4 6 7 5 5 5 5 3 3 = 43. In, 4 3 4 5 5 4 5 3 4 = 37. Gordon fair.	80
,, ,,	,, ,,	F. G. T. **v** H. S. C. Everard & W. Gordon (best of balls).	—	8	–	Played a very strong game; out 38, in 37 = 75. 5 4 4 5 4 6 4 3 3 = 38; in, 4 2 4 5 4 5 4 4 5 = 37. H. S. C. E. very fair. Gordon quite off his game. Perfect day for golf. Also 4 byes.	75

Golfing Diary

Date	Links	Match	Odds	Won	Lost	Remarks	Score
1896 Mar. 5	St. Andrews	F. G. T. **v** J. H. Blackwell.	2 strokes	4	–	Played very well, except last hole and 2nd hole. Out, 4 7 4 5 4 5 3 3 4 = 39. In, 4 4 4 4 5 4 4 5 6. J. H. B. fair, rather off his putting.	79
,, ,,	,, ,,	Same Match - - -	,, ,,	3	–	Played well on the whole, but rather slackly going out. 4 5 5 6 5 5 6 3 4 = 43. In, 4 3 4 5 6 4 4 4 4 = 38. J. H. B. not putting well.	81
,, 6	,, ,,	F. G. T. & W. Gordon **v** D. I. Lamb.	F. G. T. & W. G. receiving 3 strokes.	Halved		Played in a regular gale, and blizzard of rain, snow, and hail. Very good match. Good golf impossible.	—
,, 7	,, ,,	F. G. T. **v** W. Gordon & J. Grimond.	Best of balls and 5 strokes.	3	–	Played very well after first 4 holes. Gordon and Grimond fair. F. G. T. 5 5 5 6 5 5 4 2 4 = 41. In, 4 3 3 4 6 4 4 4 3 = 35 = 76. F. G. T. rather unfortunate in some putts.	76
,, ,,	,, ,,	Same Match - - -	Best of balls and 6 strokes.	4	–	The play all round was not so good, especially on my opponents' part. F. G. T. 81. Out 42, in 39. One or two bad holes. Beautiful day.	81
,, ,,	,, ,,	F. G. T. **v** A. H. Cochran.	10 holes A. H. C. 3 holes start	2	–	Played well, with exception of 2nd hole, 7. Out, 4 7 4 4 5. In, 4 5 5 5 3. A. H. C. off his putting.	—
,, 9	,, ,,	F. G. T. & H. S. C. Everard **v** A. H. Cochran & Andrew Kirkcaldy.	36-hole match.	0	10	Andrew and A. H. C very good, 83 with a 9. Self and Everard fair in the morning. F. G. T. very bad in the afternoon.	—
,, 10	,, ,,	F. G. T. **v** A. Aikman -	—	2	–	Aikman good out and fair in, 40 and 47. Self fair, 85. F. G. T. putting badly.	85
,, ,,	St. Andrews New Links	Same Match - - -	—	4	–	Both played very well, with exception of last 3 holes. Exceptional putting on both sides. F. G. T. 42 and 39. Score in, 4 4 3 4 4 6 4 6 = 39.	81
,, 11	St. Andrews Old Links	F. G. T. **v** C. E. Gilroy -	4 strokes	2	–	Both bad going out and bad in. Strong wind. Gilroy had not played for some time. F. G. T. putting badly.	86
,, ,,	,, ,,	Same Match - - -	,, ,,	4	–	Both a little better. Self 84, with some indifferent holes. Gilroy rather off his driving. F. G. T. 6 to last hole.	84
,, 12	,, ,,	F. G. T. **v** Jim Cunningham.	J. C. 3 holes up.	4	–	Played very badly going out, and fairly well in. Out 44, in 40. J. Cunningham off his game.	84
,, ,,	,, ,,	,, ,, ,,	,, ,,	0	4	Played badly all through, completely off my putting. Cunningham good out, but only fair in. F. G. T. 90. Beautiful day for golf. Greens a little keen.	90
,, 13	St. Andrews	F. G. T. **v** Andrew Kirkcaldy.	—	–	2	Andrew very good; out 38. Self bad and 4 down. All square and 3 to play. Andrew in the railway; self safe. Played a beautiful shot up to hole and kicked into bunker under the hole into an impossible "lie." Missed a short putt at 17th and lost match. Cruel luck!	86

F. G. Tait

Date	Links	Match	Odds	Won	Lost	Remarks	Score
1896 Mar.13	St. Andrews	F. G. T. **v** W. Greig & A. H. Cochran (best of balls).	—	1	–	A very good match. My opponents started with 4 fours. I putted badly and missed some very short putts. Greig not on his best game.	85
,, 17	Musselburgh	F. G. T. **v** W. MacFarlan.	+2 holes	4	0	Played steadily 27 holes; 35, 36 and 37. MacFarlan rather off his putting. W. MacF. holed the 1st hole in 2 the 2nd round. C. MacRae also played and was in great form.	71
,, 20	Barnton	F. G. T. **v** W. T. Armour & Angus MacDonald (best of balls).	—	Halved		A good match all through. F. G. T. putting badly, but playing the rest of the game well. Armour very good. MacD. fair.	—
,, 21	Muirfield	F. G. T. **v** L. M. B. Melville.	—	–	3	Leslie B. M. very good, but lucky. Holed a long mashie approach and 2 long putts. Self also good except two short putts. L. M. B. M. 71 without 7th hole.	—
,, ,,	,,	Same Match - - -	—	7	–	F. G. T. played a very strong game, and rather demoralized the amateur champion. F. G. T. round in 73, record of Muirfield. Out, 3 5 4 4 5 4 4 5 4 = 38. In, 4 4 4 4 4 3 4 3 5 = 35. L. M. B. M. round in 78. L. M. B. M.'s putting all day was excellent. F. G. T. very hard luck on the putting green.	73
,, 24	Mortonhall	F. G. T. **v** Colin MacRae.	18 strokes	–	1	Played well to start with, but badly at the end. Putting greens in bad order. MacRae good.	—
,, ,,	,,	Same Match - - -	,, ,,	Halved		Played better round in 73, one stroke above record. Putting very difficult. MacRae much better than in first round.	73
,, 28	New Luffness	F. G. T. **v** W. G. Bloxsom.	—	–	–	Spring Medal. Played well with exception of putting, which was atrocious. Finished in 82. Bloxsom fair. T. T. Gray won medal in 81. F. G. T. 2nd, 82.	82
Apr. 2	North Berwick	F. G. T. **v** W. MacFarlan.	+2 holes	3	–	Played a good game with exception of 17th hole and a few short putts. W. MacF. fair.	82
,, ,,	,, ,,	F. G. T. & Major D. Kinloch **v** Ben Sayers & John Penn.	—	–	–	A very fine match, but only time for 12 holes. Major and I dormie one, but putted badly at the last hole. Sayers good.	—
,, 3	,, ,,	F. G. T. **v** W. MacFarlan.	Regimental Sweepstake.	–	–	MacFarlan had one or two bad holes, and was unlucky in his putting, otherwise he played well. F. G. T. very bad luck at 17th hole ; 8 !! and 5 to the last! W. MacF. 95. Won Sweepstake.	84
,, ,,	,, ,,	,, ,, ,,	+2 holes	3	–	W MacF. good coming in. F. G. T. very steady all through.	79

Golfing Diary

Date	Links	MATCH	Odds	Won	Lost	REMARKS	Score
1896 Apr. 3	North Berwick	F. G. T. **v** Ben Sayers -	—	–	3	A very good match until the last 4 holes. Sayers very good, 77. F. G. T. 78; 11th hole in 2! 100 yds. approach! Sayers very lucky at 17th hole in a long putt which he played far too hard, but his ball hit mine away about 4 yds. and lay dead itself. F. G. T. won the last hole. The match ought to have been halved. Lost by 3 and 1 to play.	78
,, 4	,, ,,	F. G. T. **v** H. Ferrier Kerr.	+ ½	4	–	Played well against a strong wind going out. Kerr driving well, but rather wild on the greens. F. G. T. two consecutive 2's at the 13th and 14th holes. Out, 45. In, 4 5 5 2 2 4 5 – –. No time to play last two holes.	—
,, ,,	,, ,,	G. F. T. **v** H. Ferrier Kerr.	+ ½	5	–	Wind much stronger. Started at 2nd hole and played the last 16. Kerr again driving well, but erratic on the green. F. G. T. very steady.	—
,, 6	Mortonhall	F. G. T. **v** Colin MacRae.	One stroke a hole.	–	2	Very winfly, and only time for 12 holes. MacRae good. F. G. T. one very long drive over pond, going to 3rd hole. Over 200 yds. carry.	—
,, 8	,,	Same Match - - -	15 strokes	5	–	MacRae off his game. Self fair. Driving well. Putting rather badly.	—
,, 13	,,	,, ,, ,,	,, ,,	–	4	MacRae in great form, especially on the green. Self indifferent. MacRae 92, with 3 sevens.	—
,, 14	,,	F. G. T. **v** Capt. Deane & Capt. W. Campbell.	12 strokes and best of balls.	3	–	F. G. T. good, with exception of two or three holes, round in 74. Deane and Campbell rather shaky on the green.	74
,, 16	,,	F. G. T. **v** Colin MacRae.	12 strokes	0	4	MacRae very good; round in 38, with a 9 and a 7. Putting very well. Self fair, but driving badly.	—
,, 17	,,	F. G. T. **v** Capt. Campbell & Colin MacRae.	9 strokes and best of balls.	3	–	Very windy day. Played very well with exception of one hole. Campbell in good form. MacRae rather off his game.	—
,, 21	,,	F. G. T. **v** Colin MacRae.	6 strokes in 12 holes.	3	–	Only time for 12 holes. Both played badly. F. G. T. using two new drivers with little success.	—
,, 23	,,	,, ,, ,,	,, ,,	3	–	Both played badly. F. G. T. driving very badly. Very hot. Played first 7 holes behind two awfully slow players.	—
,, 25	North Berwick	F. G. T. **v** Capt. The Master of Sempill.	27 strokes and 2 holes up.	5	–	First round of a *Regimental Handicap Tournament*—F. G. T. very good until match was over. Sempill very erratic.	—
,, 29	,, ,,	F. G. T. **v** Colin MacRae.	9 strokes	6	–	MacRae very much off his game. Self in great form with exception of one or two holes. Out, 42; in, 37 = 79. Last four holes in, 14 = 3 4 4 3 = 14 !!	79

277

F. G. Tait

Date	Links	MATCH	Odds	Won	Lost	REMARKS	Score
1896 May 1	North Berwick	F. G. T. **v** W. MacFarlan.	4 strokes	3	–	Second round of a *Regimental Handicap Tournament.*—Played well, round in 80. W. MacF. good until last 5 holes. F. G. T. driving very well.	80
,, 2	Mortonhall	F. G. T. **v** Duncan MacLaren.	*Spring Medal* at Mortonhall.	–	–	Played indifferently, and went round in 78. MacLaren 81. Taylor won in 75; self second, 78. A very hot day, and had to carry my own clubs, consequently I did not play my best. Greens very bad.	78
,, 4	St. Andrews	F. G. T. **v** L. M. Balfour Melville & C. Hutchings.	|3-ball match.	4 4	– –	Played very well with exception of a few short putts. Out 41; in 40 =81. Greens very keen, and putting very difficult. Won 3 byes from L. M. B. M., and 2 from C. H. L. M. B. M. rather off his game. C. H. good until last 6 holes.	81
,, ,,	,, ,,	F. G. T. **v** J. E. Laidlay & J. B. Pease.	,, ,,	3 1	– –	Played well again with exception of two holes. Out 40; in 43, with 7 to 16th hole. Pease very good, out 38. Laidlay and Pease halved. Pease putted, and drove very well. Laidlay very fair.	83
,, 5	,, ,,	F. G. T. **v** W. N. Boase	+ 3 holes	2	–	Played the first 3 holes very badly, but after that very well, with exception of 13th and 14th holes. Round in 83 long hole; out in 3, holed a full drive of about 180 yds. Out, 7 5 6 4 3 5 4 3 3 = 40. In, 4 2 5 7 7 4 5 5 4 = 43. Boase fair, with exception of a few holes. Awfully hot day.	83
,, 5	,, ,,	F. G. T. **v** W. Greig -	—	Halved		Both played badly, with an occasionally good hole. Greig driving well but putting badly. Halved match.	
,, 6	,, ,,	F. G. T. **v** L. M. B. Melville.	*Medal Round.*	Hutchings won medal in 82, L. M. B. M. 83, A. E. MacFie 84, F. G. T. & S. Pease 86.		L. M. B. M. played well, and won second medal with a score of 83. Self very bad, 86. Out, 6 4 5 4 4 6 5 4 4 = 42; in, 5 4 4 5 7 5 5 4 5 = 44 = 86. Putting badly.	86
,, ,,	,, ,,	F. G. T. **v** J. E. Laidlay & S. M. Fergusson.	3-ball match.	4 6	–	Played good golf until the match was over. Mure Fergusson off his game. Laidlay fair. F. G. T., 39 out.	
,, 8	North Berwick	F. G. T. **v** A. R. Cameron.	24 strokes and 2 up.	4		Third round of *Regimental Handicap.*—Cameron all right going out, but went off his game coming in. Self very fair. 42 out; 39 in. Three bad holes.	81
,, 11	,, ,,	F. G. T. **v** W. Thompson (Professional).	—	7	–	Played very well, and reduced the North Berwick record by 1 stroke. Out, 4 5 4 3 4 4 4 5 3 = 36; in, 4 4 4 4 4 3 5 6 4 = 38. Rather unlucky at the 16th and 17th holes.	74

Golfing Diary

Date	Links	MATCH	Odds	Won	Lost	REMARKS	Score
1896 May 12	Muirfield	F. G. T. **v** Ben Sayers -	—	7	–	Played very well. Out 38 ; in 42 = 80. Record for extended course. Sayers very much demoralised. Also 1 bye.	80
,, 13	North Berwick	F. G. T. **v** A. G. Wauchope (Junior).	18 strokes and 1 up.	2	–	Final *Regimental Handicap Tournament.* — Played very steadily, and putted well. Round in, 80 ; might, with a little care, have been some strokes better. Wauchope putted badly, otherwise he must have won.	80
,, 16	Sandwich	F. G. T. **v** H. S. Colt -	—	6	–	Played very well. Out in 38 ; in in 38. Tees very long, as for championship. 5 3 5 5 4 3 5 4 4 = 38. 4 3 6 4 4 5 4 4 4 = 38. F. G. T. lofted 3 stimies. H. S. C. rather off his game.	76
,, ,,	,,	F. G. T. **v** H. S. Colt & J. L. Low.	3-ball match.	Halved & 4		H. S. C. much better. J. L. L. very tired and off his game. F. G. T. not so good as the previous round, and playing rather slackly. 38 and 44 = 82.	82
,, 17	,,	F. G. T. **v** S. Mure Fergusson.	—	5	–	Played a very strong game, with the exception of two holes. Mure good, with the exception of three or four tee shots. F. G. T. putting very well. Out, 4 5 3 7 3 3 5 3 5 = 38 ; in, 5 4 4 7 4 5 4 5 4 = 42. S. Mure F., 82.	80
,, ,,	,,	F. G. T. & S. Mure Fergusson **v** J. Ball & C. Hutchings.	—	4	–	Both Mure and I in good form, and a little heavy for the other two. F. G. T. and S. M. F., out, 5 4 4 5 4 4 6 3 4 = 39 ; in, 4 4 4 6 5 5 5 3 4 = 40. Ball and Hutchings very good up to the 12th hole. S. M. F. driving very well.	79
,, 18	,,	F. G. T. **v** L. M. Balfour Melville.	*St. George's Cup Competition.*	–	–	Played very well in the first round, but with bad luck ; round in, 84. L. M. B. M. played first 4 holes badly ; after that he played very well, and finished in 87. In the second round we both played very good golf. F. G. T. eventually won the cup with 84 and 81 = 165, by 2 strokes. L. M. B. M. finished in 87 and 85. There was a very fine field ; all those entered for Amateur Championship.	84 ⎫ 81 ⎭ 165
,, 19	,,	F. G. T. **v** C. G. Broadwood.	1st round *Amateur Championship.*	7	–	Played a good game. Out in 38, and 4 5 4 first 3 holes in. My opponent was evidently off his game. Very heavy rain during last part of round.	—
,, ,,	,,	F. G. T. & L. M. B. Melville **v** J. E. Laidlay & S. Mure Fergusson.	—	3	–	L. M. B. M. and I played a very steady game all through. The other two were driving very badly, but recovering very well. L. M. B. M. and F. G. T., out 39 ; in 41 = 80.	80

F. G. Tait

Date	Links	Match	Odds	Won	Lost	Remarks	Score
1896 May20	Sandwich	F. G. T. **v** C. Hutchings.	2nd round *Amateur Championship.*	4	–	A very fine match going out, but coming in C. H. went rather off his game against the wind. A beastly day, very wet and windy.	—
,, ,,	,,	F. G. T. **v** J. E. Laidlay	3rd round *Amateur Championship.*	3	–	The wind increased to a gale, with very cold rain. Golf very difficult to play. A very good match up to the 16th hole. J. E. L. not driving very well.	—
,, 21	,,	F. G. T. **v** J. Ball - -	4th round *Amateur Championship.*	5	–	Played a very strong game, and rather demoralised the ex-champion. Out, 4 4 4 4 3 3 6 3 5=36; in, 5 4 5 6 5. F. G. T. putting very well. Won the match by 5 up and 4 to play. John Ball very steady. Fairly strong wind.	—
,, ,,	,,	F. G. T. **v** H. G. Hutchinson.	5th round *Amateur Championship.*	3	–	Started badly, and was 2 down at the turn, but after that played a grand game. Holed a fine putt to win match at 16th hole. H. G. H. putted very well.	—
,, 22	,,	F. G. T. **v** H. H. Hilton	Final *Amateur Championship.* 36 holes.	8	–	Played a particularly strong game. Out, 4 4 4 5 4 2 4 4 5 =36; in, 4 3 4 5 6 5 5 4 5 =41. With the exception of a few short putts, the score could not have been improved upon. F. G. T 6 up at the end of first round. Hilton played a very plucky uphill game; 83 first round. Second round F. G. T. very steady, except 1st hole. 6 4 4 5 4 3 5 4 4 =39; in, 4 4. Hilton again very plucky, and holed some good putts.	77
,, 23	Rye	F. G. T. **v** H. S. Colt & J. O. Fairlie (best of balls).	—	–	6	H. S. C. and J. O. F. too strong for the golfed-out Champion, to whom they showed no mercy. H. S. C. and J. O. F. both played a good game, and did some very fine holes.	—
,, 25	,,	F. G. T. **v** H. S. Colt -	—	–	–	Played with Colt for the *Handicap Sweepstake.* Both played indifferently. Self, 81 and 6=87. H. S. C. made no return. Greens awfully dry and very difficult.	81
,, ,,	,,	F. G. T. & J. S. Scott **v** H. S. Colt & J. O. Fairlie.	—	3	–	F. G. T. and J. S. S. rather heavy for the other two. All played indifferently, especially on the putting greens.	—
,, 26	,,	F. G. T. **v** H. Vardon -	36-hole match.	–	4	Rather too much golf, and a little stale after the Amateur Championship, and consequently not nearly up to the last week's form. Vardon very steady. F. G. T. rather unlucky off the tee; 4 niblick shots in middle of course. Also putted badly.	—

Golfing Diary

Date	Links	MATCH	Odds	Won	Lost	REMARKS	Score
1896 June 6	Muirfield	F. G. T. **v** S. Mure Fergusson.	—	6	–	Mure completely off his driving. F. G. T. putted badly on the way out, and took 44. Played well in, 36=80.	80
,, ,,	,,	,, ,, ,,	—	0	2	Mure much better. Self a good deal worse, putting badly. Mure, 82. F. G. T., 84.	84
,, 8	,,	,, ,, ,,	—	3	0	Played well, with the exception of one or two holes. Mure driving very badly, but putting and approaching very well.	—
,, ,,	,,	,, ,, ,,	—	5	0	Played well; one bad hole. Mure still completely off his driving.	80
,, ,,	Archerfield	F. G. T. **v** G. H. Law & C. Law.	Best of balls.	2	0	Played very well, and established a record for the links. G. H. L. in great form, especially putting.	68
,, 9	Muirfield	F. G. T. **v** A. Kirkcaldy.	—		3	Played well, with the exception of 7th, 8th, and 9th holes. Andrew K. in great form, except 18th hole 8!! A. K., 80.	—
,, ,,	,,	F. G. T. **v** A. Herd	-	–	4	Played badly. Herd in good form, 79; A. H. driving very straight, F. G. T. putting very badly.	—
,, 10	,,	F. G. T. **v** Kinnell	- *Open Championship.*	–	–	F. G. T. got a very bad start; drove over the wall at the 1st hole and took 5. Played well after that, except 5th, 7th, 8th, and 9th holes. Rather unlucky in putting. Kinnell very good at beginning, but bad after.	83
,, ,,	,,	,, ,, ,,	,,	–	–	Played a very strong game all through, and rather unlucky in my putts. Kinnell very bad. Taylor led me by 3 strokes on first two rounds (77 and 78).	75
,, 11	,,	F. G. T. **v** C. Hutchings	,,	–	–	Played rather badly and with bad luck. A very hot day. Started at an inconvenient hour, 12.30. 7th, 8th, and 9th holes **very** bad. Putting badly. C. H. very fair.	84
,, ,,	,,	,, ,, ,,	,,	–	–	Started, knowing that 74 was required, and would have done it but for bad luck at 16th hole. Played a splendid game from start to finish, but the long putts would not go in. Taylor and Vardon tie for first, 316. W. Fernie and self third, 319.	77
,, 19	Mortonhall	F. G. T. **v** T. M. Berkeley & C. MacRae.	Best of balls & ½.	1	–	Played fairly well, with exception of two or three holes. T. M. B. in great form. MacRae rather off his game.	74
,, 25	,,	F. G. T. **v** D. MacLaren	—	–	–	Summer Meeting.—F. G T., 72 and 4=76, 4th. Beat record by 3 strokes. No scratch prize.	72
,, ,,	,,	F. G. T. & D. MacLaren **v** W. Taylor and MacGregor.	12 hole match.	3	–	F. G. T. and MacL. in great form. Taylor and MacGregor fair.	—
July 1	Barnton	F. G. T. **v** W. T. Armour & T. T. Gray.	Best of balls.	Halved		F. G. T. good. Beat record of green by 2 strokes.	76

281

F. G. Tait

Date	Links	Match	Odds	Won	Lost	Remarks	Score
1896 July 1	Barnton	F. G. T. **v**. W. T. Armour & T. T. Gray.	Best of balls.	–	3	Armour in great form; round in, 76. Putting and approaching beautifully. F. G. T. bad.	—
,, 8	,,	,, ,, ,,	,,	–	3	All played fairly well. Greens very heavy from the recent heavy rain.	—
,, 10	,,	,, ,, ,,	,,	Halved		Two excellent matches. Armour holed a very good putt to save first match.	—
,, ,,	,,	,, ,, ,,	,,	Halved		F. G. T. missed a yard putt to win the second match! Gray fair.	—
,, 13	,,	F. G. T. **v** A. G. Tait & W. T. Armour.	Best of balls.	2	–	A. G. T. rather out of practice, but played fairly well, especially driving. Armour and F. G. T. fair.	—
,, 15	,,	F. G. T. **v** T. T. Gray & W. T. Armour.	,,	–	1	Gray and Armour both good. Gray holed two approaches. F. G. T. missed a 6 foot putt to half match.	—
,, ,,	,,	F. G. T. & W. T. Armour **v** T. T. Gray & Lees (Barnton professional.)	—	5	–	F. G. T. and W. T. A. in great form; round in 76. Gray and Lees poor.	76
Aug. 4	Carnoustie	F. G. T. **v** W. MacFarlan & Bob Simpson.	3-ball match.	3 1	–	All played badly. Greens in a horrible condition; not worth playing on.	—
,, 5	,,	,, ,, ,,	,,	3 1	–		—
,, 7	St. Andrews	F. G. T. **v** L. M. B. Melville.	—	4	–	F. G. T. in great form; round in 77. Out, 4 5 5 4 4 7 3 3 4 =39; in, 4 3 4 4 5 4 5 5 4=38. L. M. B. M., 81.	77 Left hand course
,, 13	Carnoustie	F. G. T. **v** W. MacFarlan & Bob Simpson.	3-ball match.	4 4	–	All in good form. F. G. T., out 36. Good in, with exception of one hole.	—
,, 17	,,	F. G. T. & W. MacFarlan **v** Bob Simpson & W. Smith.	—	5	–	W. MacF. and I in great form. Fairly outclassed the professionals. Bob Simpson rather off his game.	—
,, 19	,,	,, ,, ,,	—	2	–	A very fine match. Finished at the last hole by a fine putt of W. MacF.'s. All in good form.	—
,, ,,	,,	,, ,, ,,	—	0	5	The amateurs received a horrible dressing. W. MacF. not quite up to his usual game. The professionals played well.	—
,, 29	St. Andrews	F. G. T. **v** A. G. Tait & — Firebrace.	Best of balls.	–	6	F. G. T. very bad; suffering from a fall from a bicycle. A. G. T. very fair. Firebrace indifferent.	—
Sept. 9	Ballater	F. G. T. **v** Capt. Cumming Bruce.	1 stroke a hole.	Halved		A very bad course; long grass, bad putting greens, and short holes. First—and probably the last—round at Ballater.	—
Nov. 28	Ganton	F. G. T. **v** J. Harvey -	½	2	–	Played very badly for first 9 holes; after that good. 32 for last 9 holes; equals Vardon's record. J. H. very fair.	32
,, ,,	,,	F. G. T. & T. M. Berkeley **v** J. Harvey & Maxwell Stuart.	—	Halved		Self and partner 4 up at one time, but only succeeded in getting a hard half. Other two good after first 6 holes.	—
Dec. 10	Redcar	F. G. T. **v** J. W. Taylor	—	–	1	Taylor played very well; 76. Self rather at sea on a new course, and putted badly. F. G. T., 77.	—

Golfing Diary

Date	Links	MATCH	Odds	Won	Lost	REMARKS	Score
1896 Dec. 11	Redcar	F. G. T. & Hon. G. Lascelles **v** Capt. Pennyman & C. D. Mackenzie.	⅓	Halved		My partner in great form with all his clubs. Self fair. Mackenzie and Pennyman good at the end.	—
,, ,,	,,	F. G. T. & Hon. G. Lascelles **v** Capt. Pennyman & Bob Hardie.	4 strokes.	7	–	My partner played magnificently, and together we went round in 82. Hardie very much off his game.	—
,,	Beverley	F. G. T. **v** J. Harvey	½	–	–		—
,,	,,	*Black Watch G.C.* **v** *Beverley G.C.* F. G. Tait **v** W. MacFarlan **v** J. Harvey **v** A. G. Wauchope **v**		11 6 4 4 — 25	0	————	
,,	Ganton	F. G. T. **v** A. M. Chance	⅓	4	–	————	—
,,	,,	Same Match - - -	⅓	5	–	————	—
1897 Jan. 16	Muirfield	F. G. T. **v** A. R. Paterson.	4 strokes	5	–	Both played very indifferent golf.	—
,, ,,	,,	Same Match - - -	,, ,,	Halved		Both slightly better.	—
Feb. 6	,,	F. G. T. **v** C. E. S. Chambers & D. Lyell.	Best of balls.	–	4	C. E. S. C. and D. Lyell very good. D. L. four threes going out!! Self, good out, bad in.	—
,, ,,	,,	Same Match - - -	,, ,,	–	4	Best of balls very good. F. G. T. indifferent.	—
,, 8	St. Andrews	F. G. T. **v** H. S. C. Everard, R.A. Hall, & T. Morris.	Best of balls.	5	0	Played well. The 3 balls very bad. Links in disgraceful order. Putting greens awful.	79
,, 9	,, ,,	F. G. T. **v** W. T. Armour & G. H. Law.	,, ,,	4	–	Played well. Armour and Law rather off their game.	—
,, ,,	St. Andrews New Course	Same Match - - -	,, ,,	3	–	F. G. T. very fair. Opponents rather better.	—
,, 10	St. Andrews Old Links	F. G. T. **v** H. S C. Everard & J. Oswald	,, ,,	4	–	F. G. T. good. Everard and Oswald only fair.	79
,, ,,	,, ,,	Same Match - - -	Best of balls.	1	–	F. G. T. not so good. Opponents much better. J. Oswald almost holed putt at last hole to half match.	83
,, 11	,, ,,	F. G. T. **v** C. E. S. Chambers.	+3 holes	7	–	Played very well, with exception of two holes. Chambers only halved 4 holes, and did not win any.	81
,, ,,	,, ,,	Same Match - - -	,, ,,	–	4	Played slackly, and with rather bad luck. Won 2 byes.	84
,, 12	,, ,,	F. G. T. **v** H. S. C. Everard & J. Oswald.	Best of balls.	5	–	Played well, 80. Won by 5 and 4, and 4 byes. Opponents very bad coming in.	80
,, ,,	,, ,,	Same Match - - -	,, ,,	–	2	H. S. C. E. and J. O. very good, 80. F. G. T. very fair. Missed 3 short putts.	81
,, 13	St. Andrews New Links	F. G. T. **v** Andrew Kirkcaldy.	—	–	2	A splendid match. Andrew in great form, 5 up after first 6 holes. After that, F. G. T. very good. Andrew holed a fine putt at 16th hole and got dormie. A. K., 81.	83

F. G. Tait

Date	Links	MATCH	Odds	Won	Lost	REMARKS	Score
1897 Feb.13	St. Andrews New Links.	Same Match - - -	—	1	–	Another splendid match, both in great form. F. G. T. only halved the 3rd hole by carelessly moving his ball with hand while removing a piece of grass. The hole was played out and won by F. G. T., but he had, of course, to lose a stroke, according to the rules of golf. This unfortunate accident made the difference of 1 hole. A. K., 80, a magnificent score. F. G. T., in, 4 3 5 4 4 4 5 4 4 = 37.	—
,, 15	St. Andrews Old Links	F. G. T. **v** T. Jeffrey -	½	5	–	T. Jeffrey very much out of practice. Self very fair.	—
,, 17	St. Andrews	F. G. T. **v** N. E. Playfair, R. A. Hull & I. Gardiner.	Best of balls.	2	–	F. G. T. good. N. E. P. off his game going out, but good coming in. R. A. H. very fair.	—
,, ,,	,, ,,	F. G. T. **v** N. E. Playfair & A. H. Cochran.	,, ,,	–	5	N. E. P. very good; round in 82. Self and Cochran bad.	—
,, 24	North Berwick.	F. G. T. **v** C. E. S. Chambers.	3 holes up	3	–	} Very strong wind. Both playing badly.	—
,, ,,	,, ,,	Same Match - - -	,, ,,	–	2		—
Mar. 1	St. Andrews	F. G. T. **v** N. E. Playfair.	4 holes up	5	–	⌠ F. G. T. very fair. N. E. P. { occasionally good, but not ⌡ steady.	—
,, ,,	,, ,,	Same Match - - -	,, ,,	4	–		—
,, 2	,, ,,	F. G. T. **v** H. S. C. Everard & A. H. Cochran.	Best of balls.	1	–	⌠ Both good matches. Very cold	day. Wind in afternoon a	regular gale. H. S. C. E.	played very well in both	times. A. H. C. good out. ⌡ F. G. T. good.	85
,, ,,	,, ,,	Same Match - - -	,, ,,	2	–		81
,, 3	,, ,,	F. G. T. **v** R. H. Hull & A. H. Cochran.	Best of balls and 1 up.	Halved		⌠ Hull and Cochran both good	in the morning. F. G. T. 81,	with a 7. Afternoon, F. G. T.	played first 6 holes badly,	after that, well. F. G. T.	last 12 holes 5 3 3 4 4 4 4 5 5	4 4 4. Hull and Cochran not ⌡ so good as morning.	81
,, ,,	,, ,,	Same Match - - -	,, ,,	3	–		—
,, 4	,, ,,	F G. T. & J. E. Cameron **v** N. E. Playfair (with 4 up).	—	2	–	All in good form. N. E. P. playing his long putts very well.	—
,, 5	,, ,,	F. G. T. **v** H. S. C. Everard, N. E. Playfair & A. H. Cochran.	Best of balls.	–	7	F. G. T. very bad. N. E. P. and H. S. C. E. both good, and putting very well. Best of 3 balls, 78.	—
,, ,,	,, ,,	Same Match - - -	,, ,,	–	3	F. G. T. much better. Combination rather too strong. 78 once more. H. S. C. E. and N. E. P. again very good.	—
,, 6	,, ,,	F. G. T. **v** N. E. Playfair & A. H. Cochran.	,, ,,	2	–	A fine match. F. G. T. 1 down and 6 to play. N. E. P. and A. H. C. not quite so good the last two holes. F. G. T. 42 out, 38 home = 80.	80
,, ,,	,, ,,	Same Match - - -	,, ,,	7	–	Won first 7 holes. Out in 39, back in 40. Strong wind north. N. E. P. and A. H. C. indifferent.	79

Golfing Diary

Date	Links	Match	Odds	Won	Lost	Remarks	Score
1897 Mar. 8	St. Andrews	F. G. T. **v** Andrew Kirkcaldy & W. Auchterlonie.	Medal Ground specially turned on for this match.	– Halved	1	All in good form. Andrew K. 81. F. G. T. good, with exception of a few long putts. All driving well. Holes specially lengthened for match, rather longer than medal course.	—
,, ,,	,, ,,	Same Match - - -	,, ,,	Halved	Halved	F. G. T. very good out, but very bad in. Out, 3 4 4 4 4 4 3 3 5 = 34. In, 4 4 6 5 6 5 4 6 6 = 46. F. G. T. had putts to hole every hole out in 3, except long hole. Short putt at 9th hole in and out.	80
,, 9	Elie	F. G. T. **v** J. E. Laidlay	—	–	3	First time on Elie Links. Played very badly in the morning, having left St. Andrews without breakfast.	—
,, ,,	,,	Same Match - - -	—	–	2	Laidlay fair in morning. Afternoon both very bad. Links in bad order.	
,, 20	Ganton	F. G. T. **v** A. G. Wauchope (Junior).	12 strokes and 1 up.	3	–	F. G. T. in form; 35 out, 33 in = 68. Course rather short, about 3 strokes easier than usual. A. G. W. very fair.	68
,, ,,	,,	F. G. T. **v** A. G. Wauchope & C. G. Broadwood.	,, ,,	Halved Halved		All three rather indifferent -	—
,, 30	York	F. G. T. **v** C. MacRae.	½	–	2	C. MacRae in great form. F. G. T. very fair.	—
Apr. 1	Ganton	F. G. T. **v** Major Brougham.	18 strokes	2	–	Played a very fair game both rounds, 74 each time, with 2 bad holes. Major B. very fair.	74
,, ,,	,,	,, ,,	,, ,,	2	–		74
,, 6	,,	F. G. T. **v** W. MacFarlan & C. G. Broadwood.	3-ball match.	Halved 8	–	W. Mac F. in great form. Self very fair. Broadwood most indifferent.	75
,, ,,	,,	F. G. T. & W. MacFarlan **v** H. Vardon & C. G. Broadwood.	—	–	1	A great match. Self and Mac F. 2 up and 3 to play, and lost last 3 holes. F. G. T. missed a very short putt at 17th hole.	—
,, 9	,,	F. G. T. **v** W. MacFarlan & C. G. Broadwood.	3-ball match.	–	4 1	F. G. T. very bad in both matches. W. Mac F. in great form. Vardon very good. Broadwood distinctly good in afternoon.	—
,, ,,	,,	F. G. T. & W. MacFarlan **v** H. Vardon & C. G. Broadwood.	—	–	2		
,, 15	St. Andrews	F. G. T. **v** A. H. Cochran.	4 strokes	3	–	Very windy and greens very keen. Very difficult golf.	—
,, ,,	,, ,,	F. G. T. **v** A. H. Cochran & N. E. Playfair.	Best of balls.	2	–		—
,, 16	Muirfield	F.G.T. **v** R. T. Boothby	—	–	1	R. T. B. very fair. Self good at first, but got too many up, and then got careless, with the usual result.	—
,, ,,	,,	F. G. T. **v** L. M. Balfour Melville & C. Whigham.	3-ball match.	3 6	–	Played much better. L.M.B.W. very fair. C. W. rather poor on the putting greens.	—
,, 23	,,	F. G. T. **v** J. M. Williamson & D. MacEwen.	36 holes	6 4	–	Played moderately. MacEwen and Williamson fair.	—
,, 24	,,	F. G. T. **v** W. A. Henderson & R. J. Bryce.	Best of balls.	Halved	–	Played badly. The two balls also bad.	—
,, ,,	,,	Same Match - - -	,, ,,	4	–	Played well - - - -	—
,, 26	,,	F. G. T. **v** L. M. B. Melville.	—	8	–	Played a strong game both rounds. Leslie off his putting	—
,, ,,	,,	Same Match - - -	—	4	–		—

F. G. Tait

Date	Links	MATCH	Odds	Won	Lost	REMARKS	Score
1897 Apr.27	Muirfield	F. F. T. **v** C. Dalziel -	*Amateur Cham-*	3	–	Played well. Dalziel very good towards the finish.	—
,, 28	,,	F. G. T. **v** W. Greig -	*pionship.*	–	1	Putted very badly. Greig putted very well.	—
,, ,,	,,	F. G. T. **v** H. H. Hilton & J. E. Laidlay.	—	Halved	Halved	Played last three holes very badly. H. H. and J. E. L. indifferent.	—
,, 29	,,	F. G. T. **v** J. Hornby & W. Henderson.	Best of balls.	–	1	Henderson in great form. F. G. T. very fair.	—
,, ,,	,,	F. G. T. **v** J. E. Laidlay & J. Ball.	—	5	–	J. B. played a very fine game, 75. F. G. T. also very good, except 17th hole. J. E. L. rather demoralised.	—
					2		
,, 30	,,	F. G. T. **v** J. Graham -	—	2	–	Both played well. F. G. T. got over bunker at 16th hole in two!!!!!!	—
,, ,,	,,	F. G. T. & J. Graham **v** J. Ball & H. H. Hilton.	4-ball match.	–	2	Ball very good. Other three very fair.	—
May 1	New Luffness	F. G. T. **v** G. H. Law -	*Luffness Medal.*			Played well, but with bad luck; two unplayable balls. Won the medal all right.	78
,, 3	St. Andrews	F. G. T. **v** Capt. W. Burn.	2 holes up	5	–	Out, 5 4 4 4 6 4 4 3 4 = 38; in, 4 4 4 5 4 4 3 6 4 = 38. Full medal round. Played very well.	76
,, ,,	,, ,,	F. G. T. **v** Andrew Kirk-caldy & J. E. Laidlay.	3-ball match.	–	2	Laidlay in great form. A. K. and self very fair.	—
				–	3		
,, 4	,, ,,	F. G. T. **v** N. E. Play-fair.	6 strokes	–	2	N. E. P. two good for F. G. T. with a third.	—
,, ,,	,, ,,	Same Match - - -	,, ,,	Halved		Both played well	—
,, 5	,, ,,	F. G. T. **v** N. E. Play-fair.	*St. Andrews Spring Medal.* Tie for first medal.			5 5 4 5 6 6 5 3 4 = 43; 4 3 5 5 6 5 5 4 4 = 41. Strong cross wind. Played well with exception of three holes.	84
,, ,,	,, ,,	F. G. T. **v** L. M. B. Melville.	,,	,,	,,	6 5 4 7 6 5 5 4 4 = 46; 5 3 5 5 6 4 5 5 4 = 42. F. G. T. putted disgracefully. L. M. B. indifferent.	88
,, 17	Hoylake	F. G. T. **v** C. Hutchings	—	Halved		Both in fair form - - -	—
,, ,,	,,	Same Match - - -	—	7	–	C. H. off his game, and putting very badly. F. G. T. very fair.	—
,, ,,	,,	F. G. T. **v** J. E. Laidlay	14-hole match.	2	–	Both played very steadily -	—
,, 18	,,	F. G. T. **v** W. Auchter-lonie.	—	–	2	⎫ Two good matches. F. G. T. putting badly. W. Auchter-lonie played a fine, steady game.	—
,, ,,	,,	Same Match - - -	—	–	2	⎬	—
,, 19	,,	F. G. T. **v** J. Rowe -	*Open Championship*			5 4 5 2 4 4 4 5 5; 5 4 5 4 5 4 5 4 5· Played well.	79
,, ,,	,,	,, ,, ,, -	,,	,,	,,	4 5 5 3 5 6 3 5 3; 4 3 4 3 5 5 5 5 6. Played well, but unluckily.	79
,, 20	,,	F. G. T. **v** C. R. Smith	,,	,,	,,	4 5 5 3 5 5 2 6 4; 4 5 3 3 5 5 6 3 7. Played well; putted badly at the 18th hole.	80
,, ,,	,,	,, ,, ,,	,,	,,	,,	4 4 5 3 4 5 4 4 5; 5 3 4 4 5 5 5 5 5· Played well, very unluckily. Finished third.	79
,, 21	,,	F. G. T. **v** J. Ball -	—	–	2	Both played well. J. B. holed a mashie shot out of the rushes at 3rd hole in.	—
,, ,,	,,	Same Match - - -	—	Halved		Another good match. J. B. 4-up at one time. F. G. T. nearly won the match.	—
Aug.20	St Andrews	F. G. T. **v** Ed. B. H. Blackwell.	—	–	3	Both fine matches. F. G. T. first round missed some easy putts.	80

Golfing Diary

Date	Links	MATCH	Odds	Won	Lost	REMARKS	Score
1897 Aug.20	St. Andrews	Same Match - - -	—	3	–	Ted Blackwell driving enormous balls. F. G. T. 3 up on 36 holes.	78
,, 21	,, ,,	F. G. T. **v** Harold Finch Hatton & E. R. Blackwell.	—	2 4	–	F. G. T. good with exception of a few holes. H. F. H. very fair. E. R. B. rather off his game.	—
,, ,,	,, ,,	F. G. T. **v** Harold Finch Hatton & E. R. Blackwell.	Best of balls.	–	5	F. G. T. moderate. E. R. B. very good. Combination too strong.	82
,, 23	,, ,,	F. G. T. **v** E. R. Blackwell.	—	1	–	A fine match. F.G.T. two down and five to play. E. R. B. out in 37, and round in 81.	83
,, ,,	,, ,,	Same Match - - -	—	4	–	F. G. T. fairly good, but not steady. E. R. B. not so good.	—
,, 24	,,	F. G. T. **v** L. M. B. Melville.	Tie for *May Medal.*			F. G. T. 84. L. M. B. M., 89. Out, 4 7 4 5 5 5 4 3 4 = 41. In, 4 3 4 5 7 5 5 6 4 = 43. Two bad holes.	84
,, ,,	,, ,,	F. G. T. **v** Ed. B. H. Blackwell & L. M. B. Melville.	—	1 4	–	F. G. T. in better form. Ted Blackwell also good. L. M. B. rather off his game.	82
Sep. 24	,, ,,	F. G. T. **v** Surgeon-Major Duncan & — Davidson.	Best of balls and 2 strokes.	5	–	Played well first round for a mouth. Opponents very moderate.	81
,, ,,	,, ,,	F. G. T. **v** H. Janion -	½ and 1 up.	–	2	H. J. played too well going out. F. G. T. bad all through, 92 ! ! ! !	92
,, 25	,, ,,	F. G. T. **v** C. Hutchings	—	2	–	Played well both rounds. Strong wind.	83
,, ,,	,, ,,	,, ,, ,,	—	4	–	C. H. good first round - -	83
,, 27	,, ,,	F. G. T. **v** L. M. B. Melville.	—	6	–	4 4 4 4 5 4 4 3 3 = 35; 5 3 4 5 5 4 4 5 5 = 40. F. G. T. in great form. L. M. B. very fair.	75
,, ,,	,, ,,	Same Match - - -	—		1	4 5 4 4 5 4 5 3 4 = 38; 4 4 4 4 5 4 5 6 4 = 40. L. M. B. in great form; F. G. T. also. L. M. B. M., 78, with a seven for 16th hole !!	78
,, 28	,, ,,	F. G. T. & A. G. T. **v** E. B. H. Blackwell & E. R. Blackwell.	36-hole match.	–	3	All bad first 18 holes. Second 18 holes the brothers Blackwell very good. A. G. T. rather off his game.	—
,, 29	,, ,,	F. G. T. **v** L. M. B. Melville.	*Medal Round.*	–	–	Out, 4 5 5 4 4 5 3 2 4 = 36; in, 3 4 4 5 6 5 6 6 6 = 45. F. G. T. very good for first 15 holes, last 3 holes awful. S. Mure Fergusson first with 80; F. G. T. second, 81.	81
,, ,,	,, ,,	F. G. T. & L. M. B. Melville **v** J. E. Laidlay & S. Mure Fergusson.	—	4	–	L. M. B. M. and F. G. T. in great form. J. E. L. quite off his game.	—
,, 30	,, ,,	F. G. T. & E. R. Blackwell **v** S. Mure Fergusson & Capt. W. Burn.	—	4	–	} A poor match all through; all played slackly.	—
,, ,,	,, ,,	Same Match - - -	—	Halved			
Oct. 5	Ganton	F. G. T. **v** J. Harvey & N. N. Ramsay.	Best of balls and 3 up.	–	1	} Two capital matches. J. H. and N. N. R. in great form.	—
,, ,,	,,	Same Match - - -	,, ,,	–	3		
,, 8	Brough	F. G. T. **v** — Jackson -	—	3	–	} A regimental match; four a side. We won by 14 holes in the singles, and by 10 holes in the foursomes.	—
, ,,	,,	F. G. T. & W. MacFarlan **v** — Jackson & — Harrison.	—	6	–		

287

F. G. Tait

Date	Links	MATCH	Odds	Won	Lost	REMARKS	Score
1897 Sep.12	Ganton	F. G. T. **v** J. Harvey & N. N. Ramsay.	Best of balls and 3 up.	6	—	F. G. T. in great form first round. J. H. and N. N. R. very good after lunch.	—
,, ,,	,,	Same Match - -	,, ,,	—	3		
,, 16	Muirfield	F. G. T. **v** R. H. Johnston.	36 holes 8 strokes.	3	—	Played fairly well. R. H. J. putted very well first round.	—
,, 23	Blairgowrie	F. G. T. **v** N. N. Ramsay	14 strokes	2	—	Beastly wet day. Both rather off it.	—
,, ,,	,,	Same Match - -	,, ,,	5	—	F. G. T. in great form. Established two records; one for the 9 holes, another for the 18. First round, 37=4 4 5 3 4 4 5 4 4=37. Second round, 33 =5 4 3 4 3 4 4 3 3=33. N. N. R. good second round.	70
,, 25	,,	F. G. T. **v** N. N. Ramsay	,, ,,	2	—		
,, ,,	,,	Same Match - -	,, ,,	—	5		
Nov. 4	Barnton	F. G. T. **v** A. M. Ross -	—	1	—	Both played well. A. M. R. very good on the green.	—
,, 16	Elie	F. G. T. **v** J. E. Laidlay	—	Halved		Both in good form. J.E.L. holed a fine putt to half the match.	—
,, ,,	,,	Same Match - -	—	—	4	J. E. L. in great form. F. G. T. good, except putting.	
,, 17	,,	F. G. T. **v** J. E. Laidlay	—	—	4	J. E. L. again played very well. F. G. T. also good, until the putting green was reached.	—
,, ,,	,,	Same Match - -	—	1	—	Both in great form in both rounds. F. G. T., 77. J. E. L., 76.	
,, ,,	,,	,, ,, ,,	—	—	1		
,, 18	,,	F. G. T. **v** J. E. Laidlay	—	Halved		F. G. T. 4 up and 6 to play, and only halved!!! Played the last 4 holes very badly.	—
,, ,,	,,	Same Match - -	—	—	4	J. E. L. in great form again. F. G. T. indifferent.	—
,, ,,	,,	,, ,, ,,	—	5	—	J. E. L. rather tired and quite off his game. F. G. T. fair. Strong wind.	
,, 22	St. Andrews	F. G. T. **v** A. Kirkcaldy	Short match of 6 holes.	2	—	Played well. A. K., 18th hole in 3.	—
,, ,,	,, ,,	F. G. T. **v** E. B. H. Blackwell.	—	—	7	Ted played very well. F. G. T. quite useless.	—
,, 23	,, ,,	F. G. T. **v** C. F. H. Leslie & F. M. Innes.	Best of balls.	—	5	F. G. T. worse than ever. F. M. I. very steady.	—
,, ,,	,, ,,	Same Match - -	10-hole match.	Halved		F. G. T. a little better. Very cold and windy.	
,, 26	,, ,,	F. G. T. **v** E. B. H. Blackwell.	—	2	—	Both in good form. Capital match.	—
,, ,,	St. Andrews New Links	Same Match - -	—	Halved		Another splendid match, both in great form.	—
,, 29	,, ,,	F. G. T. **v** A. Rotherham.	6 strokes	3	—	Both played indifferently	—
,, ,,	,, ,,	Same Match - -	,, ,,	3	—		—
,, 30	,, ,,	F. G. T. & E. B. H. Blackwell **v** A. Kirkcaldy & W. Auchterlonie.	4-ball match, 36 holes.	5	—	Ted in great form; F. G. T. also good. Our best ball in morning, 74. Second round both of us in great form again. Best ball, 69. Ted, 76; self, 79. Ted holed short hole in one. Our best ball was as follows: 5 4 3 4 4 4 1 4 = 33; 3 4 3 5 5 4 4 4 4 = 36 = 69. W. A. very good. A. K. rather unsteady, but brilliant. In the first round the professionals did not win a single hole!!	74

Golfing Diary

Date	Links	MATCH	Odds	Won	Lost	REMARKS	Score
1897 Dec. 3	St. Andrews New Links	F. G. T. v E. B. H. Blackwell.	—	2	–	Ground rather hard on account of frost. Approaching very difficult. Both played well under the circumstances.	—
,, ,,	St. Andrews Old Links	Same Match - - -	—	5	–		
,, 4	Muirfield	F. G. T. v R. H. Johnston & A. R. Paterson.	Best of balls, 36-hole match.	–	5	F. G. T. played well first round, but not well enough second round. R. H. J. and A. R. P. both good, especially R. H. J., second round.	—
,, 10	New Luffness	F. G. T. & J. Kerr v W. G. Bloxsom & B. Sayers.	36-hole match.	10	–	F. G. T. and J. K. in great form, especially on the putting green. Opposition demoralized slightly. F. G. T. and J. K., 82 and 79.	—
,, 18	Muirfield	F. G. T. & J. H. Aitken v L. M. B. Melville & R. H. Johnston.	—	3	–	Partner and self in great form in both rounds. L. M. B. M. good, with exception of a few short putts. R. H. J. good in morning, but rather off in afternoon.	—
,, ,,	,,	Same Match - - -	—	4	–		
,, 20	St. Andrews	F. G. T. v H. Ferrier Kerr, with a ⅓.	9-hole match.	4	–	H. F. K. driving well, but rather uncertain on the green and through the green. F. G. T. in good form, 40 and 42.	82
,, ,,	,, ,,	Same Match - - -	—	6	–		82
,, 21	,, ,,	F. G. T. v G. H. Law & H. Ferrier Kerr.	Best of balls.	3	–	G. H. L. only moderate. H. F. K. fair in the morning, but badly off in the afternoon. F. G. T. very fair both rounds.	82
,, ,,	St. Andrews New Links	Same Match - - -	,, ,,	9	–		82
,, 22	St. Andrews	F. G. T. v E. B. H. Blackwell.	—	Halved		Ground very hard with frost. Ted played well both rounds, especially in the first. F. G. T. a little off in the afternoon. Ted, 80 in morning. F. G. T., 12th hole in 2!!; Ted, 3!!!!	82
,, ,,	,, ,,	Same Match - - -	—	-	5		
,, 23	,, ,,	F. G. T. v E. B. H. Blackwell & E. R. H. Blackwell.	3-ball match.	4 / 7	–	Considering the hard ground all played well. E. R. H. B. rather off at beginning, but quite good during the second round. Ted not so good as the day before.	80
,, ,,	,, ,,	,, ,, ,,	,, ,,	4 / 3	–		
1898 Jan. 8	Ascot	F. G. T. v C. Hamilton	8 strokes	5	–	F. G. T. played well both rounds, although suffering from a stiff knee. C. H. moderate.	77 / 79
,, ,,	,,	Same Match - - -	,, ,,	4	–		
,, 9	New Zealand Byfleet	F. G. T. v C. A. W. Cameron.	6 strokes	4	–	Played well both rounds, with exception of a few short putts. My first visit to N.Z. C. A. W. C. very fair.	78
,, ,,	,, ,,	Same Match - - -	6 strokes and 1 hole up.	4	–		75
,, 15	Woking	F. G. T. v W. Carr -	36-hole match, 8 strokes.	7	–	F. G. T. played well first round; rather indifferently second round. W. Carr not in form.	—
,, 16	,,	F. G. T. v F. E. Faithful	4 strokes	4	–	F. E. F. driving badly. F. G. T. moderate. Very foggy.	—
,, ,,	,,	F. G. T. & C. A. W. Cameron v Hon. A. H. Grosvenor & F. E. Faithful.	—	8	–	F. G. T. and C. A. W. C. in great form. Opponents demoralised.	
1898 Jan. 29	Byfleet	F. G. T. v S. Mure Fergusson.	36-hole match.	5	–	First round, neither played very well. Second round, F. G. T. in great form; round in 75. Mure Ferguson not driving well.	75

F. G. Tait

Date	Links	Match	Odds	Won	Lost	Remarks	Score
1898 Jan. 30	Byfleet	F. G. T. with 1 up **v** C. A. W. Cameron & W. D. Bovill.	Best of balls.	6	–	F. G. T. very steady. Other two very bad.	—
,, ,,	,,	F. G. T. & C. A. W. Cameron **v** W. D. Bovill & A. H. Trevor	4 strokes	3	–	C. A. W. C. driving very well. F. G. T. moderate. Bovill very fair. A. H. T. rather wild.	—
Feb. 5	Wimbledon	F. G. T. **v** N. R. Foster	—	3	–	Very cold day. Both played fairly well.	—
,, 9	Woking	F. G. T. & Capt. G. Verner **v** Capt. Pennyman & Capt. F. J. Carruthers.	⅓	1	–	A capital match all through, and won by a very lucky putt on last green. G. V. in great form. Pennyman putted extremely well. F. G. T. fair.	—
,, 13	,,	F. G. T. **v** W. M. Corrie	⅓	5	–	} Played well both rounds. W. M. C. not in his best form.	76
,, ,,	,,	Same Match - -	,,	4	–		
,, 19	Richmond (Sudbrook Park).	F. G. T. **v** J. Gairdner & D. Kinloch.	3-ball match.	4 5	–	} F. G. T. in poor form both rounds. Gairdner good second round. D. K. good second round.	79
,, ,,	,, ,,	,, ,, ,,	,, ,,	– Halved	3		
,, 20	Byfleet	F. G. T. **v** J. Gairdner -	—	4	–	} J. G. rather off his driving all day, but his approaching and putting was good. F. G. T. in excellent form.	—
,, ,,	,,	Same Match - - -	—	4	–		
,, ,,	,,	Same Match (11 holes) -	—	2	–		
,, 25	Woking	F. G. T. & Capt. F. J. Carruthers **v** Capt. Pennyman & Major J. Reid.	¼	–	2	Carruthers a little off his game. Pennyman driving badly but putting very well. F. G. T. and Reid steady.	—
,, 27	Byfleet	F. G. T. **v** R. Graham Murray & F. E. Baddeley.	Best of balls and ⅓.	–	4	} R. G. M. and F. E. B. good in the morning, but not so good after lunch. F. G. T. very fair all through.	
,, ,,	,,	Same Match - - -	,, ,,	4	–		
Mar. 4	Woking	F. G. T. **v** E. M. Young	12 strokes	5	–	F. G. T. putting very well. E. M. Y. rather unsteady, but driving well.	—
,, 5	Wimbledon	F. G. T. **v** F. E. Faithful.	4 strokes	Halved		F. G. T. very fair, with exception of last four holes. F. E. F. in good form.	—
,, ,,	,,	F. G. T. & F. E. Faithful **v** J. H. Taylor & C. A. W. Cameron.	—	–	7	J. H. T. and C. A. W. C. in great form. F. E. F. quite off his game. F. G. T. moderate.	—
,, ,,	,,	Same Match - - -	—	–	2	F. E. F. rather better. F. G. T. rather worse. C. A. W. C. putting in great style. Taylor very straight and well.	
,, 6	Woking	F. G. T. **v** F. E. Faithful.	4 strokes	5	–	F. G. T. in great form; 76, with two *sevens*. F. E. F. very fair.	76
,, ,,	,,	F. G. T. & F. E. Faithful **v** E. R. H. Blackwell & C. A. W. Cameron.	—	–	3	E. R. H. B. and C. A. W. C. very steady. F. E. F. simply awful. F. G. T. good under the circumstances.	
,, 12	,,	F. G. T. **v** F. T. Welman & W. Carr.	Best of balls.	2	–	{ W. Carr and F. T. Welman both fair in the first round, but very indifferent second round. F. G. T. good all through.	78 76
,, ,,	,,	Same Match - - -	,, ,,	7	–		
,, 19	,,	F. G. T. **v** J. S. Paton -	4 strokes	5	–	Strong wind. F. G. T. in great form, 75 (record of Woking). J. S. P. very fair.	75

Golfing Diary

Date	Links	Match	Odds	Won	Lost	Remarks	Score
1898 Mar.19	Woking	F. G. T. v W. A. Henderson.	—	6	–	Woking v Oxford University, 9 a side.—F. G. T. in great form. W. A. H. a little off. Woking won all the matches except two halved.	—
,, 25	Duddingston	F. G. T. v L. M. Balfour Melville.	—	1	–	Both played well considering the awful day (snow, sleet, and wind).	—
,, 26	,,	Same Match - - -	—	–	3	Same beastly weather. L. M. B. M. in good form. F. G. T. very fair.	—
,, ,,	,,	F. G. T. & L. M. B. Melville v W. Auchterlonie & B. Sayers.	—	–	3	F. G. T. and L. M. B. M. started badly, and were 4 down after 6 holes, but after that both played well. W. A. and B. S. both good. Awful day; snow, sleet, and a gale blowing.	—
,, 31	Byfleet	F. G. T. v F. E. Baddeley & — Woodroffe.	Best of balls and ⅓.	Halved		Woodroffe in great form, especially putting. F. E. B. very fair. F. G. T. steady.	—
Apr. 1	Woking	F. G. T. v Capt. G. Verner.	1 stroke a hole.	4	–	Verner driving very well. F. G. T. very fair.	—
,, ,,	,,	F. G. T. & Capt. G. Verner v Capt. W. Sellar.	⅓	–	4	W. S. in good form. Verner rather off his game. F. G. T. moderate.	—
,, 8	Sandwich	F. G. T. v J. Oswald & E. Lehman.	Best of balls.	4	–	4 4 4 7 3 3 3 3 6 = 37; 4 5 5 5 6 5 3 4 4 = 41. Strong wind. J. O. very fair.	78
,, ,,	,,	F. G. T. v A. D. Blyth -	—	–	1	Both in good form. F. G. T. missed some short putts.	—
,, ,,	,,	Same Match - - -	11-hole match.	3	–	F. G. T. better. A. D. B. not so good.	—
,, 9	,,	F. G. T. & S. S. Schultz & T. R. Mills.	*Handicap round by strokes.*	–	–	Very strong wind. S. S. S. rather off his game. T. R. M. very steady. F. G. T. fair.	90
,, ,,	,,	F. G. T. v S. S. Schultz & T. R. Mills.	Best of balls.	Halved		S. S. S. in great form; out in 36. T. R. M. holed a very fine putt on the last green to half match. F. G. T. good.	—
,, 10	,,	F. G. T. getting 1 hole and 1 bisque v W. D. Bovill, E. Lehman & J. Oswald.	36-hole match.	–	5	F. G. T. rather tired after 36-hole match with A. D. B., W. D. B. and J. O. in great form.	—
,, ,,	,,	F. G. T. v A. D. Blyth -	—	1	–	Both played very well, especially in the first round. Very strong wind made putting very difficult.	—
,, 11	,,	F. G. T. v F. A. Booth -	36-hole match.	6	–	F. G. T. 5 up after first round (81). F. A. B. very good second round up till 10th hole. F. G. T. very steady both rounds.	81
,, 12	,,	F. G. T. v T. R. Mills & S. S. Schultz.	Best of balls.	6	–	Very strong cold wind. F. G. T. in great form. T. R. M. and S. S. S. both rather off.	—
,, ,,	,,	Same Match - - -	,, ,,	Halved		A good match all through; all played well.	80
,, ,,	,,	F. G. T. with 1 up and 1 bisque v J. Oswald, Murray Smith, & W. D. Bovill.	,, ,,	–	1	The best ball very good. F. G. T. very fair, rather unlucky on the putting green.	81
,, 13	,,	F. G. T. v T. R. Mills -	4 strokes	5	–	T. R. M. quite off his game. F. G. T. in great form.	78
,, ,,	,,	F. G. T. v S. S. Schultz	,, ,,	–	3	F. G. T. not so good. S. S. S. in great form.	—

T 2

F. G. Tait

Date	Links	MATCH	Odds	Won	Lost	REMARKS	Score
1898 Apr.14	Sandwich	F. G. T. **v** S. S. Schultz & W. M. Grimshaw.	1 hole up and best of balls.	1	–	F. G. T. 3 down at the turn, and home in 39. S. S. S. putting very well.	—
,, ,,	,,	Same Match - - -	,, ,,	–	2	S. S. S. again in great form. F. G. T. good. Home in 39.	79
,, ,,	,,	F. G. T. & J. Robertson Walker **v** S. S. Schultz & C. H. P. Carter.	15-hole match.	5	–	F. G. T. and J. R. W. in great form out; in, 38. C. H. P. C. quite out of form.	—
,, 15	,,	F. G. T. **v** S. S. Schultz & T. R. Mills.	Best of balls.	–	5	T. R. M. very fine out; S. S. S. very good in. Best ball, 74!!! F. G. T. very good bar 4th hole.	—
,, ,,	,,	Same Match - - -	,, ,,	–	2	S. S. S. in irresistible form, 76. T. R. M. also good. F. G. T. very good except 3 holes. Best ball, 75.	78
,, 16	,,	F. G. T. & C. H. P. Carter **v** T. R. Mills & S. S. Schultz.	4-ball match.	3	–	F. G. T. and C. H. P. C. in great form, and rather strong for T. R. M. and S. S. S.	—
,, ,,	,,	Same Match - - -	—	2	–	Best ball of C. H. P. C. and F. G. T. (74). F. G. T., 75, record of Sandwich; 35 and 40.	75
,, 17	,,	F. G. T. **v** S. S. Schultz	4 strokes	2	–	⎧S. S. S. not putting up to form. F. G. T. good both rounds. The last round of 77 ought to have been a 72 had the putting been even ordinary. Greens rather fiery.	79
,, ,,	,,	Same Match - - -	,, ,,	4	–	⎩	77
,, 22	Woking	F. G. T. **v** Hon. H. H. Finch Hatton.	3 strokes	7	–	H. Finch Hatton quite off his game. F. G. T. in good form. Two short holes in two each.	—
,, 23	Byfleet	F. G. T. **v** S. S. Schultz & F. T. Welman.	Best of balls.	8	–	36 holes.—F. G. T. very steady, other two not in form.	—
,, 30	St. Andrews	F. G. T. **v** Hon. S. Finch Hatton.	2 strokes	7	–	⎧S. Finch Hatton quite off his game. F. G. T. indifferent.	—
,, ,,	,, ,,	Same Match - - -	,, ,,	3	–	⎩	—
May 2	,, ,,	F. G. T. **v** S. Mure Fergusson.	—	–	2	⎧F. G. T. putted very badly in the morning. Both good in the afternoon. S. M. F. made some wonderful recoveries.	80
,, ,,	,, ,,	Same Match - - -	—	1	–	⎩	—
,, 4	,, ,,	F. G. T. **v** Hon. H. H. Finch Hatton.	—	Halved		*Medal Round.*—F. G. T. putted abominably. H. H. F. H. in great form.	86
,, ,,	,, ,,	F. G. T. & Hon. H. H. Finch Hatton **v** A. F. Macfie & C. Hutchings.	—	Halved		3 up and 3 to play and only halved the match! H. H. F. H. in great form until the last 3 holes.	—
,, 7	Wimbledon	F. G. T. **v** Lord E. Hamilton & F. E. Faithful.	Best of balls.	–	10	F. G. T. dead off. Opponents very steady, especially before lunch. 36-hole match.	—
,, 8	Byfleet	F. G. T. **v** F. E. Faithful.	4 strokes	7	–	F. G. T. once more in form. F. E. F. quite off.	—
,, ,,	,,	F. G. T. & F. E. F. **v** Harold Finch Hatton & W. Carr.	4-ball match, best of two against best of two.	4	–	F. G. T. and F. E. F. rather strong for other two.	—
,, ,,	,,	Same Match (10 holes) -	—	3	–	Same thing again. F. G. T. and F. E. F. rather strong.	—
,, 14	Woking	F. G. T. & A. T. Lawrence **v** J. S. Paton & A. F. Burr.	—	5	–	F. G. T. and partner in good form. J. S. P. and A. F. B. indifferent.	—

Golfing Diary

Date	Links	Match	Odds	Won	Lost	Remarks	Score
1898 May 14	Woking	F. G. T. **v** J. S. Paton & A. F. Burr.	4 strokes 9 strokes	4 5	– –	F. G. T. in great form, 74, equals record of Woking. Out, 36; in, 38.	74
,, ,,	,,	F. G. T. with 2 holes **v** J. S. Paton, A. F. Burr, Sir T. Parkyns & A. E. Balfour.	Best of 4 balls, 14-hole match.	5	–	The four balls quite out of form. F. G. T. very fair.	—
,, 15	,,	F. G. T. **v** A. D. Blyth -	—	3		Both in good form. F. G. T. home in 36!! 4 3 4 4 5 6 2 5 3 =36.	
,, 18	,,	F. G. T. **v** J. S. Paton & C. A. Sugden.	Best of balls and 1 hole up.	2	–	Very windy day. F. G. T. in good form, especially in putting. J. S. P. not quite in form. C. A. S. played well.	79
,, 20	Hoylake	F. G. T. **v** E. D. Prothero.	—	3	–	⎱ F. G. T. played badly both rounds. E. D. P. fair.	
,, ,,	,,	Same Match - - -	—	3		⎰	
,, 21	,,	F. G. T. **v** J. Ball, jun. -	36-hole match.	5	–	⎧ F. G. T. in great form both rounds. J. B. very good second round. F. G. T. 5 up first round; all square second. All played well.	—
,, 23	,,	F. G. T. **v** Hon. O. Scott & Hon. D. Scott.	4 strokes	–	3 1	⎨	—
,, ,,	,,	F. G. T. & J. Graham **v** J. Ball & H. H. Hilton.	Best of two against best of two.	5	–	⎩ 4 4 3 2 4 4 2 5 4=32; 4 3 3 3 5 4 5 4 5=36. F. G. T., J. G., and H. H. H. in great form. H. H. and J. B. did not win a single hole!!!! Best ball of F. G. T. and J. G.	68
,, 24	,,	F. G. T. **v** J. Wilson -	—	4	–	First round of *Amateur Championship.*—F. G. T. not putting well. J. W. played very pluckily.	—
,, 25	,,	F. G. T. **v** C. Hutchings	—	1	–	A very fine match; both in great form. C. H. finished magnificently. F. G. T. won at the 19th hole.	—
,, ,,	,,	F. G. T. **v** H. H. Hilton	—	6	–	The Open Champion quite demoralised, and totally incapable of playing any kind of shot. F. G. T. very steady. H. H. H. did not win a single hole!!!	—
,, 26	,,	F. G. T. **v** J. Graham -	—	1	–	Both putted badly. J. G. missed a very short putt to half the match.	—
,, ,,	,,	F. G. T. **v** J. L. Low -	—	1	–	A great struggle. F. G. T., although rather off his game, managed to win the match at the 22nd hole, after a series of great recoveries. J. L. not at his best.	—
,, 27	,,	F. G. T. **v** S. Mure Fergusson.	Final, 36 holes.	7	–	F. G. T. 3 up at half time (putting extraordinarily well). S. M. F. in great form, but unlucky on the green. Second round, F. G. T. in great form. S. M. F. very good up till the 9th hole.	—
,, 29	Sandwich	F. G. T. **v** S Mure Fergusson.	—	–	4	F. G. T. very slack. S. M. F. very fair, and putting well.	—
,, ,,	,,	F. G. T. & S. Mure Fergusson **v** A. D. Blyth & F. E. Faithful.	2 holes up in 11 holes.	3	–	The two finalists much too good for opponents.	—
,, 30	,,	F. G. T. **v** F. E. Faithful & Murray Smith.	Best of balls.	5	–	F. G. T. in great form. Opposition feeble.	—

Amateur Championship. (bracketed across rows May 24–27)

F. G. Tait

Date	Links	MATCH	Odds	Won	Lost	REMARKS	Score
1898 May30	Sandwich	F. G. T. & E. Hambro v S. Mure Fergusson & A. D. Blyth.	—	4	–	F. G. T. and E. H. started badly by losing the first 4 holes, but won 8 out of the next 9!!!!	—
,, ,,	,,	F. G. T. & S. Mure Fergusson v E. Hambro & A. D. Blyth.	4-ball match.	5	–	S. M. F. and F. G. T. in great form. E. H. rather off his game. Best ball.	72
,, 31	,,	F. G. T. v J. Gairdner -	3 strokes	3	–	F. G. T. quite good. J. G. very fair.	—
,, ,,	,,	F. G. T. v J. Gairdner & Martin Smith.	Best of balls.	–	4	The two balls rather good for F. G. T. Only 11 holes played.	—
,, ,,	,,	F. G. T. & S. Mure Fergusson v E. Hambro & A. D. Blyth.	4-ball match.	5	–	F. G. T. and S. M. F. again in great form. E. H. quite off his game. A. D. B. very good.	—
June 1	,,	F. G. T. v S. Mure Fergusson.	*St. George's Challenge Cup Competition.*	–	–	F. G. T. played well, but was very lucky to beat S. M. F., who played very fine golf on a beastly day of wind and rain.	84 79
,, ,,	,,	Same Match - - -	,,	–	–		
,, 4	Byfleet	F. G. T. v C. H. P. Carter.	⅓	–	2	C. H. P. C. fairly on the spot.	—
,, ,,	,,	F. G. T. & A. G. Wauchope v C. H. P. Carter & R. Graham Murray.	4 strokes	–	2	F. G. T. and A. G. W. were set an impossible task, but came out of it fairly well. R. G. M. putting very well.	—
,, 5	,,	F. G. T. v C. H. P. Carter.	4 holes up.	1	–	F. G. T. in great form. C. H. P. C. started badly, but finished well.	—
,, ,,	,,	F. G. T. & A. G. Wauchope v C. H. P. Carter & R. Graham Murray.	2 holes up.	Halved		A great match. A. G. W. a little indisposed.	—
,, ,,	,,	F. G. T. & R. Graham Murray v W. Carr & C. H. P. Carter.	4-ball match.	2	–	F. G. T. and R. G. M. 1 down and 3 to play!!	—
,, 7	Prestwick	F. G. T. v H. H. Finch Hatton.	2 strokes	2	–	Both played fairly well.	—
,, ,,	,,	Same Match - - -	,, ,,	Halved		Both played indifferently.	—
,, ,,	,,	F. G. T. & H. H. Finch Hatton v S. Mure Fergusson & E. Hambro.	—	–	4	F. G. T. played very badly. S. M. F. and E. H. good. H. H. F. H. good, but not supported by F. G. T.	—
,, 8	,,	F. G. T. v J. G. MacFarlan.	*Open Championship.*			Played very well going out, but badly and with bad luck in. Out, 36; in, 45. Seven to the 17th hole!! Missed five short putts!	81
,, ,,	,,	Same Match - - -	,,	,,	,,	Played well - - - -	77
,, 9	,,	F. G. T. v C. Neaves -	,,	,,	,,	Played very well, but rather unlucky in my long putts.	75
,, ,,	,,	Same Match - - -	,,	,,	,,	Came to awful grief in the "Cardinal," but played well and finished fifth. H. Vardon, Park, Hilton, Taylor, Tait, was the order.	82
,, 11	Byfleet	F. G. T. v S. Mure Fergusson & W. S. Fothringham.	3-ball match (6).	1 5	–	S. M. F. good first round, but rather off the second. W. S. F. quite off his usual game.	
,, ,,	,,	,, ,, ,,	3-ball match, 6 strokes.	4 5	–		

Golfing Diary

Date	Links	Match	Odds	Won	Lost	Remarks	Score
1898 June 12	Woking	F. G. T. **v** J. S. Paton & W. Carr.	Best of balls.	–	4	Three very fine matches. J. S. P. and W. C. rather hot for F. G. T.	–
,, ,,	,,	Same Match - - -	,, ,,	–	1		–
,, ,,	,,	,, ,, ,,	,, ,,	1	–		
,, 18	,,	F. G. T. **v** J. L. Ridpath.	2 up and ½.	5	–	J. L. R. rather off his game. F. G. T. very fair.	–
,, ,,	,,	F. G. T. & J. L. Ridpath **v** C. A. W. Cameron & W. Carr.	—	3	–	F. G. T. and J. L. R. three down and seven to play, but won next six holes.	
,, 19	Byfleet	F. G. T. **v** J. L. Ridpath.	1 up and ½.	7	–	J. L. R. quite off his game; F. G. T. playing well.	–
,, ,,	,,	Same Match - - -	2 up and ½.	2	–	J. L. R. much better. F. G. T. in great form; round in 74.	74
,, 24	,,	F. G. T. **v** H. H. Finch Hatton.	2 strokes.	6	–	Played for the *New Zealand Cup*, and came in second, 76 + 4 = 80 ; winning score, 93 − 16 = 77.	76
,, ,,	,,	F. G. T. **v** H. H. Finch Hatton & Rand.	,, ,,	5	2	H. H. F. H. quite off his game both rounds. F. G. T. not good second round.	–
,, ,,	,,	F. G. T. **v** Rand - -	1 stroke in 10 holes.	1	–	Both in good form - - -	–
,, 25	,,	F. G. T. **v** H. H. Finch Hatton.	*New Zealand Annual Meeting.*			F. G. T. in great form; won Medal, *Brookland's Cup*, and Sweepstake. H. H. F. H. not good.	73
,, 25	,,	F. G. T. & H. H. Finch Hatton **v** Major D. Kinloch & Rand.	—	–	1	F. G. T. rather feeble both rounds. Rand in great form. Finch Hatton very fair.	–
,, ,,	,,	F. G. T. & Newton **v** Major D. Kinloch & E. G. Rand.	—	–	1		
,, 26	,,	F. G. T. **v** S. Mure Fergusson & H. H. Finch Hatton.	3-ball match, 2 strokes.	1 / 3	–	S. M. F. and self in good form both rounds. H. H. F. H. good first round, rather off his game the second.	–
,, ,,	,,	,, ,, ,,	,, ,,	– / 5	2 / –		
,, 29	,,	F. G. T. & J. Mellor **v** D. A. Kinloch & Newton.	4-ball match.	3	–	Major Kinloch rather off his game. Mellor indifferent. Self and Newton very fair.	–
,, ,,	,,	Same Match - - -	,, ,,	2	–		
,, ,	,,	F. G. T. **v** Newton -	3 strokes in 7 holes.	1	–	Both very fair - - -	–
July 7	Frinton	F. G. T. **v** Major Lindsay.	½	3	–	F. G. T. rather out of form in all these matches. Major Lindsay sometimes outdrove the champion.	–
,, 13	,,	F. G. T. & Caldwell **v** Major Lindsay & Capt. Stewart.	—	6	–		
,, 15	Woking	F. G. T. **v** J. S. Paton -	4 strokes and 1 up.	3	–	Finished in the dark in 76 -	76
,, 16	,,	F. G. T. **v** J. S. Paton & R. H. Balloch.	Best of balls and 2 up.	–	6		–
,, ,,	,,	F. G. T. & R. H. Balloch **v** J. S. Paton & Hon. A. Lyttelton.	2 holes up.	2	–	Very hot. F. G. T. very slack.	
,, ,,	,,	Same Match - - -	10-hole match, 1 hole up.	2	–		–
,, ,,	,,	F. G. T. **v** R. H. Balloch, F. E. Cuming & J. S. Paton.	Best of balls.	1	–		

F. G. Tait

Date	Links	MATCH	Odds	Won	Lost	REMARKS	Score
1898 July 17	Woking	F. G. T. & R. H. Balloch **v** F. E. Cuming & J. Braid.	36-hole match.	–	7	R. H. B. quite off his usual game. F. E. C. and J. B. distinctly good. F. G. T. very fair.	—
,, ,,	,,	F. G. T. with 1 hole up **v** F. E. Cuming, J. S. Paton & A. E. Balfour.	Best of balls.	2	–	A very close and exciting match; won at last hole.	—
,, 22	Felixstowe	F. G. T. **v** A. E. Kennedy	6 strokes	Halved		Strong wind both days. F. G. T. played one good round, 78. A. E. K. in very fair form. Greens very dry and bumpy.	—
,, 23	,,	Same Match - - -	,, ,,	3	–		—
,, ,,	,,	,, ,, ,,	6 strokes and 1 bisque.	6	–		—
,, 24	,,	F. G. T. **v** A. E. Kennedy & J. Hutchinson Driver.	Best of balls and 3 strokes.	2	–	All fairly bad.	—
,, 29	Old Luffness	F. G. T. **v** L. R. Gray & R. C. Kitto.	—	2	–	Played badly all day.	—
,, ,,	,, ,,	,, ,, ,,	Best of balls.	5 –	1		—
,, ,,	,, ,,	Same Match - - -	,, ,,	2	–		—
,, 30	,, ,,	F. G. T. & W. T. Armour **v** J. Brotherston & H. Cunningham.	—	2	–	*County Cup Competition.*–Won by New Luffness, represented by W. T. Armour and F. G. Tait, and A. M. Ross and T. T. Gray. New L. beat Dirleton Castle, first round; New L. beat Honourable Company, second round; New L. beat Tantallon, final round.	—
,, ,,	,, ,,	F. G. T. & W. T. Armour **v** J. E. Laidlay & A. O. MacKenzie.	—	–	3		—
,, ,,	,, ,,	F. G. T. & W. T. Armour **v** T. M. Hunter & C. L. Dalziel.	—	–	3		—
Aug. 16	Great Bentby	F. G. T. **v** Major Lindsay, R.A.	½	2	–	Both played well. The Major in great driving form.	—
,, 19	Woking	F. G. T. **v** J. S. Paton -	4 strokes and 1 up.	Halved		Both played well, but finished last four holes in the dark.	—
,, 20	,,	,, ,, ,,	,, ,,	5	–	Record of Woking. Out, 4 3 5 3 4 4 3 4 5=35; in, 4 4 4 5 4 5 4 4 4=38.	73
,, ,,	,,	F. G. T. & J. S. Paton **v** J. H. Outhwaite & C. Rowe.	36-hole match.	Halved		A very fine match. C. Rowe in very fine form. All played well.	—
,, 21	,,	F. G. T. **v** J. S. Paton -	—	4	–	F. G. T. with a driver and an iron played Paton with all his clubs. F. G. T. came home in 36!!!!	78
,, ,,	,,	F. G. T. **v** J. S. Paton -	A 10-hole match. 4 strokes.	2	–	J. S. P. not in his best game. F. G. T. very fair.	—
,, ,,	,,	F. G. T. & J. S. Paton **v** J. H. Outhwaite & C. Rowe.	—	–	2	C. Rowe again in great form. Paton quite off his game.	—
,, 26	Byfleet	F. G. T. **v** S. Finch Halton.	2 strokes	Halved		Both played well - - -	—.
,, ,,	,,	Same Match (8 holes) -	—	–	2		—
,, 27	,,	Same Match - - -	2 strokes	2	–	S. F. H. not so good - - -	—
,, ,,	,,	,, ,, ,,	—	3	–		—
,, 28	,,	F. G. T. **v** S. Finch Halton.	—	8	–	S. F. H. quite off his game. F. G. T. very fair.	—
,, ,,	,,	Same Match - - -	—	5	–		—
,, ,,	,,	Same Match (7 holes) -	—	4	–		—
Sep. 22	St. Andrews	F. G. T. **v** R. Whyte & C. A. W. Cameron.	Best of balls.	3	–	All rather out of form - - -	—

Golfing Diary

Date	Links	MATCH	Odds	Won	Lost	REMARKS	Score
1898 Sep.23	St. Andrews	F. G. T. **v** R. T. Boothby.	—	2	–	Both putted badly - - -	—
,, ,,	,, ,,	F. G. T. & R. T. Boothby **v** J. Low & A. F. Macfie.	—	–	2	R. T. B. quite off his game. J. L. and A. F. M. fair.	—
,, 24	,, ,,	F. G. T. **v** W. Greig -	—	–	2	F. G. T. putted very badly. W. Greig in great form.	—
,, ,,	,, ,,	F. G. T. **v** A. G. Tait & C. A. W. Cameron.	Best of balls.	1	–	All played badly - - -	—
,, 26	,, ,,	F. G. T. & A. G. Tait **v** C. Hutchings & J. Graham.	—	5	–	The opposition, although round in 81, were simply smothered. The Brothers Tait made the foursome record of St. Andrews, 74!!! Out, 4 6 4 4 6 4 4 3 3 = 38; in, 3 2 4 5 6 5 4 4 3 = 36 = 74.	74
,, ,,	,, ,,	Same Match - - -	—	2	–	The play in the afternoon was not so good.	—
,, 27	,, ,,	F. G. T. **v** L. M. B. Melville.	—	–	2	F. G. T. not putting well. L. M. B. M. very steady.	—
,, ,,	,, ,,	F. G. T. & J. O. Fairlie **v** L. M. B. Melville & W. J. Mure.	—	3	–	A good match up to the 14th hole.	—
,, 28	,, ,,	F. G. T. **v** Capt. W. Burn.	*Medal Round.*	–		Very wet and windy, putted badly all the way out, and lost at least 6 strokes. Played well in, except 17th hole, 7!!! Out, 42; in, 40. Tied with L. M. B. M. for 2nd.	82
,, ,,	,, ,,	F. G. T. & Capt. W. Burn **v** S. Mure Fergusson & J. E. Laidlay.	—	Halved		F. G. T. and Capt. W. B. dormie two, and only halved!!	
29	,, ,,	F. G. T. **v** L. M. B. Melville.	Tie for *Gold Medal.*	F. G.T.78, L.M.B.M. 83.		F. G. T. in great form, only missed one putt, and holed no long ones. Out, 4 5 4 4 5 4 4 3 4 = 37; 4 3 5 6 5 4 4 6 4 = 41 = 78.	78
,, ,,	,, ,,	F. G. T. & L. M. B. Melville **v** S. Mure Fergusson & J. E. Laidlay.	—	4	–	F. G. T. and L. M. B. M. in great form; round in 77. L. M. B. M. putted very well. Out, 37; in, 40 = 77.	77
,, 30	,, ,,	F. G. T. & L. M. B. Melville **v** S. Mure Fergusson & C. Whigham.	—	2	–	F. G. T. and L. M. B. M. rather slack. S. M. F. not in his best form.	—
Oct. 6	Prestwick	F. G. T. **v** R. H. Balloch & C. Whigham.	½	1 Halved		Played with strange and borrowed clubs, and played very badly. C. Whigham off his putting. R. H. B. very fair.	—
,, 8	New Luffness	,, ,, ,,	*New Luffness Autumn Meeting.*			F. G. T. in great form, with exception of half-a-dozen short putts. Won medal by 7 strokes. G. H. L. not in form, 92.	79
,, 15	Muirfield	F. G.T. **v** L. M. Balfour Melville & R. H. Johnston (2 holes up).	15th hole in 3!!	4	1 –	R. H. J. in good form. L. M. B. M. not quite in form. F. G. T. very fair.	—
,, ,,	,,	Same Match - - -	15th hole in 2!!!!	Halved 4		L. M. B. M. and F. G. T. in great form on a very difficult day; strong wind and rain. R. H. J. not quite so good as in the morning.	—
,, 22	New Luffness	F. G. T. & A. R. Paterson **v** A. G. Tait & R. H. Johnston.	4-ball match.	5		⎧F. G. T. in great form both ⎪ rounds. A very difficult day ⎪ to play, strong wind and ⎨ rain. A. G. T. and A. R. P. ⎪ not in form. R. H. J. good.	76 77
,, ,,	,, ,,	F. G. T. with 1 hole up **v** A. G. Tait, R. H. Johnston & A. R. Paterson.	Best of balls.	Halved		⎪ F. G. T. equalled record first ⎪ round, and holed 11th hole ⎩ in 3!!!!	

297

F. G. Tait

Date	Links	Match	Odds	Won	Lost	Remarks	Score
1898 Nov.12	Barnton	F. G. T. v A. Mac-Donald.	—	5	–	⎫	
,, ,,	,,	F. G. T. with 2 holes up v A. MacDonald & T. T. Gray.	Best of balls.	4	–	⎬ Putted well all day. Mac-donald and Gray very fair.	
,, ,,	,,	F. G. T. with 1 hole up v A. MacDonald & T. T. Gray.	Best of balls, 9-hole match.	2	–	⎭	
,, 14	Muirfield	F. G. T. v J. E. Laidlay	—	5	–	⎱ F. G. T. in good form all day.	81
,, ,,	,,	Same Match - - -	—	4	–	⎰ J. E. L. not putting well.	79
Dec.20	North Berwick	F. G. T. v W. T. Armour & Angus Mac-Donald.	Best of balls.	5	–	F. G. T. in good form. W. T. A. a little off. A. MacD. very fair.	—
1899 Jan. 4	New Luffness	F. G. T. v J. McL. Marshall & A McL. Marshall.	Best of balls.	4	–	⎫ 12th hole in 2!! First round, J. Marshall in good form, especially putting.	—
,, ,,	,, ,,	Same Match - - -	Best of balls and 3 holes up.	Halved			—
,, 20	Barnton	F. G. T. v C. E. S. Chambers.	3 holes up	2	–	Chambers' brother also played. I lost to him by 1, giving ½. Very wet day.	—
Feb.11	New Luffness	F. G. T. v G. H. Law & J. M. Bow.	Best of balls.	3	–	⎰ F. G. T. in great form. G. H. L. and J. M. B. not quite in form. 75 record, after a very bad start for first 6 holes. Out, 5 5 4 6 4 5 3 3 3 = 38 ; in, 4 4 5 3 4 6 3 3 5 = 37.	78 75*
,, ,,	,, ,,	Same Match - - -	,, ,,	4	–		
,, 16	North Ber-wick.	F. G. T. v H. Ferrier Kerr.	2 up and ½.	5	–	⎰ Strongish wind. H. F. K. quite out of form. F. G. T. "bang on it."	—
,, ,,	,, ,,	Same Match - - -	,, ,,	4	–	⎱	
,, 17	,, ,,	F. G. T. & G. Younger v J. E. Cree & H. Ferrier Kerr.	36-hole match.	7	–	F. G. T. and G. Y. rather strong for J. E. C. and H. F. K., neither of whom were in form.	
,, 20	St. Andrews	F. G. T. v Tom Morris & F. H. Woodroffe.	Best of balls and ½.	4	–	⎱ T. M. and F. H. W. not quite in form. F. G. T. in great form, especially driving. Bunkers full of water.	80 81
,, ,,	,, ,,	Same Match - - -	Best of balls and ½.	3	–		
,, 21	,, ,,	F. G. T. v W. N. Boase	3 holes up.	5	–	W. N. B. quite off his game. Out, 4 3 3 5 4 5 4 3 4 = 35 ; in, 4 4 4 6 7 4 5 5 4 = 43.	78
,, ,,	,, ,,	Same Match - - -	,, ,,	4	–	F. G. T. in great form. Links very wet and heavy, and bunkers full of water. Out, 4 3 4 4 5 4 5 3 5 = 37, in, 45. Strong wind from the south both rounds.	82
,, 22	St. Andrews New Links	F. G. T. v Ned Scratton & F. H. Woodroffe.	4 strokes, 12 strokes and 1 up.	Halved 3		——	—
,, ,,	St. Andrews Old Links	,, ,, ,,	,, ,,	3 4	–	F. H. W. rather off his game. Ned occasionally very good, but rather unsteady. F. G. T. in fine form, with exception of a few holes. 6 4 4 5 6 5 5 3 4 = 42 ; 5 4 4 5 4 4 4 4 4 = 38.	80
,, 23	St. Andrews	F. G. T. v G. H. Law & H. Ferrier Kerr.	Best of balls.	5	–	5 4 4 4 5 5 5 3 4 = 39 ; 4 3 4 4 4 4 3 6 5 = 37. Played very well.	76
,, 24	,, ,,	F. G. T. v H. L. Puxley & R. A. Gordon.	Best of balls and 7 bisques.	2	–	Played a good, steady game all through.	—

Golfing Diary

Date	Links	MATCH	Odds	Won	Lost	REMARKS	Score
1899 Feb.24	St. Andrews	Same Match - - -	Best of balls and 7 up.	3	—	H. L. P. and R. A. G. played some excellent holes.	—
,, ,,	,, ,,	F. G. T. **v** H. L. Puxley	36-hole match, 26 holes up.	Halved		This match was played at the same time as the 3-ball match.	—
,, 25	,, ,,	F. G. T. **v** H. Ferrier Kerr & J. Kerr.	Best of balls.	2	—	Very foggy in the morning; only played 10 holes. H. F. K. in good form.	—
,, ,,	,, ,,	Same Match - - -	Best of balls and 4 strokes.	2	—	Beautiful afternoon. J. K. putted very well. F. G. T. in great form; 3 bunkers going out and 6 to short hole in, and round in 81. H. F. K. not quite so good.	81
Mar.10	Oxford	F. G. T. **v** H. C. Ellis -	—	—	5	F. G. T. could not putt at all. Ellis very good. F. G. T. lost one bye as well.	—
,, ,,	,,	F. G. T. & R. H. Johnston **v** T. M. Hunter & E. C. Lee.	—	4	—	F. G. T. and R. H. J. began to understand the links a little better, and played rather well.	—
,, 12	Byfleet	F. G. T. & B. H. Blyth **v** R. H. Johnston & A. R. Paterson.	—	2	—	All played rather moderately. Also played 10 holes v A. R. P. and R. H. J. (best of balls and 1 up), and halved.	
,, ,,	,,	Same Match - - -	—	3	—		
,, 14	,,	F. G. T. **v** Earl of Winchelsea.	—	5	—	Both played rather skittles.	
,, ,,	,,	Same Match - - -	—	2	—		
April 1	North Berwick.	F. G. T. **v** H. Ferrier Kerr.	¼ and 2 holes up.	4	—	H. F. K. not in form. F. G. T. very fair.	—
,, ,,	,, ,,	Same Match - - -	,, ,,	4	—		
,, 7	,, ,,	F. G. T. **v** H. Ferrier Kerr.	2 holes up and ⅓.	—	1	Both in very fair form, with the exception of putting.	—
,, 8	,, ,,	F. G. T. **v** J. E. Laidlay	*Tantallon Medal*			Played a perfectly stinking game; 3 putts on every green. J. E. L. very wild, but putting well. J. E. L. won in 85; F. G. T., 94.	—
,, ,,	,, ,,	,, ,, ,,	—	Halved		F. G. T. a little better. J. E. L. much the same.	
,, 13	Prestwick	F. G. T. **v** H. Ferrier Kerr.	2 up and ⅓.	1	—	Played very well. H. F. K. also very good, but three or four of his strokes were of no use.	77
,, 14	North Berwick	F. G. T. **v** R. H. Johnston.	—	1	—	R. H. J. in great form.	—
,, 20	Prestwick	F. G. T. **v** Dr. Bryce -	4 strokes	Halved		Dr. Bryce drove very well.	—
,, ,,	,,	F. G. T. **v** J. Neilson & E. D. Prothero.	Best of balls.	6	—	In great form first 14 holes. In, 68. Opposition demoralised.	—
,, 22	New Luffness	,, ,, ,,	New Luffness Spring Meeting.			Played well, but with rather bad luck; 78. A. W. Robertson won medal in 77.	—
,, 25	Prestwick	F. G. T. **v** J. Hunter -	—	—	3	Putted badly. Hunter in good form. Only played 14 holes.	—
,, 26	,,	Same Match - - -	—	4	—	Played good golf. Hunter not driving very well, but putting beautifully.	—
,, ,,	,,	,, ,, ,,	—	2	—		
,, ,,	,,	F. G. T. **v** Gilbert Whigham.	—	1	—	Played rather slackly. G. W. first 5 holes very good.	—
,, 27	,,	F. G. T. **v** R. Maxwell -	—	4	—	Played well, with exception of two holes. R. M. very fair.	80

F. G. Tait

Date	Links	Match	Odds	Won	Lost	Remarks	Score
1899 May 1	St. Andrews	F. G. T. v Major P. C. J. Livingston.	2 holes up.	6	–	———	—
,, ,,	,, ,,	F. G. T. & P. C. J. Livingston v C. Hutchings & W. H. Burn.	—	–	1	———	—
,, ,,	,, ,,	F. G. T. v J. E. Laidlay & Earl of Winchilsea.	8-hole match.	2 3	– –	———	—
,, 2	,, ,,	F. G. T. v Capt. W. H. Burn.	4 strokes	2	–	———	—
,, ,,	,, ,,	F. G. T. & Capt. W. H. Burn v L. M. B. Melville & S. Mure Fergusson.	—	Halved		———	—
,, 3	,, ,,	F. G. T. v F. M. Orr -	1 stroke and 3 holes up.	3	–	New Links. A round before medal.	—
,, ,,	,, ,,	F. G. T. v J. L. Low -	Spring Meeting.	–	–	———	80
,, ,,	,, ,,	F. G. T. v J. L. Low & C. E. Hambro.	—	1 1	–	———	—
,, 4	,, ,,	F. G. T. v Earl of Winchilsea.	—	2	–	———	—
,, ,,	,, ,,	F. G. T. & Earl of Winchilsea v H. G. Hutchinson & C. Hutchings.	—	2	–	———	—
,, ,,	,, ,,	F. G. T. & Earl of Winchilsea v S. Mure Fergusson & C. E. Hambro.	—	3	–	———	—
,, 5	North Berwick.	F. G. T. & E. Mitchell Innes.	Conservative Club Medal.			———	87
,, ,,	,, ,,	F. G. T. & E. Mitchell Innes v C. E. S. Chambers & Angus Macdonald.	—	4	–	———	—
,, 9	Prestwick	F. G. T. v E. D. Prothero.	—	1	–	———	—
,, ,,	,,	Same Match - - -	6 strokes	–	1	———	79
,, 13	Duddingston	F. G. T. & L. M. B. Melville v J. E. Laidlay & C. Dalziel.	36-hole match.	6	–	———	—
,, 16	Prestwick	F. G. T. v J. L. Low & C. Whigham.	—	6 6	– –	———	—
,, ,,	,,	F. G. T. & H. H. Hilton v J. L. Low, C. Whigham & E. D. Prothero.	Best of two v best of three.	1	–	———	—
,, 17	,,	F. G. T. & C. Whigham v H. H. Hilton & J. L. Low.	—	–	2	———	—
,, ,,	,,	F. G. T. & C. Whigham v H. ·H. Hilton & J. L. Low.	—	–	5	———	—
,, 18	,,	F. G. T. v C. Gilroy -	1 hole up in 9 holes.	3	–	————	—
,, 19	,,	F. G. T. v C. Gilroy & G. H. Law.	3 up 4 up	6 6	– –	——––	—
,, 20	,,	F. G. T. v H. H. Hilton.	—	3	–	———	—
,, ,,	,,	F. G. T. & J. E. Laidlay v J. Ball & H. H. Hilton.	—	Halved		———	—
,, 22	,,	F. G. T. & J. L. Low v H. H. Hilton & J. Graham.	—	Halved		———	—
,, ,,	,,	Same Match - - -	—	–	4	———	—

Golfing Diary

Date	Links	MATCH	Odds	Won	Lost	REMARKS	Score
1899 May 23	Prestwick	F. G. T. v A. R. Aitken	—	4	–		
,, ,,	,,	F. G. T. v H. M. Balingall.	—	3	–		
,, 24	,,	F. G. T. v. S. H. Fry -	—	2	–		
,, ,,	,,	F. G. T. v G. F. Smith	—	5	–	*Amateur Championship.* Lost on playing off tie.	—
,, 25	,,	F. G. T. v H. H. Hilton.	—	1	–		
,, ,,	,,	F. G. T. v J. M. Williamson.	—	3	–		
,, 26	,,	F. G. T. v J. Ball -	Final, 36 holes.	Halved			
June 3	Sandwich	F. G. T. v H. Finch Hatton.	2 strokes	1	–		—
,, ,,	,,	Same Match - -	,, ,,	3	–		—
,, 4	,,	F. G. T. & C. E. Hambro v J. Ball & S. Mure Fergusson.	4-ball match.	2	–		—
,, ,,	,,	F. G. T. & C. E. Hambro v J. Ball & S. Mure Fergusson.	—	–	1		
,, 5	,,	F. G. T. & W. Mure v H. G. Hutchinson & H. Finch Hatton.	—	8	–		—
,, 6	,,	F. G. T. v H. H. Finch Hatton.	*St. George's Cup Competition.*	–	–		76 79
,, 7	,,	F. G. T. v H. G. Hutchinson.	*Open Championship.*	–	–		81 82
,, 8	,,	F. G. T. v — Herd -	,, ,,	–	–		79 82
,, 10	Byfleet	F. G. T. v Earl of W. & R. G. Murray.	6	3	–		—
				–	1		
,, ,,	,,	F. G. T. & R. G. M. v Earl of W. & Whigham.	Best of balls v best of balls.	6	–		—
,, 11	,,	F. G. T. v Earl of W. & R. G. Murray.	6 strokes	2	–		—
				–	4		
,, ,,	,,	,, ,, ,,	,, ,,	4 7	–	4 5 3 2 4 4 4 4 3 ; 5 5 5 4 4 4 3 4 3	—
,, 17	Muirfield	F. G. T. v H. F. K. & E. Mitchel Innes.	Best of balls.	4	–		—
,, 21	Carnoustie	F. G. T. v MacLean & R. A. Gordon.	Best of balls and 4 strokes.	2	–		—
,, ,,	,,	Same Match - -	5 strokes and best of balls.	4	–	4 4 4 5 3 4 4 4 5=37; 4 5 3 4 5 5 4 3 4=37.	74
,, 22	,,	F. G. T. v R. A. Gordon, Wemyss, & MacLean.	Best of balls and 2 strokes in 36 holes.	2	–		—
,, 23	North Berwick	F. G. T. v H. F. Kerr -	6 strokes	2	–		—
,, 24	,, ,,	F. G. T. v H. Ferrier Kerr & J. E. Cree.	Best of balls.	–	2		—
,, ,,	,, ,,	Same Match - -	,, ,,	2	–		—
,, ,,	,, ,,	,, ,, ,,	,, ,,	2	–		—

F. G. Tait

Date	Links	Match	Odds	Won	Lost	Remarks	Score
1899 July 5	North Berwick.	F. G. T. ▼ J. E. Cree & G. L. MacEwen.	Best of balls.	4	–	Played well - - - -	—
,, ,,	,, ,,	Same Match - - -	,, ,,	–	1	Only played 14 holes - -	—
,, 7	New Luffness	F. G. T. ▼ Rev. J. Kerr	1 stroke a hole.	2	–	——	77
,, 15	Archerfield	F. G. T. ▼ G. H. Law	4 holes	–	–	——	—
,, ,,	,,	,, ,, ,,	,, ,,	8	–	F. G. T. in great form. 4 4 3 3 3 4 3 4 3 = 31 ; 3 4 3 4 3 4 4 3 4 = 32. Record of Archerfield.	63
,, 21	Ganton	F. G. T. ▼ W. Park -	—	4	–	F. G. T. in great form ; lost a few shots through not knowing greens. Park driving badly.	70
,, ,,	,,	F. G. T. & J. Ball ▼ T. Vardon & C. G. Broadwood.	4-ball match.	–	2	F. G. T. and J. B. rather feeble. T. Vardon good for 11 holes.	—
,, 22	,,	F. G. T. ▼ C. Dalziel & H. M. Brown.	Best of balls.	3	–	Played well. C. Dalziel and H. M. B. played with borrowed clubs.	—
,, 24	,,	F. G. T. & W. Park ▼ J. Ball & H. Vardon.	36-hole match.	–	5	——	—
,, 27	Muirfield	F. G. T. & R. Maxwell ▼ C. Dalziel & Mansfield Hunter.	—	–	2	——	—
,, 28	,,	F. G. T. & R. Maxwell ▼ T. Brotherston & H. Cunningham.	County Cup.	1	–	Our other foursome lost by 2 -	—
,, 29	,,	F. G. T. & R. Maxwell ▼ C. L. Dalziel & M. Hunter.	36-hole match.	10	–	——	—
,, 31	St. Andrews	F. G. T. ▼ A. H. Cochran & E. C. P. Boyd.	4 holes. 5 holes.	4 5	– –	New Links - - - -	—
Aug. 1	St. Andrews New Links	F. G. T. ▼ J. H. Wilson	7 holes	4	–	⎫	—
,, ,,	,, ,,	F. G. T. ▼ D. I. Lamb -	4 holes	2	–	⎪	
,, 2	,, ,,	F. G. T. ▼ A. F. Macfie	3 holes	4	–	⎪	
,, ,,	,, ,,	F. G. T. ▼ E. C. P. Boyd	5 holes	3	–	⎬ Calcutta Cup - - - -	
,, 3	,, ,,	F. G. T. ▼ J. O. Fairlie	4 holes	2	–	⎪	
,, 4	,, ,,	F. G. T. ▼ Dr. A. H. Vassie.	5 holes	3	–	⎪	
,, ,,	,, ,,	F. G. T. ▼ J. L. Low -	2 holes	Halved		⎪	
,, 5	,, ,,	,, ,, ,,	,, ,,	4	–	⎭	
,, ,,	St. Andrews Old Links	F. G. T. & J. O. Fairlie ▼ J. L. Low & H. C. Ellis.	—	Halved		——	—
,, 18	,, ,,	F. G. T. ▼ J. O. Fairlie	6 strokes	3	–	——	—
,, 25	St. Andrews New Links	F. G. T. ▼ E. B. H. Blackwell & E. R. H. Blackwell.	—	7 7	– –	Played well. Also won 3 byes from Ted. Ted and Ernley both off their game.	82
,, ,,	,, ,,	F. G. T. ▼ E. R. H. Blackwell.	3 holes up.	3	–	——	82
,, 26	,, ,,	F. G. T. ▼ G. H. Law, J. M. Bow & C. J. Currie.	Best of balls.	3	–	⎫	80
,, ,,	,, ,,	Same Match - - -	,, ,,	3	–	⎬ Played excellently - - -	79
,, 31	St. Andrews Old Links	F. G. T. ▼ A. H. Cochran.	⅓	2	–	Played indifferently. A. H. C. very feeble.	—

Golfing Diary

Date	Links	Match	Odds	Won	Lost	Remarks	Score
1899 Aug.31	St. Andrews Old Links	F. G. T. **v** A. H. Cochran & G. Mellor.	Best of balls.	2	–	Played very well. Out, 4 6 4 4 5 4 4 3 3 = 37; in, 4 4 4 4 6 4 4 5 4 = 39. Best of balls very good, 78. Right hand course long.	76
Sep. 1	St. Andrews New Links	F. G. T. **v** A. G. Tait, J. R. Hutchison & J. Stott.	,, ,,		Halved	F. G. T. last 10 holes in 39, a record; 3 4 4 5 2 5 4 4 4 4 = 39. Best of balls very good.	81
,, ,,	,, ,,	,, ,, ,,	,, ,,	4	–	F. G. T. again in great form. J. S. not in form. A. G. T. did most of the work.	79
,, 2	St. Andrews Old Links	F. G. T. **v** C. Hutchings.	–	4	–	First 5 holes bad; after that, excellent golf. C. H. fair.	80
,, ,,	,, ,,	,, ,, ,,	–	2	–	Played moderately well. C. H. very fair.	–
,, 4	,, ,,	F. G. T. **v** W. H. Fowler.	5 strokes		Halved	Played well most of the way round. Fowler in good form.	–
,, ,,	,, ,,	F. G. T. & W. H. Fowler **v** J. L. Low & A. G. Tait.	–	5	–	F. G. T. and W. H. F. very hot, with exception of two holes. 17th hole on top of Old Station !!!	–
,, 5	,, ,,	F. G. T. **v** J. T. Cathcart.	14 strokes	3	–		
,, ,,	,, ,,	F. G. T. **v** J. B. Grimond.	12 strokes	8	–		
,, 6	,, ,,	F. G. T. **v** R. H. Johnston.	5 strokes	4	–	*Jubilee Cup* - - - -	–
,, ,,	,, ,,	F. G. T. **v** W. E. Fairlie	,, ,,	3	–		
,, 7	,, ,,	F. G. T. **v** C. A. W. Cameron.	9 strokes	–	3		
,, ,,	St. Andrews New Links	F. G. T. **v** A. G. Tait -	3 holes	2	–	Played very well; 79 with a 7 to 6th hole. Alec very fair.	–
,, 8	St. Andrews Old Links	F. G. T. **v** C. Hutchings.	2 strokes	1	–		–
,, ,,	,, ,,	Same Match - - -	,, ,,	2	–		–
,, 9	North Berwick	F. G. T. & C. F. Whigham.	*Tantallon Medal.*			Strong wind; putted badly. J. E. Laidlay won with 87.	89
,, ,,	,, ,,	F. G. T. & C. F. Whigham **v** T. M. Hunter & P. Wynne.	Best of two v best of two.	–	2	F. G. T. and C. F. W. only moderate. P. Wynne putted very well.	–
,, 21	St. Andrews Old Links	F. G. T. & Osmand Williams **v** E. R. H. Blackwell & C. A. W. Cameron.	–	–	4	F. G. T. played badly first round, and well second. O. W. quite off his putting. C. A. W. C. and E. R. H. B. both in good form.	–
,, ,,	,, ,,	Same Match - - -	–	–	3		–
,, 22	St. Andrews	F. G. T. & C. A. W. Cameron **v** L. M. B. Melville & C. Hutchings.	2 strokes	3	–	L. M. B. M. and C. H. not in good form. C. A. W. C. played well.	–
,, ,,	,, ,,	Same Match - - -	,, ,,	–	1		–
,, 23	,, ,,	F. G. T. **v** R. H. Johnston & C. A. W. Cameron.	1 up and 2 strokes, 1 up and $\frac{1}{3}$.	6 5	–	Played well; 80. Strong wind and keen greens.	80
,, ,,	,, ,,	F. G. T. & R. H. Johnston **v** A. G. Tait & C. A. W. Cameron.	3 holes up.	1	–	F. G. T. and R. H. J. 4 down and 5 to play, and won match.	–
,, 25	,, ,,	F. G. T. & A. G. Tait **v** C. Hutchings & Ed. Blackwell.	–	–	2	All played well. Very wet, especially in afternoon. Taits 3 down and 4 to play.	–
,, ,,	,, ,,	Same Match - - -	–		Halved		–

F. G. Tait

Date	Links	Match	Odds	Won	Lost	Remarks	Score
1899 Sep.26	St. Andrews	F. G. T. & A. J. Balfour **v** Ed. Blackwell & Ernley Blackwell.	Receiving 4 strokes.	–	3	——	—
,, ,,	,, ,,	Same Match - - -	,,	Halved		——	—
,, 27	,, ,,	F. G. T. **v** Ed. Blackwell.	*Autumn Medal*			——	83
,, ,,	,, ,,	F. G. T. & Ed. Blackwell **v** C. Hutchings & L. M. B. Melville.	Best of two and best of two.	3	–	——	—
,, 28	,, ,,	F. G. T. & A. G. T. **v** L. M. B. Melville & C. F. Whigham.	—	–	2	——	—
,, ,,	,, ,,	Same Match - - -	—	–	5	Won 4 byes.	—
Oct. 1	Lytham and St. Anne's.	F. G. T. **v** J. Ball - -	—	Halved		——	—
,, 2	,, ,,	,, ,, ,,	36-hole match.	1	–	——	—

EYRE AND SPOTTISWOODE, HER MAJESTY'S PRINTERS, LONDON.

Afterword
by
Ross Goodner

Freddie Tait played his championship golf during a period of history that could be called the Age of the Amateur. That age began with the first British Amateur, in 1885, and ended—depending on one's point of view—either in 1916, when Chick Evans won both the U.S. Open and U.S. Amateur, or in 1930 with the retirement of Bob Jones after he had won the Grand Slam. Jones, of course, was the dominant player of the 1920s, but he was by that time the only amateur who was a consistent threat to the professionals. Evans, on the other hand, became in 1916 the third amateur in four years to win the U.S. Open, following Francis Ouimet in 1913 and Jerry Travers in 1915. (Evans had finished only a stroke behind Walter Hagen in 1914.)

When Tait appeared, there were in Scotland and England a broad range of amateurs who could hold their own with the professionals. First among these were the two Hoylake stars, John Ball and Harold Hilton. Ball, who grew up on that golf course, tied for fourth in the British Open as a teenager back in 1878, but didn't really hit his stride until 1890, when he won the Open by three strokes at Prestwick. Ball had won the British Amateur in 1888 and was to win it a record eight times in a span of twenty-four years. Hilton, eight years younger than Ball, won the Open twice—in 1892 and 1897—before winning the first of his four Amateurs. He added the U.S. Amateur in 1911.

Only a cut below Ball and Hilton were a number of other outstanding amateurs: John Laidlay, the inventor of the overlapping, or Vardon, grip, and a two-time Amateur champion who was runnerup in the 1893 Open; Ted Blackwell, a prodigious driver, who was a player of championship calibre for three decades, despite two periods of six and five years when he lived in California and played no golf at all; Horace Hutchinson, the winner of two Amateurs, and a man who wrote about the game at least as well ashe played it; and Leslie Balfour-Melville, an all-rounder who represented Scotland at rugby football and cricket, won the Scottish tennis championship, and took time out from cricket for golf only when the competitions were held on convenient courses.

Tait didn't move into such heady company immediately. Blackwell recalled playing a lot of golf with the teen-aged Tait during the late 1880s and giving him several strokes. However, when Blackwell returned from his first stay in California, in 1892, he found Tait a vastly improved player. Hilton felt the same way. He later wrote: "In 1893, Fred Tait commenced business as the slaughterer of Hilton. I met him in the first round (of the Amateur), and he downed me three and two. I was rather sick about it at the time, but I got quite used to these defeats in after years, and I always think that poor Fred must have been very disappointed when other men took the liberty of knocking me out. In 1894 he again repeated the offence, but on this occasion he only beat me on the last green . . . in 1896 I did better. I reached the final and there had to meet mine old enemy, Fred Tait. He had trampled on nearly every other opponent he had met, and he did not fail to maintain this unkindly spirit when we met. It was the fairest and most honest slogging I ever received in my life. I played good, sound honest golf, but I could not live with him at any point in the game."

The words fair and honest appear in almost every account of Tait's behavior, either on or off the course. He was indeed a high-spirited man who had absolute belief in himself. His occasional pranks may have been a source of irritation to some, but he was unfailingly cheerful and without guile. While he was a formidable competitor, he realized that it was a game he was playing, and he took no joy from winning on a rules technicality.

Hal Ludlow, a leading amateur of the day, recalled watching the 1898 Amateur final, at Hoylake, between Tait and Mure Fergusson, who was always a tough man to beat: "At the long hole, Fergusson hit on an adjacent green from a long slice; his opponent was straight down the course. When Fergusson came up, he asked the referee (I think Charles Hutchings) the rule. Freddy called out, 'Place it.' Hutchings explained that the local *rule was to drop. Fergusson did so, dropping into a bad lie. Freddy, seeing this, immediately ran across, and without a word teed it up. His opponent got in a fine shot and halved the hole. I fancy that it was this generous spirit that made Freddy Tait so loved by the crowd, making his wins just as popular in England as in Scotland."*

Another testimonial came from Jack White, the 1904 Open champion. In recalling the Open of 1892 at Muirfield, when he was only nineteen, White wrote " . . . I got into the prize-list at Muirfield, but had a lot to thank poor Mr. Freddy Tait for. He was my partner, and he was driving a terrific ball, but let me keep the honor the whole way round."

The best description of Tait's style of play comes, naturally, from Bernard Darwin: "He was certainly an illustration of fortune favoring the brave, but because he could bring off such prodigious recoveries, I think those who never saw him have misconstrued his game. Such epithets as 'slashing' are to my mind inappropriate. They do no justice to the drowsy ease of his swing and the control under which he kept his strength. He could make wild shots, possibly owing to his curious underhand grip of the right hand, but not to any reckless abandon. On his best days, when no recoveries were needed, it would have been difficult to imagine anyone playing more smoothly and easily and more within himself."

At match play, Tait's mastery over Hilton was complete. He beat the Englishmen five times in the Amateur and it wasn't until after Tait's death that Hilton started winning the championship. Against Ball, however, he had all he could handle. Ball beat Tait, 5 and 3, in the 1895 Amateur semifinals, but Tait avenged that with a 5-and-4 fourth-round triumph on his way to the title in 1896. Then came the historic 1899 final at Prestwick, won by Ball at the 37th hole. It was perhaps fitting that in the last match Tait played, at Lytham St. Annes, he defeated Ball on the 36th hole only days before leaving for South Africa.

One could hardly find a more suitable biographer for Freddie Tait than John Low, a frequent rival of his on the links as well as a thoughtful writer whose philosophy of life and golf must have been similar to Tait's. In 1907, Low wrote: "Even in the most straightforward shots one golfer will vary his treatment of the ball greatly from another; if it were not so, golf would be a stale business, and the watching of it a monotony to the eye. I think it may fairly be contended that the finest games are those which allow of the greatest variety of maneuver."

A full quarter of a century before Grantland Rice, Low wrote, "I determined that for the amateur the playing of the game, not the winning of it, is the greatest good."

In 1934, Darwin looked back on Tait's impact on the game: "In his day and in his own Scotland he was a national hero. I do not think I have ever seen any other golfer so adored by the crowd—no, not Harry Vardon or Bobby Jones in their primes. It was a tremendous and, to his adversaries, an almost terrifying popularity. He was only thirty when he was killed: a brave young man, like many others who were killed, a very good specimen of the plucky, cheerful, open-airy regular soldier; a thoroughly friendly creature, who made friends with all sorts and conditions of men, but not in any way possessed of an outstanding mind or character.

"He was just a thoroughly good fellow who played a game very skillfully, and in a cheery and chivalrous spirit. Yet, when he died, it is hardly too much to say that Scotland went into mourning, and his old friend John Low wrote a full-sized biography of him that was widely read. This is a remarkable state of things, and there was some remarkable quality about this otherwise ordinary man which, in the language of the theatres, 'got across,' so that he had only to step on to the links for everyone to follow him."

Let us hope that this new edition of Low's work will be as widely read as the original. Freddie Tait is worth the effort.

Ross Goodner